The University of Law

This book must be returned to the library on or before the last date
stamped below. Failure to do so will result in a fine.

Bloomsbury Library
T: 01483 216387
library-bloomsbury@law.ac.uk

Moorgate Library
T: 01483 216371
library-moorgate@law.ac.uk

Contract Law

Contract Law

A COMPARATIVE INTRODUCTION

SECOND EDITION

Jan M. Smits

Professor of European Private Law, Faculty of Law, Maastricht University, The Netherlands

Edward Elgar
Cheltenham, UK • Northampton, MA, USA

Published by
Edward Elgar Publishing Limited
The Lypiatts
15 Lansdown Road
Cheltenham
Glos GL50 2JA
UK

Edward Elgar Publishing, Inc.
William Pratt House
9 Dewey Court
Northampton
Massachusetts 01060
USA

A catalogue record for this book
is available from the British Library

Library of Congress Control Number: 2017939798

ISBN   978 1 78536 876 9 (cased)
ISBN   978 1 78536 878 3 (paperback)
ISBN   978 1 78536 877 6 (eBook)

Typeset by Servis Filmsetting Ltd, Stockport, Cheshire
Printed and bound in Great Britain by TJ International Ltd, Padstow

Contents in brief

Contents in full

Boxes

Preface to the second edition

Any newcomer on the already well-served market for contract law books must explain itself. Over the last two hundred years or so, contract law has been mainly national in contents and outlook. This is reflected in the abundance of textbooks on the contract law of national jurisdictions. These textbooks introduce students to the national contract law of their own country in their own language. Next to these traditional books, there is an increasing number of texts available that offer a comparative, European or even global perspective on the law of contract – invariably designed to cater for the needs of students who are already familiar with the fundamentals of contract law. This book seeks to combine the two: it introduces students to the field of contract law by way of a comparative approach. It assumes that contract law is an international discipline that can be taught on the basis of common principles and methods, just like economics, psychology or any other field of academic study. There are two reasons why this approach is adopted.

First, substantive law is no longer the exclusive product of the nation-state and introductory textbooks should reflect this. In particular in the context of the European Union, law is shaped as much by the national legislators and courts of the 28 Member States as it is by the European legislature and the Court of Justice of the European Union. At a global scale, the role of private regulation and of the Convention on Contracts for the International Sale of Goods is increasing, as is the potential for choice of the legal regime applicable to the contract. All this reduces the self-evidence of teaching contract law on the basis of the intricacies of one national law alone. Most of today's law students will spend their professional life in a world in which knowledge of only one jurisdiction is not enough.

Second, learning the law is as much about learning a *method* as it is about mastering the substantive law. It is arguably more important to learn to 'think like a lawyer' than it is to know about the details of a court case or a statute that is likely to change anyway. In a similar way as economists do not focus on the study of one particular economy but adopt a method of analysis ('the economic approach'), law is ideally regarded not as a subject but as a method. Under this view, students no longer study German, English or Polish contract law, but simply 'contract law' by applying the legal approach towards the questions they are confronted with. This does not mean that the details of, or differences between, various legal systems are not discussed. To the contrary: it is exactly by looking at these similarities and differences among jurisdictions that one learns that much of the law is about exploring and contrasting the implications of conflicting views of what is right. It is this approach, focusing on arguments and policies that is at the core of this book. National laws are presented as variations on common themes and as alternative ways of dealing with some common problem.

This book thus caters to the needs of the international classroom. It was originally written for use in the first-year contract law course of Maastricht University's European Law School. This explains why the main materials used in the book come from German, English, French and Dutch law and from international instruments, but there is also ample attention for other jurisdictions, including those of Central and Eastern Europe. Background knowledge of comparative law is not required. Throughout the book separate textboxes provide information essential to understanding the background to the substantive law, as well as on other salient issues.

I am immensely grateful to colleagues and students who commented on a draft version of this textbook or provided essential support in other ways. These are, in alphabetical order, Bram Akkermans, William Bull, Caroline Calomme, Jiangxiu Ge, Catalina Goanta, Jonas Hinrichsen, Hester van der Kaaij, Theano Karanikioti, Mark Kawakami, Nicole Kornet, Liuhu Luo, Eve Meurgey and Omar Salah. I had the privilege of trying out a first version with the Maastricht European Law School class of 2013–16. It is difficult to find more talented and motivated law students than in this programme.

This second edition takes into account the most important developments over the past three years. In particular, the long-anticipated reform of the French law of obligations (introduced on 1 October 2016) and the enactment of the UK Consumer Rights Act 2015 prompted a revision of several parts of this book. In addition, the entire text has been revised and updated and a new chapter on contracts and third parties has been added. The purpose of the book remains as it was: to be a rewarding and stimulating tool in the study of contract law. Comments are most welcome at jan.smits@maastrichtuniversity.nl.

Maastricht/Liège, January 2017

How to use this book

An academic textbook like this cannot be read like a novel. Although each student has their own technique of studying, some suggestions on how to master this book may be helpful.

This book consists of **six parts**, each asking a central question of contract law:

Part 1: What is contract law and what are its sources?

Part 2: How does a contract come into being?

Part 3: What are the contents of the contract?

Part 4: Can a validly formed contract be 'avoided' (set aside) and if so, for what reason?

Part 5: What are the contractual remedies in case of breach of contract?

Part 6: How can third parties be affected by the contract?

Each part of the book consists of several chapters. Both the parts and the chapters are preceded by an **outline** that highlights the key themes. It is a good idea to get acquainted with the topics of a certain part or chapter by first reading these outlines, followed by a first read of the chapter, skipping the separate textboxes. After reading the list of **Topics for review** at the end of each chapter, reread the chapter more slowly, making sure that you understand each step of the argument. The law is often about structuring a topic (a problem and its possible solutions) in a certain way; you need to make sure that you are able to reproduce this structure and it usually helps a lot if you try to make your own summary of the topic. It can be immensely useful to make this summary by drawing your own table. You will find ready-to-use tables in some parts of the book, but is highly advisable to build your own ones when you go through the materials.

Each chapter highlights significant issues in separate **textboxes**. Their aim is to provide background knowledge to the main text or to explore topical issues. The textboxes will often make the main points fall into place. A **glossary** with definitions and key points is provided at the end of the book. If you come across a concept that you are uncertain about, it is likely that you will find it in the glossary. Remember that studying law is not about *memorising* these definitions and key points, but about *understanding* them. If the glossary does not provide you with an answer, check the **index** to see where a concept is discussed in more detail. The **table of statutes** and **table of cases** refer you to legislation and case law.

At the end of each chapter suggestions are made for **further reading**. If reference is made to case law or to non-reproduced statutory provisions, it is highly advisable to consult these yourself. Links to English translations are provided on the **companion website**, which is available at https://www.e-elgar.com/textbooks/smits

Abbreviations

ABGB	Allgemeines Bürgerliches Gesetzbuch (Austrian Civil Code)
AGBG	Gesetz zur Regelung des Rechts der Allgemeinen Geschäftsbedingungen (German Act on General Conditions)
All ER	All England Law Reports
Art(s.)	Article(s)
B2B	Business-to-business
B2C	Business-to-consumer
BGB	Bürgerliches Gesetzbuch (German Civil Code)
BGH	Bundesgerichtshof (German Federal Supreme Court)
BGHZ	Entscheidungen des Bundesgerichtshofs in Zivilsachen (Decisions of the German Supreme Court in Civil Cases)
Bull. cass.	Bulletin des arrêts de la Cour de Cassation (Journal of decisions of the French Court of Cassation)
BVerfG	Bundesverfassungsgericht (German Constitutional Court)
BW	Burgerlijk Wetboek (Dutch Civil Code)
C2C	Consumer-to-consumer
CC	Code Civil (French Civil Code)
CISG	Convention on Contracts for the International Sale of Goods
Civ.	Cour de Cassation, Chambre civile
CJEU	Court of Justice of the European Union
CRA	Consumer Rights Act 2015
D.	Recueil Dalloz
DCFR	Draft Common Frame of Reference of European Private Law
DM	Deutsche Mark
€	Euro
ed(s).	editor(s)
ECHR	European Convention on Human Rights and Fundamental Freedoms
e.g.	exempli gratia (for example)
et al	et alii (and others)
EU	European Union
ff	following pages/articles
FF	French Franc
Fl	Dutch guilder
HGB	Handelsgesetzbuch (German Commercial Code)

HL	House of Lords
HR	Hoge Raad (Dutch Supreme Court)
J	Judge, Justice
L	Partie législative (of the French Consumer Code)
LJ	Lord Justice
NGO	Non-Governmental Organisation
NJ	Nederlandse Jurisprudentie
OR	Obligationenrecht (Swiss Law of Obligations)
p(p)	page(s)
PECL	Principles of European Contract Law
PICC	UNIDROIT Principles of International Commercial Contracts
R	Partie réglementaire (of the French Consumer Code)
RG	Reichsgericht (highest German court until 1945)
RGZ	Entscheidungen des Reichsgerichts in Zivilsachen (Decisions of the German Reichsgericht in Civil Cases)
TEU	Treaty on European Union
TFEU	Treaty on the Functioning of the European Union
UCC	Uniform Commercial Code (USA)
UCTA	Unfair Contract Terms Act 1977
vol(s)	volume(s)
ZPO	Zivilprozessordnung (German Code of Civil Procedure)
§	Paragraph

Table of cases

Netherlands

United Kingdom

Other

Table of legislation and international instruments

Part One

Contracts

Part 1 of this book discusses two main issues: what is contract law and what are its sources.

- The question of what is **contract law** is answered by reference to which types of contracts exist, why we need contract law, what its main principles are, and how it relates to other fields of private law (Chapter 1);
- The question of where to find contract law is asking about the **sources** of rights and obligations of the contracting parties. The rules and principles that govern a contract can be found in the party agreement, in official sources (such as national and European legislation and case law and international treaties) and in informal rules (Chapter 2).

1

Introduction

 CHAPTER OVERVIEW

This chapter explains:
- The **need** for contract law in a well-functioning society;
- The **types** of contracts that are usually distinguished;
- The **place** of contract law in the system of private law as a whole;
- The **main principles** of contract law;
- The **historical development** of these principles since Roman times.

Contract

A contract is usually associated with a piece of paper through which one buys a house, takes up a job or ensures access to a mobile phone network, for example. Although these transactions can in most cases indeed be qualified as binding contracts, the law uses a broader definition. In any given jurisdiction, contracts are defined as legally binding agreements, irrespective of whether they are written down or not. This means that, in law, people conclude contracts when they buy products in a supermarket, take out insurance, download software, are treated by their doctor or go to the hairdresser. Contracts can even come about in cases where no word is spoken at all, as in case of putting money into a machine to buy a cup of coffee and of computerised derivatives trading. Each agreement that qualifies as legally binding – and therefore as a contract – needs to meet certain requirements, that are discussed in Part 2 of this book. This chapter discusses the concept of a contract in general and seeks to introduce the main principles of contract law.

Why contract law?

Voluntary exchange

The need for a well-functioning contract law follows from the type of society that we live in. A market economy as is now prevalent in almost the entire world – with the possible exception of North Korea – is based on the premise that people and companies should make their own bargains on the basis of a voluntary exchange of goods and services. It is not the government that decides how many goods are produced or how much money a person is to pay for the product they desire. Instead, within certain limits, it is left to the needs of the people and therefore to the market's price mechanism to

Contract law

ensure that supply and demand correspond to each other. Such a market economy – no matter if it comes in the version of continental Rhineland, the Nordic social model, Anglo-American capitalism or China's socialism – cannot do without contracts. Contract *law* in turn ensures that these contracts are binding, and can therefore be enforced in the courts in case the other party does not perform. This turns contract law – the rules and principles that govern transactions among parties – into the cement of modern society: it enables market actors (individuals and companies, but also government bodies, municipalities, NGOs, charities, etc.) to participate in economic and social life. A manufacturer would not be able to run its business if customers could simply renege on their orders. I would not be able to lead a normal life if my landlord were allowed to evict me from my apartment any time she received a better offer from a potential tenant. Contract law thus allows planning by individual members of society. Aristotle, in his *Rhetorics* (I, 14, 22), already saw this: '… so that if you destroy the authority of contracts, the mutual intercourse of men is destroyed'. This does not mean that no alternative ways of organising society are available (see Box 1.1), but they are difficult to reconcile with today's views of what a society must look like.

Types of contracts

Most rules and principles of contract law are designed to apply to any contract, regardless of the type of party and the type of obligations the parties take upon them. In principle, it does not matter whether the contract concerns the purchase of a pen or a one billion euro takeover: as will become clear in this book, both transactions are governed by the same principles (such as the freedom to decide what the conditions are) and rules (notably on the formation of the contract through offer and acceptance, interpretation, performance, damages, etc.). This is not just a matter of systematic rigidity: the implicit assumption behind it is that the law must treat all contracts and parties equally, no matter what they contract about or who they are. What one party is entitled to, must also be afforded to the other party.

General character of contract law

Classification

Despite this general character of contract law, lawyers usually distinguish between different types of contracts. One can classify contracts on basis of the parties involved, the main characteristics of the contract, and the reason why parties want to be bound.

It is obvious that not all contracting parties are the same. A multinational company aiming to build a new factory does not have much in common with a student looking for a new pair of shoes. This is why contracts are usually

BOX 1.1

CONTRACTS AND THE ECONOMY

It is surely imaginable how an individual person could survive without making contracts: he or she could live off charity or obtain the necessities of life (such as food and housing) from his or her own resources. It is more difficult to conceive of a *society* in which the need to contract with other people is completely absent. One could think of the type of community that existed in prehistoric times before any division of labour occurred: small groups of nomadic people who shared what they found by hunting, fishing and gathering had no need for contract law. It may be true that one good was bartered for another (e.g. wool for hops), but this exchange typically took place on the spot, allowing the parties to immediately inspect the goods, and not accept them if necessary. The nature of the goods also made it unnecessary to have rules on hidden defects: it is easy to see whether wool and hop or an axe are suited for their intended use. Rules on *future* performance and on non-performance of the contract were therefore not needed.

This example makes us realise that contracts are superfluous as long as rights and obligations arise from one's personal status as a member of the tribe or family of which one remains a member during one's entire life. In a feudal society, as prevalent in Europe until around 1400, one's inherited status as a vassal or a landowner was decisive for one's legal position; the intention to leave the group was irrelevant. And if one worked as an employee, there was no such thing as an employment contract setting the working hours and pay. Instead, obligations followed from the status of servant, who had to do virtually everything the master asked. The master in turn had to supply food and offer protection. This only changed with increasing division of labour and the ensuing development of the economy, prompting the need for binding contracts that free people could make with each other. The German author Hein Kötz put it like this: 'People who specialise, like the farmer in producing food, the trader in distributing goods, and the tailor in making clothes, or the haulier, the moneylender, the construction worker, the teacher, the doctor, and others who provide specialist services, all such people must be able to exchange their products or services for money and then use the money to procure the goods or services they need to live on: they have to make contracts.' In Europe it took until the eighteenth and nineteenth centuries before this development 'from Status to Contract' (as the English scholar Henry Sumner Maine famously called it in his book *Ancient Law*) was completed. Two factors were responsible for this: 1. The move away from an agricultural to an industrial economy; and 2. A fundamental change in how society was regarded. Liberalism emphasised that everyone should be allowed to shape one's life as he wished. Freedom of contract was seen as the necessary tool to make this *laissez-faire* possible.

distinguished on the basis of *who* concludes them. Commercial contracts (contracts between two or more commercial parties, sometimes also referred to as business-to-business or B2B-contracts) thus stand next to consumer contracts (contracts between a business and a consumer, or B2C-contracts). Contracts concluded between two individuals (not a business) are sometimes referred to as consumer-to-consumer (or C2C-contracts). As we shall see, the relevance of these distinctions is that legislators and courts sometimes make rules specifically designed for B2B- or B2C-contracts.

Type of parties

Contracts can also be distinguished on the basis of their main characteristics: what parties need to *do* under the contract depends on the type of contract they concluded. The seller and buyer in a contract for sale of goods need to do something different than the employer and employee in an employment contract, for example. While in a sales contract, the seller needs to deliver the good and the buyer undertakes to pay the price, an employment contract requires the employee to perform the contractually agreed work and the employer to pay the required remuneration. These so-called *specific contracts* are all governed by their own specific rules, laid down in national civil codes or developed by the courts. Typical specific contracts one can find in civil codes are sale of goods, barter, lease, mandate, donation and the employment contract. Other specific contracts do have a name (and therefore share with sale, barter, etc. that they are *nominate contracts*), but are not dealt with in detail in statutory law. Examples are franchise and distribution contracts.

Type of performance

Specific contracts

A third categorisation of contracts is based on *the reason why* parties want to be bound. In his *Traité des Obligations* of 1761, the famous French jurist Pothier defined contract as an agreement 'by which two parties reciprocally promise and engage, or one of them singly promises and engages, to the other to give some particular thing, or to do or abstain from doing some particular act.' The distinction made here between contracts in which each party assumes an obligation in order to obtain the performance to which the other party, in exchange, obliges itself towards the first party (bilateral contracts) and contracts in which a party is not promised anything in return for its performance (unilateral contracts) has found its way to many civil codes, including the French (Art. 1106 *Code Civil*: *contrat synallagmatique* and *unilatéral*)), the German (*gegenseitiger* (§ 320 BGB) and *einseitiger Vertrag*) and the Dutch (Art. 6:261 Dutch Civil Code: *wederkerige* and *eenzijdige overeenkomst*). In case of a bilateral contract, party A only wants to be bound to party B because party B is also willing to oblige itself towards party A. Ally promises Bob to pay a price for the bike he is selling to her. This element of exchange (*do ut des* in lawyers' Latin) is clearly present in contracts such as sale, lease, employ-

Reason for performance

Bilateral contract

ment, franchising and insurance, but not in the contract of donation. Catalina's promise to Mark to give him her iPad when her newly bought Samsung Galaxy has arrived is at best a unilateral contract (if binding at all: see Chapter 4). The presumed reason why the donor agrees to gratuitously transfer ownership of a good to the donee is not because she receives anything in return, but because she intends to benefit the donee.

Unilateral contract

Contract law as part of private law

System

In the civil law tradition, to which most countries on the European continent belong (see in more detail Box 2-1), contract law is seen as only one part of a more comprehensive 'system' of private law. Private law consists of the rules and principles that deal with the relationships between private actors such as individuals and companies. Next to contract law, also the fields of tort law (sometimes referred to as the law of 'delict' or law of 'civil wrongs'), restitution, property law, trust law, inheritance law, family law and company law are part of the overall system of private law.

Law of obligations

The law of contract, tort and restitution are often lumped together under the heading of 'law of obligations.' This is because they can all give rise to so-called 'obligations', a legal term indicating that a (usually) enforceable duty exists of one person vis-à-vis another person or several other persons. In a bilateral contract, such as sale, typically two obligations come into being: the obligation of the buyer to pay the price and the obligation of the seller to deliver the good. While in case of a contract, this obligation arises voluntarily because a party intends to be legally bound, in case of a tort the obligation is imposed upon a person independent of its intention, usually because the law wants to attach consequences to wrongful behaviour causing damage to the victim. Typical tort cases concern victims claiming damages for personal injury (as in case of assault, medical negligence or liability for defective products such as exploding iPhones) or for defamation (think of publishing false statements damaging someone's reputation). This distinction between voluntary (self-imposed) and non-voluntary obligations is as old as the civil law tradition itself: it was already set out as the *summa divisio* (ultimate partition) in the *Institutes*, a textbook for law students written by the Roman jurist Gaius around the year 160.

This classification of different areas of law into one system of private law, as well as of different types of obligations into one law of obligations, is typical for the civil law tradition. German, French or Polish textbooks, for example, only tend to deal with contract law as part of book series on the law of obligations, if not on private law as a whole. This is different in the English common

English law

BOX 1.2

THE GARMENT INDUSTRY SUPPLY CHAIN: A CASCADE OF CONTRACTS

The importance of contracts in the global economy can be illustrated by reference to the supply chain in the garment industry, an industry worth 1000 billion euro in 2016. The typical supply chain consists of Europe- or US-based clothing companies that place orders with big manufacturers in Asia, which in turn subcontract to smaller factories in their home country, which again may outsource to homeworkers. It is not difficult to imagine the high number of widely diverse contracts required to make this supply chain work. In a typical example, we find four contracts at the core of the chain:

- Angelina buys a V-neck chiffon blouse at her local Primark shop (consumer sale);
- Primark concludes a two-year 'clothing manufacturing agreement' with manufacturer Shanghai Globaltex Inc. (SG), requiring SG to manufacture a set quantity of clothes in accordance with the quality and design standards prescribed by Primark. This contract typically entails provisions on quality control (such as a duty to furnish to Primark a sample of each product to be approved before production starts), on delivery ('60 days net term'), on contractual remedies ('shipment delivered with a delay of ten days or more: 20 per cent deduction from the price; shipment delivered with a delay of 30 days or more: 100 per cent deduction from the price'), on payment, on termination of the contract, on ownership of design rights and on use of subcontractors.
- Shanghai Globaltex Inc. concludes subcontracts with several local companies in Shanghai (including China Jiajia Co.) for the delivery of materials, for cutting and sewing and for packing and transport;
- China Jiajia Co. hires homeworkers who are paid by the piece.

Next to this core supply chain, other contracts that Primark will have to conclude, include those for design, distribution and marketing of the clothing, lease of offices, hiring of employees, insurance of the stock against the risk of fire, printing of catalogues and web design. The retailer in turn will have to lease shop space and employ staff, while the manufacturer has to purchase or lease machinery. Most of these parties are likely to have concluded credit agreements with banks (ranging from the credit card that Angelina uses to buy her blouse to an extended loan facility granted to Primark by an international consortium of banks). All in all, a true cascade of contracts is behind the simple purchase by Angelina.

law, in which such scientific rationalisation has long been absent. The first comprehensive book on the English law of obligations was only published in 2010 and is seen as an outlier. What one does find, however, are separate textbooks on contract law, the law of torts, property law, etc. This different mentality was well captured by the English judge Macmillan who in 1947 called upon his fellow-judges not to rationalise the law of England: argu-

BOX 1.3

THE CONTRACT AS JURIDICAL ACT

The law is not only shaped by legislators and courts. An equally important role is played by legal academics who analyse and systematise the products of the official law-makers. In particular in the civil law tradition law professors have had a profound influence on the present system of private law. The high tide of this influence was in nineteenth-century Germany when the so-called Pandectists, working on the basis of the then still applicable Roman law, developed sophisticated doctrines that subsequently found their way into legal practice as they were taken over by legislators and courts. This influence was not limited to Germany alone, but can be seen throughout the civil law world (and sometimes beyond).

One of these doctrines is the so-called juridical act (*Rechtsgeschäft* in German, *acte juridique* in French, *rechtshandeling* in Dutch). Its main intellectual father is Friedrich Carl Von Savigny (1779–1861), a Berlin law professor who was to become one of the most famous jurists of his time.

What Von Savigny sought to collect under one umbrella term were acts that have legal consequences because of the fact that these consequences are intended by the person acting. Art. 3:33 of the Dutch Civil Code formulates it like this: 'A juridical act requires an intention to create legal relations, which intention becomes manifest in a declaration.' A contract is the most important example of a juridical act (sometimes also called a 'legal transaction'), but also the making of a will ('testament') and the decision to start a company, to quit one's job or to legally recognise a child only have legal consequences because these are intended.

The juridical act has a prominent place in civil codes. In the Dutch Code, a whole title (Arts. 3:32–59) is devoted to the *rechtshandeling*, dealing with questions of its formation and validity. The German Code places the *Rechtsgeschäft* even in the very first Book, devoting almost 100 articles to it, while the French Code codifies the concept in Art. 1100-1.

ments 'based on legal consistency are apt to mislead for the common law is a practical code adapted to deal with the manifold diversities of human life, and as a great American judge has reminded us, "the life of the law has not been logic; it has been experience"' (*Read v J Lyons & Co*).

Main principles of contract law

Principles

When lawyers say that a field of law is governed by certain principles, they intend to refer to the main values or goals that underlie this field. It may be that these principles are laid down in legislation or court cases, but this need not be the case. Sometimes principles are seen as so self-evident that the official institutions do not bother to put them into writing. Thus, both the

French and the Dutch Constitution lack an explicit provision on the rule of law, while the German Civil Code does not codify the binding force of contract. As principles all refer to fundamental standards, it is difficult to prioritise one principle over another: they can contradict each other. In addition, principles are so broad that they are never without exceptions. Given this meaning, we can say that contract law is governed by four principles: freedom of contract, binding force, the absence of formalities and contractual fairness.

Freedom of contract has already been mentioned as an essential part of the liberal politics of *laissez-faire*: it gives legal application to the idea that each individual should be allowed the autonomy to make the choices they desire. If parties are best able to decide what is in their own interest, they are also in the best position to make the contract they prefer: the law presumes that a party will not choose contract terms that are unfavourable to it. Article 19 of the Swiss Code of Obligations puts this succinctly in one sentence: 'Within the limits of the law, the parties may determine the terms of their contract as they please.' But the principle of freedom of contract not only entails that a person is allowed to conclude a contract on whatever terms it deems fit (choice of contents), but also *whenever it* desires (freedom to contract at all) and with *whomever* it wants (freedom to choose the other party).

Freedom of contract

It must be clear that this principle can never be applied across the board. In the messy reality of daily life, many parties do not have the bargaining power needed to choose the terms they like best. The reality is that consumer-buyers, insurees, tenants, employees and smaller businesses often simply have to accept the terms dictated to them by their economically stronger and more experienced counterparts. Often, these terms come in the form of general conditions (see Chapter 8) that the other party is indifferent about and simply accepts without bothering to read them. This is why legislators and courts tend to intervene to protect the interests of the weaker party: contracts like employment, residential lease, consumer credit and consumer sale are governed by a myriad of mandatory laws that set limits to the freedom of the professional party. This means that sometimes so little is left of the freedom to contract that one speaks of *regulated contracts* (see Box 1.5 below).

General conditions

The second main principle of contract law is that the contract is binding upon the parties (*binding force*). Each party has to perform the obligations it took upon itself and if it fails to do so, the court can intervene at the request of the other party. We will see in Part 5 that the law can react in different ways to ensure the binding force of the contract: it can force the defaulting party to

Binding force

perform the contract (as is the normal remedy in civil law jurisdictions), or it can prefer to have the debtor pay damages (as in the common law). Both reactions, however, are evidence of the principle that a contract must be upheld. No one is forced to enter into a contract, but if one *does*, one is bound by it in the same way as if the rules therein had been made by the legislator. The French Civil Code of 1804 – drafted at the peak of the autonomy of the individual citizen – encapsulates this succinctly in its famous Art. 1103: 'Agreements lawfully entered into have the force of law for those who have made them.' This elevates a contract to the same level of bindingness as a democratically enacted statute. However, as no principle is without exceptions, here too it is possible that the binding force might be set aside, for example if the contract contains a clause that the law considers to be unfair or prohibited (Chapters 8 and 10).

The third principle is that contracts do not require any particular form (*principle of informality*). This is the necessary corollary of the rule we briefly
Informality   encountered before: if parties are legally bound to the contract because they *intend* to be bound, their intention is apparently sufficient and there is, as a matter of principle at least, no need to put the contract into writing, to utter solemn words, to visit a notary, to have a witness present, or to hand over the good in order to make it binding. Lawyers speak of the mere agreement that suffices for a contract to exist, or *consensus ad idem*. Although this principle may be self-evident to us, it has taken 2000 years of legal history to accept that most contracts can do without formalities (see Box 1.4). Throughout this book, we will encounter exceptions to the principle (see also Chapter 6).

The fourth and final main principle of contract law is that of *contractual fairness* (*Vertragsgerechtigkeit; justice contractuelle*). Of the four principles discussed in this chapter, it is the one that is the least precise. This is because views of what is 'fair' fundamentally differ. One extreme is to apply the idea that a fair contract consists of simply following what the contracting parties agreed upon when they exercised their autonomy. If an individual is in a better position than anyone else – including a judge – to decide what is in their own interest and they conclude a contract conscious of its consequences, it is fair to hold this individual to what he or she agreed upon. The famous French aphorism to describe this view is: 'Qui dit contractuel dit juste' ('the contractual is fair out of itself'). In this view the law is not concerned with the fairness of the outcome or with the extent to which a contract is in line with the public interest. The English judge George Jessel in 1875 explained it like this: 'if there is one thing more than another which public policy requires, it is that men of full age and competent understanding shall have the utmost liberty of contracting and that their contracts, when entered into freely and voluntarily,

BOX 1.4

FROM ROMAN TO MODERN LAW: *PACTA SUNT SERVANDA*

In the heyday of the Roman civilisation, in which its law reached its greatest degree of sophistication (roughly between the years 0 and 250 AD), only certain types of contract could be enforced. The abstract principle that all agreements intended to have legal effect are binding was absent. There were contracts, such as sale, lease and partnership, for which the consent of parties was indeed sufficient ('consensual contracts'), but others only became binding if some formality was fulfilled. The most frequently used formality was the so-called *stipulatio*, originally consisting of a formal question-and-answer ritual. The promisee was to ask the promisor 'Do you promise such-and such?', on which the promisor had to answer in exactly the same wording 'I do promise such-and-such.' In later Roman times, a document would be drawn up stating that the stipulatio had been observed, which practically replaced the difficult Q&A-ritual. A third category of contracts became binding on the delivery of the good ('real contracts' or *contractus re*), such as a gratuitous loan of a good for use

(*commodatum*: borrow a lion and give back the same lion) or consumption (*mutuum*: borrow wine and give back a similar quantity of a comparable wine), pledge (*pignus*) and *depositum* (deposit a good to be looked after gratuitously by somebody else). This so-called *closed system of contracts* (only those contracts that fell under one of the accepted categories were binding, whereas 'naked' agreements were not: *ex nudo pacto actio non oritur*) was taken over when Roman law was rediscovered in the eleventh century (see Chapter 2) and remained influential until the seventeenth century. Under the influence of increased commerce, Canon law (which regarded the breaking of a promise as morally wrong) and Natural law writers (such as Hugo Grotius (1583–1645), who claimed in *De iure belli ac pacis* (2,11,4,1) that 'the duty to keep promises flows from the very nature of eternal justice'), the general principle was gradually accepted that *any* agreement voluntarily entered into is sufficient to count as a binding contract.

shall be held sacred and shall be enforced by Courts of Justice' (*Printing and Numerical Registering Co v Sampson*, 1875).

Two types of fairness

This view still largely forms the basis for our present-day contract law, be it that even the most liberal of contract lawyers accept that the conditions under which contractual autonomy is exercised are often flawed, and that the law therefore needs to intervene to protect one party against the other. It could be that a party misleads another by lying about the qualities of the sold product, preventing the latter from forming his intention in the right way (Chapter 9). It could also be that a party is presumed to lack the necessary judgment

BOX 1.5

REGULATED CONTRACTS

Although the main principles of contract law discussed in this chapter adequately describe the great majority of commercial (B2B) contracts and contracts among individuals (C2C), it is beyond doubt that most contracts relevant to the average person are heavily regulated by the public authorities. There is a good reason for this: despite the presumption that everyone is free to conclude the contract he or she wants, reality is different. Economic and societal factors can have a grave impact on the freedom to choose. Some contracts are even so much constrained by mandatory laws that one can speak of 'regulated contracts'. In these contracts the main decision to be taken by parties is whether to enter into the contract, while the freedom left to decide upon its terms is severely curtailed. Good examples are employment contracts and residential leases. Both contracts are characterised by the strong bargaining position of employer and landlord – in particular in times of

shortage of labour and housing – and most jurisdictions therefore lay down detailed rules aiming to protect the employee (on dismissal, sick leave, safety at the workplace, etc.) and the tenant (on access to the property, notice, maintenance, etc.) In some cases the law sets maximum prices (as in some jurisdictions with public housing, health care, certain insurance contracts, electricity and gas), or even forces people to enter into a contract (as in countries that require their citizens to have mandatory health insurance). In particular the liberalisation of markets for energy, infrastructure (such as railways) and telecom in the 1990s opened up a wide potential for the use of contracts as regulatory instruments: what used to be public law was turned into (heavily regulated) private law. The regulation aims to ensure access to these basic services and to avoid abuse of position by suppliers.

because of age or mental illness (legal incapacity: Chapter 5). In consumer contracts, the law often requires the professional party to give all kinds of information to the consumer so that the latter can take an informed decision before entering into the contract (Chapter 6). In other words: this type of fairness (often called *procedural fairness*) requires that an unequal position among the parties is remedied, mostly by obliging a party to put the weaker one in the same position in order to allow it to make an informed decision. But once this has happened, it no longer matters that a party agrees to sell something far below its value. That contract law must in any event be concerned with this procedural fairness, as opposed to *substantive fairness*, is accepted everywhere.

Distributive function

At the other extreme, we find the view that a contract should also be an instrument to (re)distribute wealth in society. It should help the poor and the weak at the expense of the rich and the strong. If a contract clearly favours one party over the other, the law should intervene and either declare the contract void or adapt it to meet requirements of social justice. This would first require a political choice that best reflects the collective goals of society, but once this choice is made the courts should apply it when being confronted with 'unfair' contracts. It is not difficult to criticise this view. Redistribution of wealth is traditionally the domain of politics, which does so by way of progressive taxation. But when it comes to a contract, it is difficult for a judge to assess whether it contributes to social justice or not. It would turn the court into a highly political institution. What is more, it is probable that no 'stronger' contracting party will still be willing to conclude a contract with a weaker one if its bindingness is debatable. As Kötz states:

> Of course some people will fare better than others. A person is obviously going to prosper if nature has endowed him with greater abilities and talents, if his parents provide him with more capital or superior education, or if Lady Luck smiles on him more frequently. But the adjustment of differences in income and wealth in a manner consonant with standards of fairness and social justice is surely the role of tax laws and the social services which taxes pay for, rather than the mission of the law of contract.

This does not mean that no elements of substantive contractual fairness can be found in contract law. We will encounter some of these in Chapter 8.

 TOPICS FOR REVIEW

The need for contract law
Contract law and society
Voluntary exchange
The development 'from status to contract'
The different categorisations of contracts
Bilateral and unilateral contracts
The importance of contracts in the supply chain
The place of contract law in the law of obligations and in private law in general in civil law and
    common law
Juridical acts
The four main principles of contract law
The historical development towards the principle of *pacta sunt servanda*
Formal and substantive contractual fairness
Regulated contracts

 FURTHER READING

– Catherine Elliott and Frances Quinn, *Contract Law*, 10th ed., Harlow (Pearson) 2015.
– Hein Kötz, *European Contract Law Vol. 1* (translated by Tony Weir), Oxford (Oxford University Press) 1997.

– Anthony Kronman, 'Contract Law and Distributive Justice,' *Yale LJ* 89 (1980), 472
– Henry Sumner Maine, *Ancient Law*, London (John Murray) 1861.
– Study Group on Social Justice in European Private Law, 'Social Justice in European Contract Law: A Manifesto,' *European Law Journal* (2004), 661.
– Reinhard Zimmermann, *The Law of Obligations: Roman Foundations of the Civilian Tradition*, Cape Town (Juta) 1990 (paperback edition with Oxford University Press, Oxford 1996).

2

Sources of contract law

 CHAPTER OVERVIEW

This chapter examines where to look for the rules and principles of contract law. It shows that contract law flows from a variety of sources:

- the **agreement** of the parties;
- the **official national, European and supranational sources**, including national legislation and case law, European directives and international treaties;
- **informal sources**, such as European principles.

National jurisdictions differ with regard to the hierarchical place they give to each of these sources. The main rift in Europe is the one between **civil law**, which places legislation (in particular codification) at the top of the pyramid, and **common law**, which gives a predominant role to judge-made law.

Contract law is the set of rules and principles that governs transactions among parties, thereby establishing those parties' enforceable rights and obligations. This chapter investigates where we find these rules and principles. It is obvious why this is an important question: if one is not able to distinguish between the relevant contract *law* and other types of norms, either every norm could be enforced in the courts (including, for example, the rule that one must eat with knife and fork and rules and customs of the Mafia), or none at all (with a lawless society as a result). It will be seen that, while each jurisdiction recognises the same sources of law, the relative weight of these sources differs from one jurisdiction to another.

Sources

The various rules of contract law are widely diverse in nature. This chapter presents these rules on the basis of their origins. Such a categorisation on the basis of *sources* allows us to distinguish between three types of rules relevant to contract law: rules that are made by the contracting parties themselves (the party agreement), rules that emerge from the official national, European and supranational sources (official sources) and, finally, informal rules that are made by others than the official institutions, including non-state organisations and academics (informal rules). Together, these rules of contract law originating at different geographical (national, European, supranational) and actor-specific (parties, legislators, courts and other actors) levels form what is often referred to as a 'multi-level' legal system. Any lawyer should be able to find their way through this system in order to identify the precise and detailed rules needed to solve a case or advise a client. If, for example, the seller of a good is confronted with a buyer who refuses to pay the price, one needs to be able to locate the relevant statutory rules and judicial decisions.

The party agreement

Compared to many other fields of law, contract law is special in at least one important respect: the question of what is the law (in the sense of the enforceable rights and obligations of the parties) can – to a large extent – be decided by the parties themselves. Freedom of contract entails that parties are not only free to decide whether they want to contract at all, and with whom, but also that they can determine the contents of their contract. The party agreement, consisting of what the parties expressly agreed upon when entering into the contract, typically includes the price of the good or service and the qualities it must possess. For the rest, it depends heavily on the type of contract and the relationship between the parties what it is that they add to these essentials. In a commercial setting of parties who have been dealing with each other for a long time (think of a transport company that has served one particular customer for over 20 years), it is not uncommon that in the course of dealing parties only still need to agree upon the price for each transport. On the other hand, the end result of long negotiations on an international merger or takeover is usually laid down in a document of several hundred pages.

Contractual rules need not be made for one contract only. In practice commercial parties often make use of standardised sets of rules that are suited to their own interests. These so-called general conditions, or standard forms, are used by almost all professional parties (including supermarkets and retailers) for the contracts they conclude with consumers or other professional parties. The advantages of this are clear: it saves a party from having to negotiate and draft contract conditions for every new contract it wants to conclude. When used in a B2C-contract the law has always been suspicious of standard terms. In so far as the consumer is even willing to read and understand the standard terms, he is hardly ever in the position to renegotiate them: it is a matter of accepting the conditions or not contracting with this party at all.

This is why legislators and courts have developed mechanisms to avoid that the consumer is confronted with general conditions that are too one-sided (Chapter 8).

Official sources

It is clear that in most cases the party agreement alone cannot set all rights and obligations under the contract. Often, parties only discuss those elements of the contract that they consider essential (such as the price and the time of delivery), not saying anything about other aspects (such as the place of delivery or what will happen if the other party does not perform the contract). In so far as such matters are not covered by general conditions, the law should provide so-called default (or 'facilitative') rules that are auto-

Default rules matically applicable if the parties have not made any other arrangements. Default rules are thus rules that parties can deviate from: they are applicable subject to agreement otherwise and fill the gaps left open by the parties (see Chapter 7). It may also happen that parties would like to contract in a way that is considered contrary to law, public policy or good morals (such as hiring someone to steal a painting, or – to give a more disputed example – paying someone to give birth to a baby, discussed in Chapter 10). In such cases, the law may have to intervene with so-called mandatory rules that

Mandatory declare such a contract void, or at least avoidable by one of the parties. Both
rules facilitative and mandatory laws can flow from the 'official' national, European and supranational sources.

National law

Official contract law at the national level is primarily produced by the legislature and the courts. In civil law countries, general rules on contract law are typically found in the Civil Code. Thus, the French *Code Civil* (CC) of 1804 places contract law in its Book III on the different ways of acquiring property, whereas the German *Bürgerliches Gesetzbuch* (BGB) of 1900 has general provisions on juridical acts (see Box 1.3) in Book 1 and specific rules on contracts in Book 2. The Dutch *Burgerlijk Wetboek* (BW) of 1992 places the provisions on juridical acts in Book 3, on contracts in general in Book 6 and on specific contracts in Book 7. To get a better picture of the central place of contract law in these three codes, their tables of contents are reproduced below.

French Code Civil
Preliminary Title: Of the Publication, Effect and Application of Laws in General (art. 1–6)

BOOK I. OF PERSONS (ART. 7–515-13)
(...)
BOOK II. OF PROPERTY AND OF THE DIFFERENT MODIFICATIONS OF
PROPERTY (ART. 515-14–710-1)
(...)
BOOK III. OF THE DIFFERENT WAYS TO ACQUIRE PROPERTY (ART.
711–2279)
  TITLE I OF SUCCESSIONS
  TITLE II OF DONATIONS
  TITLE III OF THE SOURCES OF OBLIGATIONS
  TITLE IV OF THE GENERAL REGIME OF OBLIGATIONS
  TITLE V OF THE CONTRACT OF MARRIAGE AND OF MATRIMONIAL
  REGIMES
  TITLE VI OF SALES
  TITLE VII OF BARTER
  TITLE VIII OF THE CONTRACT OF HIRING
  TITLE VIII BIS OF THE CONTRACT OF REAL ESTATE PROMOTION
  TITLE IX OF THE CONTRACT OF PARTNERSHIP AND COMPANIES
  TITLE IX BIS OF AGREEMENTS RELATING TO THE EXERCISE OF
  UNDIVIDED RIGHTS
  TITLE X OF LOANS
  TITLE XI OF DEPOSIT AND SEQUESTRATION
  TITLE XII OF CONTRACTS OF CHANCE
  TITLE XIII OF MANDATE
  (...)
BOOK IV. OF SECURITIES (ART. 2288–2488)
(...)

GERMAN *BÜRGERLICHES GESETZBUCH*
BOOK 1. GENERAL PART (§§ 1–240)
  DIVISION 1 PERSONS
    TITLE 1 NATURAL PERSONS, CONSUMERS, BUSINESSES
    TITLE 2 LEGAL PERSONS
  DIVISION 2 THINGS AND ANIMALS
  DIVISION 3 JURIDICAL ACTS
    TITLE 1 CAPACITY TO CONTRACT
    TITLE 2 DECLARATION OF INTENT
    TITLE 3 CONTRACT
    TITLE 4 CONDITIONS AND SPECIFICATION OF TIME
    TITLE 5 AGENCY AND AUTHORITY
    TITLE 6 CONSENT AND RATIFICATION
  DIVISION 4 PERIODS OF TIME AND FIXED DATES

TITLE 11 PROMISE OF A REWARD
TITLE 12 MANDATE, CONTRACT FOR THE MANAGEMENT OF ANOTHER'S AFFAIRS AND PAYMENT SERVICES
TITLE 13 MANAGING ANOTHER'S AFFAIRS
TITLE 14 DEPOSIT
TITLE 15 BRINGING THINGS ONTO THE PREMISES OF INNKEEPERS
TITLE 16 PARTNERSHIP
TITLE 17 CO-OWNERSHIP
TITLE 18 LIFE ANNUITY
TITLE 19 IMPERFECT OBLIGATIONS
TITLE 20 SURETYSHIP
TITLE 21 SETTLEMENT
TITLE 22 PROMISE TO FULFIL AN OBLIGATION; ACKNOWLEDGEMENT OF DEBT
TITLE 23 ORDER
TITLE 24 BEARER BOND
TITLE 25 PRESENTATION OF THINGS
TITLE 26 UNJUSTIFIED ENRICHMENT
TITLE 27 TORTS
BOOK 3 LAW OF PROPERTY (§§ 854–1296)
(...)
BOOK 4 FAMILY LAW (§§ 1297–2385)
(...)

DUTCH *BURGERLIJK WETBOEK*
BOOK 1 FAMILY LAW AND THE LAW OF PERSONS
(...)
BOOK 2 LEGAL PERSONS
(...)
BOOK 3 PATRIMONIAL LAW IN GENERAL
  TITLE 1 GENERAL PROVISIONS
  TITLE 2 JURIDICAL ACTS
  TITLE 3 POWER OF ATTORNEY
  TITLE 4 ACQUISITION AND LOSS OF PROPERTY
(...)
BOOK 4 INHERITANCE LAW
(...)
BOOK 5 PROPRIETARY RIGHTS
(...)
BOOK 6 GENERAL PART OF THE LAW OF OBLIGATIONS
  TITLE 1 OBLIGATIONS IN GENERAL
  TITLE 2 TRANSFER OF CLAIMS AND DEBTS

Title 3 Torts
Title 4 Obligations from A Source Other than Tort or Contract
Title 5 Contracts in General
Book 7 Specific Contracts
Title 1 Sale and Barter
Title 2 Financial Collateral Contracts
Title 3 Donation
Title 4 Lease and Hire
Title 5 Agricultural Tenancies
Title 7 Services
Title 7A Travel Contracts
Title 7B Payment Services
Title 9 Deposit
Title 10 Employment Contracts
Title 12 Contracts for Works
Title 14 Suretyship
Title 15 Contract of Settlement
Title 17 Insurance
Title 18 Annuities
Book 7A Specific Contracts, Continued
Title 5A Instalment Sales
Title 9 Partnerships
Title 13 Loans for Use
Title 14 Loans of Consumables
Title 15 Vested or Perpetual Annuities
Title 16 Contracts of Chance
Book 8 The Law of Carriage and Means of Transportation
(…)
Book 10 Private International Law

These tables of contents of three major European civil codes reveal a number of differences in their treatment of contract law. The oldest code, that of France, is sometimes referred to as 'the code of the owner': the fact that it places contract law in the book on ways to acquire property is clear evidence of the post-revolutionary focus on property (a right 'sacred and inviolable' as the French Constitution says) as the most important right of the citizen. Until the grand reform of 2016 (see below), the French Code lacked a general part on the law of obligations. The French lawmaker sought to repair this deficiency by revamping and renaming Titles III and IV of Book III. However, it would be an overstatement to say that this led to a whole new system of French contract law: the reform was more the work of a carpenter than of an architect.

Layered
structure

The German and the Dutch Code are much more systematised: they are drafted as a coherent whole with a high level of abstraction. They both have a so-called *layered structure*, which means that the more general provisions precede the more specific ones, thus avoiding repetition. The reverse of this internal economy of the Code is that only trained lawyers are able to find their way through the scattered provisions. In the Dutch Code, for example, a contract of sale is governed by the provisions in Title 2 of Book 3 on juridical acts, by Title 5 of Book 6 on contracts in general, and by the provisions specific to the sales contract in Title 1 of Book 7 (with even more specific rules on consumer sales within this Title). A similar need to go through the entire Code exists in the German case, where one finds the juridical act in the General part of Book 1 (containing rules relevant for all areas of private law, including the law of obligations, property, succession and family law) and a whole range of different rules on the law of obligations in general (Divisions 1–7) and on specific contracts (a large part of Division 8) in Book 2.

Reforms

The French, German and Dutch Civil Codes have undergone significant changes in the last two decades. The German *Schuldrechtsmodernisierungsgesetz* (Act on the Modernisation of the Law of Obligations) of 2002 incorporated doctrines developed by the courts and academia (such as precontractual liability) and made important changes to the law of contractual remedies and consumer protection, partly to incorporate law of European origin. In the Netherlands, the change was even more radical as the country adopted a whole new Civil Code that replaced the old Code of 1838, which was based on the French *Code Civil*. The nine books of the new Code have gradually entered into force since 1970 when Book 1 was introduced (Book 10 on Private International Law became law in 2012; Book 9 on Intellectual Property is yet to be introduced and the same is true for some specific contracts that are still covered by the Code of 1838 and that are brought together in the provisional Book 7A). Partly inspired by these modernisation efforts, as well as by the wish to re-establish the French Code as an attractive model abroad, the French Ministry of Justice introduced a major reform of French contract law in 2016. Next to a reformulation and renumbering of existing provisions, this reform brought some changes in the existing law. These changes will be dealt with in the subsequent chapters.

Specific statutes

Next to the civil code, many civil law countries have more specific statutes in which contract law can be found. France, for example, has adopted a separate Consumer Code (*Code de la Consommation*) that collects and consolidates laws on consumer protection, as well as a Commercial Code that provides additional rules on B2B-contracts. Germany also keeps some laws outside

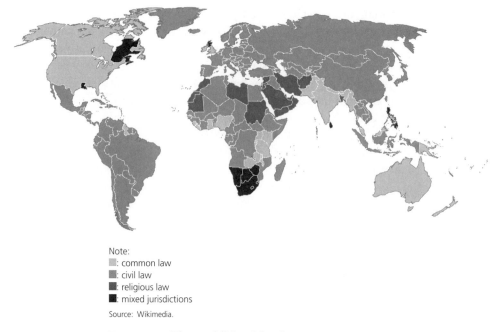

Note:
▓: common law
▪: civil law
▪: religious law
▪: mixed jurisdictions

Source: Wikimedia.

Figure 2.1 The world's legal families

the BGB, such as the Product Liability Act (*Produkthaftungsgesetz*) of 1989 and statutory implementations of recent European directives (see below).

The dominant source of contract law in the common law family is not legislation but the case law developed by the courts. The primary reaction of an English judge or lawyer when confronted with a contract case is to consult the decisions of the Supreme Court of the United Kingdom (until 2009 the judicial division of the House of Lords) and of the Court of Appeal of

English law   England and Wales. This does not mean that specific statutes on contract law are absent in England. They just do not aim to comprehensively systematise the existing law, nor do they make it redundant to consult judicial decisions. In most cases statutes only attempt to amend the common law on a particular point. The most important statutes on contract law are the Sale of Goods Act 1979, the Misrepresentation Act 1967, the Unfair Contract Terms Act 1977 and the Contracts (Rights of Third Parties) Act 1999. In 2015 the Consumer Rights Act (CRA) was introduced. This statute, essentially consolidating the English implementations of EU directives, is generally considered as the biggest overhaul in consumer law in a generation. It remains to be seen how a potential Brexit will affect the CRA.

BOX 2.1

LEGAL FAMILIES: CIVIL LAW

The world's legal systems can be categorised into groups on the basis of characteristics such as their common history, characteristic mode of legal thought, dominant sources of law and 'mentality.' The two best known of these 'legal families' are the civil law and common law family. Although this is undoubtedly a Eurocentric approach that neglects the law that existed in many parts of the world before European colonisation, it is a useful tool to map the diverse global legal landscape of today. The only national jurisdictions that are not covered by the dichotomy are so-called *mixed jurisdictions* (such as Scots and South African law, that constitute a mixture of civil law and common law elements) and countries that declare Islamic law to be the law of the State (as in for example Saudi Arabia and Iran: see Box 2.6).

The civil law family, predominant in Europe, Africa and South America, is characterised by a number of common features. First, almost all jurisdictions within the civil law tradition have a civil code as the dominant source of law. The prime examples of such codes are the French *Code Civil* of 1804, adopted under Napoleon, and the German *Bürgerliches Gesetzbuch* of 1900. Both codes were introduced after revolutionary events, namely the French Revolution of 1789 and the German unification in 1871. In both cases, the Code put an end to the legal diversity that had existed both in France and in the 39 independent German states. This reveals two important aspects of codification. It is not only a way to unify previously diverse laws, but it is also the instrument through which a national

legislator restates, simplifies, consolidates and changes the existing law, and is able to make a new start. Codification abolishes the old law. The telling story is that of the French law professor Bugnet who in the early nineteenth century told his students: 'I know nothing of civil law; I only teach the Code Napoleon.' And Napoleon himself is claimed to have said when the first commentary on his code was published that 'his' Code was now lost for good ('Mon Code est perdu').

A second feature of the civil law is that its historical roots lie in the so-called *ius commune*. Most jurists agree that one of the great lasting achievements of Roman civilisation was the private law they developed. The sixth-century compilation of this law by Emperor Justinian, now known as the *Corpus Iuris Civilis*, was rediscovered in Italy in the late eleventh century, which led to a 'second life' of Roman law. It formed the basis for law teaching at the newly founded European universities, first in Italy and later elsewhere, and was subsequently applied in practice (the so-called 'reception' of Roman law). By the seventeenth century, this reworked Roman law had become the *ius commune* (literally 'common law') of much of Europe and was applicable unless local statutes or customs ruled differently on a certain point. It was only from the end of the eighteenth century onward that Roman law was gradually replaced by national codifications. It may seem at odds with the idea of the Code as making a fresh start that its substantive rules are still based on the Roman legacy, but it is not: codification fundamentally changes the hierarchy of sources

➡

to the benefit of the (democratic) legislator, but it may still make use of the substantive rules, arguments and principles of the pre-codified time.

A third essential element of the civil law tradition is its overall mentality. This is well captured in Schlesinger's textbook on *Comparative Law*: 'The very idea of codifica-tion rests on the (…) belief that the human mind could use reason to project the solu-tion of future controversies in a systematic and comprehensive manner. (…) … a true code [is] a systematic, authoritative and direction-giving statute of broad coverage (…).' The civilian mentality is thus one of trying to systematise the law by developing principles and concepts with a view to their application in future cases. If there is any jurisdiction in which this comes out, it is German law, on which the comparatist Markesinis once wrote:

> German private law is a meticulous piece of legal engineering which, by use of concepts, attributes legal solutions to legal problems as precisely and mercilessly as a Swiss chronom-eter ticks away the years, hours, and seconds of a human life from the cradle to the grave. German law, it has been suggested, is forever prepared to sacrifice notions of justice to the altar of the concept.

In line with this, academic writing has great persuasive authority in Germany and is often quoted by the courts (in contrast to England, where at least until recently only deceased authors could be cited under the rule: 'Better read when dead').

It would be a grave mistake to assume that the dominant role of the Civil Code in civil law jurisdictions means that case law is not important. This was the naïve view of eighteenth-century legislators that indeed tried to cover every possible situation, the Prussian civil code of 1794 (the *Allgemeines Landrecht*) being a frightening example with no less than 19,000 articles. We still find a reminiscence of this in Art. 5 of the French *Code Civil* stating that 'The courts shall be prohibited from issuing rules which take the form of general and binding deci-sions on those cases which are submitted to them.' Reality is different. The Code is sometimes not only silent, but also needs interpretation in the light of the circum-stances of the case and changed views in society of what is right. The older the Civil Code, the more important it therefore is to take note of the decisions of the highest national court in civil law matters, such as the German *Bundesgerichtshof*, the French *Cour de Cassation* and the Dutch *Hoge Raad*. Art. 1 of the Swiss Civil Code (1907) well reflects how important the task of the court can still be as it assigns to the court the task of acting as a substitute legislator:

> The Code governs all questions of law which come within the letter or the spirit of any of its provisions. If the Code does not furnish an applicable provision, the judge shall decide in accordance with customary law, and failing that, according to the rule which he would establish as legislator. In this he shall be guided by approved legal doctrine and judicial tradition.

BOX 2.2

RECODIFICATION IN CENTRAL AND EASTERN EUROPE

Although this chapter discusses codification primarily in Germany, France and the Netherlands as representative jurisdictions (much of what is said for Germany applies *mutatis mutandis* to Austria, Switzerland and Greece, what is said for France often also applies to Belgium, Italy, Spain and Portugal), special attention must be paid to codification in the EU-Member States in Central and Eastern Europe. Despite the wide variety of countries involved, they all have in common that they were for several decades under communist rule and all (except for Romania, which kept its – amended – Code of 1864) adopted a new Code that was true to socialist values. In many of these countries the whole period between 1939 and 1991 is seen as one of discontinuity and all have made (or are still making) efforts to amend or replace their

Civil Codes. This was partly inspired by the wish to adapt the law to meet the needs of a market economy and attract foreign investment, but certainly also by the wish to make a fresh start, of which a new Code is typically a symbol. Thus, new Civil Codes were adopted in Lithuania (2000), Romania (2011), the Czech Republic (2014) and Hungary (2014), while efforts to develop an entirely new Code are under way in Poland (that still has its Code of 1964) and Slovakia. Estonia gradually adapted its existing Code (1993–2002) while Latvia simply re-enacted an amended version of its old Code of 1937. Outliers are Bulgaria and Croatia: they lack a comprehensive Civil Code (but have introduced separate statutes on contract law and the law of obligations) and have no plans to draft one.

European law

Contract law also flows from European sources. In the last 25 years, the European legislature has promulgated over 15 'directives' with relevance for contract law. Article 288 of the Treaty on the Functioning of the European

Directives Union (TFEU) describes a directive as a European legislative instrument that 'shall be binding, as to the result to be achieved, upon each Member State to which it is addressed, but shall leave to the national authorities the choice of form and methods'. This means that, unlike the name suggests, a

Rationale directive obliges each of the 28 EU-Member states to implement its rules into national law. After this implementation, the directive's rules are in force as if they had been created by a national legislator, be it that the Court of Justice of the European Union (CJEU) is competent to interpret the directive at the request of a national court (in the so-called preliminary reference procedure). The reason why the EU is active in the field of contract law is directly

BOX 2.3

LEGAL FAMILIES: COMMON LAW

The common law prevails in England and in almost the entire English-speaking world beyond Britain, including the United States, Australia and India. Apart from England and Wales and Northern Ireland, the other two common law jurisdictions in Europe are Ireland and Cyprus. Scotland is a mixed jurisdiction with considerable civil law influence. Scotland has its own court of appeal (the Inner House of the Court of Session), but its decisions can be challenged before the UK Supreme Court.

The most important difference between the civil law and common law tradition is the way in which the unity of (and thereby equality before) the law is maintained. In the common law, this is not primarily the task of the democratically elected legislator, but of the courts. The dominant source of private law is therefore the case law of the highest courts. The main explanation for this lies in history. Unlike on the European continent, a reception of Roman law did not take place in England. After the Norman Conquest of 1066 William the Conqueror found in place a highly fragmented law: local statutes and customs differed from one place to another and were enforced by a variety of courts. The King (and later the Royal Courts at Westminster in his name) assumed the role of highest court, which gradually led to the development of one uniform law for the whole of England. This centralisation and unification was completed around 1500, and from that time onwards it was possible to speak literally of a 'common law.' Nineteenth century attempts to replace the common law by a codification failed. In England, codification was not needed as a weapon against legal diversity (which had ceased to exist a long time before) and neither was it necessary to use it to build a nation. In addition, the ruling class regarded the idea of codification as too revolutionary. The result is that the English common law could develop uninterrupted: old case law was never 'abolished', leading to some 350,000 published cases being, in principle, still relevant today. The only way to make this mass of cases practically workable is by applying the doctrine of *stare decisis* or binding precedent, meaning that precedents coming from a court further up the hierarchy are binding for the lower court. In the UK, there is a small Supreme Court of only 12 justices that can efficiently render well-balanced decisions that become binding precedent. The court usually decides no more than 80 cases each year, dealing only with matters that the judges regard as of 'general public importance'.

Next to the emphasis on case law, a second characteristic of English law is the distinction it makes between common law and 'equity'. This distinction goes back to the Middle Ages, when the common law courts came to interpret the law in a rather strict manner. Justice-seeking individuals who were confronted with a common law court unwilling to give them what they wanted, could complain to the Lord Chancellor (later the Court of Chancery) who was allowed to grant them relief on the basis of 'equity'. Over the centuries, the case law of this equity court became a whole separate legal system side by side with the common law. It was only with the Judicature Act of 1873 that the two

←

jurisdictions were merged procedurally: the common law and equity courts were combined in one and the same court that from then on had to apply both sets of rules. The plaintiff was also no longer required to indicate whether he was seeking a common law or equitable remedy. Substantively, however, both systems have continued to exist beside each other. This is for example clearly visible in the law of contractual remedies: while the action for damages is a common law remedy, the claim for specific performance is an equitable one (see Part 5).

Also in its overall mentality, the common law is different from the civil law. English lawyers do not tend to look at the law as a coherent system, but rather as a set of *practical* rules. The German-American comparatist Max Rheinstein once put it like this:

> policies are not always followed with consistency, nor are concepts always clean-cut; the law is thought of less as a body of norms of

social conduct than as a set of rules of decision for the relatively few disputes that cannot be settled extra-judicially. (. . .) Those exbarristers who occupy the bench are close to the course of affairs and know how to decide a concrete case that is presented to the court in oral contradictory trial by the members of a highly experienced bar.

Unlike their civil law colleagues, English judges are often prepared to discuss and balance the policy considerations that underlie a particular rule in all openness. By doing so the court gives insight into the reasons for making a particular decision. English judges often adopt a personal, sometimes even literary, style, which is naturally promoted by the possibility of delivering dissenting and concurring opinions. This is consistent with the scepticism in England concerning the proposition that there is only one outcome logically considered to be correct.

related to the main aim of the EU: the development of a European single market in which the free movement of goods, services, capital and persons is ensured and in which European citizens are free to live, work and do business wherever they want. However, unlike national legislators, the EU can only act in so far as a competence to do so is provided in one of the European treaties. For contract law the source of this competence is usually found in Art. 114 TFEU, which allows the European legislator to adopt measures harmonising national provisions 'which have as their object the establishment and functioning of the internal market'. The European Commission has always been keen to argue that differences among the contract laws of the Member States hinder this internal market. In the words of the Commission itself in a Communication it issued in 2001:

> For consumers and SMEs in particular, not knowing other contract law regimes may be a disincentive against undertaking cross-border transactions. (...)

BOX 2.4

EU DIRECTIVES ON CONTRACT LAW

The coverage of contract law by EU directives is sector-specific: the European legislator never deals with contract law as a whole, but only with specific contracts (such as package travel, sale of consumer goods or timeshare), and with certain aspects of these contracts (often on information requirements vis-à-vis the consumer and contractual remedies). The great majority of the directives aim for so-called *minimum-harmonisation*: they set a minimum level of protection for the consumer and leave it to each individual Member State to offer more protection if it considers this appropriate.

The most important directives with relevance for contract law are:

- Directive 85/374 on liability for defective products
- Directive 86/653 on self-employed commercial agents
- Directive 93/13 on unfair terms in consumer contracts

- Directive 1999/44 on sale of consumer goods
- Directive 2000/31 on electronic commerce
- Directive 2002/47 on financial collateral arrangements
- Directive 2002/65 on distance marketing of financial services
- Directive 2005/29 on unfair commercial practices
- Directive 2008/48 on credit agreements for consumers (formerly Directive 87/102)
- Directive 2008/122 on timeshare (formerly Directive 94/47)
- Directive 2011/7 on combating late payment in commercial transactions (formerly Directive 2000/35)
- Directive 2011/83 on consumer rights (replacing directive 85/577 on door-to-door sales and Directive 97/7 on distance contracts)
- Directive 2015/2302 on Package Travel (formerly Directive 90/314)

Suppliers of goods and services may even therefore regard offering their goods and services to consumers in other countries as economically unviable and refrain from doing so. (…) Moreover, disparate national law rules may lead to higher transaction costs (…).

By harmonising at least some of these rules, the EU hopes that more businesses and consumers will be willing to contract across borders. If a Spanish trader would like to buy goods from a party in Germany, it may refrain from doing so because it does not know German law. A diligent party will in any event have to obtain expensive legal advice before entering into the contract. Creating a level playing field of one harmonised law must help to avoid this. Likewise, a consumer in Liège wishing to buy a TV at the Mediamarkt in Maastricht may be less inclined to do so because of diverging laws – or at least this is how the European Commission reasons.

BOX 2.5

EU POLICY INITIATIVES ON EUROPEAN CONTRACT LAW: TOWARDS A EUROPEAN CONTRACT CODE?

The European Commission, strongly supported by the European Parliament, has initiated a discussion on the future of contract law in the EU. This discussion is inspired by the criticism on the present approach of harmonisation by way of minimum-directives. This method is seen as slow, fragmentary and not very effective in view of the different national implementation techniques. In addition, the European *acquis* in this field is criticised for its inconsistencies: there is, for example, no good reason why a withdrawal right should be 14 days in one directive and only seven days in another. In 2001, the European Commission therefore published a *Communication on European Contract Law*, which sketched four options for the future:

1. no EU action, and leave problems to be resolved by the market (consumers, NGOs and businesses);
2. draft common contract law principles such as the PECL (see below), providing guidance to legislators, courts and parties, but not binding them in any way;
3. improve the quality of existing European directives;
4. adopt new EU-legislation that is not sector-specific, for example by adopting the far-going option of a European Contract Code that would replace the existing national laws.

Instead of choosing only one of these options, progress was made on each of them in the last decade:

1. retailers increasingly commit themselves to codes of conduct, allowing consumers to rely on the standards these codes set. Examples are the safety certificates issued by associations of e-commerce retailers, such as the Dutch label <www.thuiswinkel.org> and the French label <www.fevad.com>;
2. next to the PECL, several other sets of principles were drafted, including principles for specific contracts such as franchise and distribution contracts as part of the DCFR (see below);
3. the important Directive 2011/83 on consumer rights consolidates and modernises two existing directives;
4. in 2011, exactly ten years after its first communication on European contract law, the European Commission published a Proposal for a Regulation on a Common European Sales Law (CESL). This draft did not propose to introduce a full-fledged European contract code that would replace the existing national contract laws (as early as 1989 the European Parliament even suggested introducing a whole European Civil Code, but the Member States have never supported this idea), but a so-called 'optional code': a European set of rules on cross-border contracts of sale that can be chosen by the contracting parties if they prefer this over the applicability of a national law. Criticism of increasingly Eurosceptic Member States led the Commission in 2014 to withdraw the CESL proposal.

It is characteristic of EU directives that their method of implementation is left to the Member States. This leads to significant differences in implementation. While Germany and the Netherlands usually give effect to directives by inserting them into their civil codes, France collects them in its separate Consumer Code (*Code de la Consommation*). In the UK directives are transposed into the Consumer Rights Act 2015 as well as (in so far as the Consumer Rights Directive is concerned) into the Consumer Contracts (Information, Cancellation and Additional Charges) Regulations 2013/3134. It is clear that these different implementation techniques can endanger the goal of harmonisation.

Supranational law

A third source of official contract law consists of supranational rules. Long before the EU had such a pervasive influence on national contract laws by issuing directives, there have been efforts to unify parts of the law on a regional or even global scale. A successful example is the unification of conflict-of-laws rules in the context of the Hague Conference on Private International Law (established in 1893). Also parts of substantive trade law have been unified, led by the United Nations Commission on International Trade Law (UNCITRAL). Its most important achievement is the *Convention on Contracts for the International Sale of Goods* (CISG), concluded in Vienna in 1980 and in force since 1988. The CISG has been ratified in 85 states and contains rules that apply to commercial cross-border sales contracts. If both contracting parties are a business and they reside in a country that has ratified the CISG, the rules of the convention are applicable to the contract unless the parties have explicitly excluded it. For example: because Israel and the Netherlands are both a party to the CISG, an Israeli company selling oranges to a Dutch business is governed by the rules of the convention on, e.g. formation of contract and remedies in case of non-performance.

Just like the European directives discussed in the above, the CISG is inspired by the idea that the adoption of uniform rules promotes the development of international trade. This is in fact facilitated by the fact that the CISG is applicable in the world's largest economies, including the United States, China, Japan, Germany, Brazil and Russia. The most notable European trading country where the CISG is not applicable is the UK. It is said that the main reason for this lies in a lack of interest of domestic business and in the fear that London may lose its edge as one of the world's leaders in international arbitration and litigation if inroads are made on the applicability of English law. This fits in with the criticism that is sometimes expressed about the CISG. Critics argue that the CISG does not reach much uniformity in practice: despite the existence of one uniform text (be it in six authentic language versions), there is not one international court that is able to give definitive interpretations of this text. In reality, the national courts of the 80 ratifying countries all adopt diverging approaches to interpretation of the CISG, even though Art. 7(1) of the Convention requires that 'regard is to be had to its international character and to the need to promote uniformity in its application.'

Informal rules

Soft law

As is the case in many other areas of law, contract law is increasingly influenced by rules that are not officially binding, but have the status of *soft law*. Soft law can take the form of, for example, guidelines, codes of conduct, resolutions, action plans, principles and model rules. Although it is by definition not binding 'hard' law, it is important in practice for various reasons. One is that soft law is often a first step towards adopting a binding instrument: legislators tend to look at soft law as a blueprint for future statutory rules. Another is that soft law often reflects the more progressive *opinio juris*, the direction in which the law is to develop according to the cutting-edge opinion makers. This aspirational aspect of soft law can make it a very useful source in interpreting and criticising existing laws as well as in teaching the law. In the field of contract law, it can also be a reference point for parties having to draft a contract.

Principles

The best-known soft law rules in the field of contracts are so-called 'principles'. Unlike the four substantive principles of contract law identified in Chapter 1, these principles aim to identify rather detailed commonalities among different jurisdictions and put these down in the form of a rule. In so far as commonalities are difficult to find, the principles make a choice for what their drafters consider to be the 'best' rule. The three most important examples of such 'restatements' of the law are the UNIDROIT Principles of International Commercial Contracts (PICC), the Principles of European Contract Law (PECL) and the Draft Common Frame of Reference of European Private Law (DCFR).

PICC

The PICC are drafted by UNIDROIT (International Institute for the Unification of Private Law), an intergovernmental organisation founded in 1926 and located in Rome. The UNIDROIT Principles (originally published in 1994, but now in their third edition of 2010) are intended to provide a system of rules especially tailored to the needs of international commercial transactions by offering rules designed for use throughout the world 'irrespective of the legal traditions and the economic and political conditions of the countries in which they are to be applied'. The Preamble to the PICC makes clear how they can be used:

> These Principles set forth general rules for international commercial contracts.
> They shall be applied when the parties have agreed that their contract be governed by them.
> They may be applied when the parties have agreed that their contract be governed by general principles of law, the *lex mercatoria* or the like.
> They may be applied when the parties have not chosen any law to govern their contract.
> They may be used to interpret or supplement international uniform law instruments.
> They may be used to interpret or supplement domestic law.
> They may serve as a model for national and international legislators.

The PICC have come to play an important role in international commercial arbitration. If a business party from Kenya and its counterpart from the UK find it difficult to reach agreement on the law that should be applied by arbitrators in case of a dispute, they may be able to agree on the PICC as a neutral set of rules.

A comparable document are the Principles of European Contract Law, often referred to as the 'Lando Principles' after their initiator, the Danish law professor Ole Lando who assembled a group of academics from European countries to draft the text. Unlike the PICC, the PECL are a private initiative, drafted between 1982 and 1996 with the financial help of the European Commission. They have a wider scope of application than the PICC as they are intended to reflect the common core of contract law *in general* (also covering B2C- and C2C-contracts); on the other hand, they only mean to restate the contract laws of the EU Member States, and not of the entire world. As Art. 1:101 PECL makes clear, their aims are very similar to those of the PICC:

PECL

> (1) These Principles are intended to be applied as general rules of contract law in the European Union.
> (2) These Principles will apply when the parties have agreed to incorporate them into their contract or that their contract is to be governed by them.
> (3) These Principles may be applied when the parties:
> (a) have agreed that their contract is to be governed by 'general principles of law', the 'lex mercatoria' or the like; or
> (b) have not chosen any system or rules of law to govern their contract.
> (4) These Principles may provide a solution to the issue raised where the system or rules of law applicable do not do so.

BOX 2.6

ISLAMIC CONTRACT LAW

Islamic law stands apart from the civil law and common law tradition in not having a codification or accepting binding precedent. The religious law of Islam (the so-called *sharia*) consists of the norms of the *Quran* and the *Sunnah* (both seen as divine, supposedly going back directly to the prophet Muhammad) and their interpretation by Islamic scholars (*fiqh*). Judicial decisions by judges (*qadis*) – from which appeal is not possible – are not a main source of Islamic law. The best-known rules of the sharia are those that clearly deviate from Western secular values because they violate women's rights, allow stoning for adultery, or go against human rights such as freedom of expression and of sexual orientation. However, only a few countries (notably Saudi Arabia, Iran, Pakistan and Sudan) have promulgated the sharia as the exclusive law of the state. Most countries with a dominantly Muslim population (such as Egypt and Indonesia) adopt only some aspects of the sharia, while other countries (such as Turkey) do not accept it at all.

An interesting question is whether sharia contract law is any different from secular contract laws. The main principles of contract law are not. Thus, verse 5:1 of the Quran explicitly adopts the binding force of contract ('O you who believe! Fulfill [all] contracts') and verse 2:282 states that contracts can be made in any form ('But if it be a transaction which you carry out on the spot among yourselves, there is no blame on you if you reduce it not to writing'). The most important difference with non-religious contract laws concerns the question which contracts are prohibited. While secular laws prohibit contracts contrary to public policy and good morals (see Chapter 10), Islamic law prescribes that contracts should be permitted by religion (or, in other words, should be *halal*). This means that contracts relating to, for example, alcohol, tobacco, pork, pornography, gambling or prostitution are not allowed (and are therefore *haram*). Islamic market indices (see e.g. www.djindexes.com/islamicmarket) therefore provide lists of stocks in companies that comply with the sharia.

A remarkable difference between Islamic law and national jurisdictions is the prohibition of claiming interest on loans. Verse 2:275 of the Quran states: 'those who consume interest cannot stand [on the Day of Resurrection] except as one stands who is being beaten by Satan into insanity. (…) Allah has permitted trade and has forbidden interest.' Islamic jurists argue about the exact reason for this prohibition (that can, by the way, also be found in the Old Testament in Deuteronomy 23:19). Some say that a loan in Islam is always a charitable act, which therefore does not allow the making of profit. Others simply hold that if Allah imposes a rule one should not look for any worldly explanation. But regardless the reason for the rule, banks in both the Islamic and Western worlds have developed *halal* alternatives for loans bearing interest. One of these alternatives is *musharaka*, a form of joint venture in which both the lender and the borrower participate in profits and losses alike. In the last two decades many Western banks have opened *Islamic windows* facilitating Islamic banking, including interest-free Islamic mortgages.

DCFR The third set of principles worth mentioning consists of the *Draft Common Frame of Reference of European Private Law.* The so-called Study Group on a European Civil Code, the main drafter of the DCFR, sees itself as the successor body to the Commission on European Contract Law that drafted the PECL. The DCFR published in 2009 builds upon the PECL, partly because it covers other fields of private law (mainly torts and property) and partly because it deals with a range of specific contracts that are not dealt with in the PECL (sale, lease of goods, contracts for services, mandate, agency, franchise, distributorship, loan contracts, personal security and donation). Much more than the PICC and PECL the DCFR aims at being a model for the European legislator. This is evident from the – German law inspired – structure of the DCFR that consists of ten books, including a general part. The DCFR can easily be read like a civil code. But much more important is the use that can be made of the DCFR and other sets of principles in *teaching* the law: it is now common practice in many European countries to compare the national law with PECL and DCFR, thus providing a true common frame of reference for European teaching.

 TOPICS FOR REVIEW

Sources of contract law
Contract law as a multi-level legal system
Default rules
The place of contract law in the French, German and Dutch Civil Code
The layered structure of the German and Dutch Civil Code
Contract law outside the Civil Code in civil law jurisdictions
Legal families and where to find them
The main differences between the civil law and common law family
Codification in Central and Eastern Europe
The aim, form and problems of European legislation on contract law
Minimum harmonisation
Policy initiatives on European contract law
The aim and scope of application of the CISG and the extent to which it is successful
The relevance of soft law for the law of contract
The various sets of principles of contract law and their functions
Islamic contract law

 FURTHER READING

– Hugh Beale et al, *Cases, Materials and Text on Contract Law, Ius Commune Casebooks for the Common Law of Europe,* 2nd ed., Oxford (Hart Publishing) 2010, Chapter 3.
– Raoul van Caenegem, *Judges, Legislators and Professors,* Cambridge (Cambridge University Press) 1987.
– James Gordley and Arthur Taylor Von Mehren, *An Introduction to the Comparative Study of Private Law: Readings, Cases, Materials,* Cambridge (Cambridge University Press) 2006.
– Basil S. Markesinis, Hannes Unberath and Angus Johnston, *The German Law of Contract: A Comparative Treatise,* 2nd ed., Oxford (Hart) 2006.

– Ugo A. Mattei et al, *Schlesinger's Comparative Law: Cases-Text-Materials*, 7th ed., New York (Thomson Reuters) 2009.
– Matthias Reimann and Reinhard Zimmermann (eds.), *Oxford Handbook of Comparative Law*, Oxford (Oxford University Press) 2006.
– Max Rheinstein, *Gesammelte Schriften Vol. 1*, Tübingen (Mohr) 1979.
– Jan Smits, *The Making of European Private Law*, Antwerp-Oxford-New York (Intersentia) 2002.
– Jan Smits and Caroline Calomme, 'The Reform of the French Law of Obligations: Les Jeux Sont Faits', *Maastricht Journal of European and Comparative Law* 23 (2016), 1040.
– Omar Salah, 'Islamic finance: the impact of the AAOIFI Resolution on equity-based *sukuk* structures', *Law and Financial Markets Review* (2010), 507.
– Konrad Zweigert and Hein Kötz, *An Introduction to Comparative Law* (translated by Tony Weir), 3rd ed., Oxford (Oxford University Press) 1998, Part B.

Part Two

The formation of a contract

Three main requirements need to be met before a contract is validly concluded:

- **Agreement of the parties**, usually consisting of an offer by one party (the offeror) and acceptance of this offer by the other party (the offeree) (Chapter 3)
- **An intention to create legal relations**; under English law supplemented by the requirement of **consideration** to be provided by each party, and in the French legal tradition by the requirement of **causa** (Chapter 4)
- **Legal capacity of the parties** (Chapter 5)

Although a contract is in principle binding without any form, sometimes certain **formalities** have to be fulfilled in addition to these requirements (Chapter 6).

3

Offer and acceptance

Civil codes, legal doctrine and case law of any jurisdiction in the world define a contract as a legally binding agreement. The two following definitions of the French *Code Civil* and the European DCFR express the same thought:

> **Art. 1101 CC**: 'A contract is an agreement of wills among two or more persons intended to create, modify, transfer or extinguish obligations.'

> **Art. II-1:101 (1) DCFR**: 'A contract is an agreement which is intended to give rise to a binding legal relationship or to have some other legal effect. (…)'

The question when exactly the necessary agreement exists (sometimes referred to with the Latin phrase *consensus ad idem*) is usually answered by dissecting the contracting process in terms of offer and acceptance. A contract only exists if one party (the offeror) has made an offer (*offre, Antrag, aanbod*) and the other party (the offeree) has accepted this offer by way of an acceptance (*acceptation, Annahme, aanvaarding*). This model is a convenient way of analysing the negotiations or any other previous contacts between the parties: by identifying an offer and a corresponding acceptance, it becomes clear from which exact moment in time the contract comes into existence. *Before* the acceptance, no one is bound to do anything under the contract, while *after*

BOX 3.1

THE RELATIVE IMPORTANCE OF THE OFFER AND ACCEPTANCE MODEL

The model of offer and acceptance is universally applied in both civil law and common law jurisdictions. It was developed in the seventeenth and eighteenth centuries when trade and travel expanded and more and more contracts were made among people who could not see each other face-to-face. It must be remembered that the question of when an offer is made and acceptance is sent does not arise as long as contracts are concluded between bystanders. In that case, the communication is instantaneous and it is immediately clear if parties have reached agreement or not. Offer and acceptance as the *mechanics* of contract formation only become indispensable when the parties are at a distance from each other and time lapses between their declarations of offer and of acceptance (because they send letters or exchange e-mails). This rationale makes it somewhat artificial to identify offer and acceptance in case parties are in each other's presence, as when a customer buys something in a shop or when a notary drafts a deed that is signed simultaneously by the parties.

Despite the universal use of the offer and acceptance model by courts and academics, not all civil codes use the terms. The French *Code Civil* (Art. 1113) only does so since 2016. Art. 6:217 (1) of the Dutch Civil Code resolutely states that 'A contract is concluded by an offer and the acceptance thereof.'

acceptance one party (in case of a unilateral contract) or both parties (in case of a bilateral contract) are bound. This offer is often made explicit, as when Adelina tells her twin sister Viorelia that she can buy her wedding dress for € 150, but it can just as often be inferred from the circumstances of the case, as when a supermarket puts products on the shelf in order to be bought by its customers.

There are five important issues that need to be discussed concerning offer and acceptance:

Five questions

- What is an offer and how to distinguish it from a mere invitation to enter into negotiations?
- Can an offer be revoked before it is accepted by the offeree?
- How long does the offer last?
- What are the requirements that the acceptance must meet?
- What is the time of conclusion of the contract?

This chapter addresses these five questions.

What is an offer?

A. General

Article 2:201 (1) PECL states the following:

> A proposal amounts to an offer if:
> (a) it is intended to result in a contract if the other party accepts it, and
> (b) it contains sufficiently definite terms to form a contract.

Invitation

This provision represents what all European systems have in common when defining an offer. The offer must be such that it creates a contract if accepted by the other party. This requires that the offer indicates both the *intention* of the offeror to be bound and the *terms* by which the offeror is willing to be bound (think of the price of the goods and possibly the time of delivery). If both these requirements are not met, there is no offer at all, but at best an invitation to the other party to enter into negotiations (also called an invitation to treat in England, an *invitatio ad offerendum* in Germany, an *offre de pourparlers* in France and a *uitnodiging om in onderhandeling te treden* in Dutch). Only if the invitee finds such an invitation attractive enough, it can decide to make an offer itself, leaving it to the original invitor to either reject or accept it.

Binding offer

It is not difficult to tell an offer from an invitation if the proposal itself indicates that it is to be seen as a 'binding offer'. Things are also easy if the offer contains the clause that it is made 'subject to agreement', 'subject to confirmation', 'without any obligation', 'freibleibend' or 'sans engagement', or makes use of similar wording. Often, however, the statements made by the offeror are more vague and may incite the other party to think that an offer was made. In such a case, it is decisive how the proposal would be understood by a reasonable person in the position of the offeree: could such a reasonable person believe that an offer was made? It cannot be denied that this is a vague criterion. As the English legal historian John Baker once wrote: 'Despite many judicial expeditions to find him, the reasonable man has not been reduced into captivity.' This means that the criterion needs to be substantiated by reference to case law.

A good example is provided by the English case *Gibson v Manchester City Council* (1979). Mr. Gibson was the tenant of a house who was interested in buying it. After having completed an application form, the City Council sent him a letter stating that it 'may be prepared to sell the house to you' for £1,180. When Mr. Gibson said he found the price too high because of the bad condition of the path to the house, the Council replied it did not want to change the price. On 18 March 1971 Mr. Gibson wrote to the Council to 'carry on with the purchase as per my application'. Shortly after, the political winds in Manchester changed and the Council decided to no longer sell municipal property. Mr. Gibson claimed that the letter of the Council constituted an offer that he had accepted on 18 March. However, the court did not find an offer in the Council's letter: this was only an invitation to the tenant to make an offer. Mr. Gibson had subsequently done so on 18 March, but the Council had not accepted it. A reasonable person in the position of Mr. Gibson could not have believed that the Council's letter, only containing the price of the house, was an offer that only needed to be accepted by the offeree in order to form a contract.

Definitiveness
The offer must also contain sufficiently definite terms. This is the logical consequence of the very nature of an offer: if an offer can bring about a contract by a simple 'Yes, I accept', it must contain all essential elements by which the parties will be bound. If I propose to sell you three paintings from my art collection, this would usually not qualify as an offer: we will first need to know which specific paintings you are interested in. Any agreement that is too vague or incomplete will therefore not be regarded as a binding contract. This does not mean that the parties need to have reached agreement on all possible details, but they do need to agree on what they consider as vital. In case of a sales contract, this will include the good to be sold and the price (Art. 1583 of the French *Code Civil* even requires this explicitly). For the rest, Art. 6:227 of the Dutch Civil Code well expresses what any jurisdiction would accept: 'The obligations the parties take upon them, must be determinable.' If Julieta sells Argentinian beef to William, they will have to agree on the quantity and the price and anything else they find essential (such as, perhaps, that the meat emanates from eco-friendly cows). But they are free to say that they leave for example the place and time of delivery to be decided upon by a third party ('Delivery on future dates as indicated by the restaurants mentioned in the annex to this contract').

B.   Offers to the public: advertisements

An offer does not have to be directed towards a specific person. It can also be addressed to the general audience. Many products are put up for sale in advertisements, ranging from a used study book advertised by a student who no longer needs it, to clothing, food and consumer electronics advertised in magazines or leaflets distributed door-to-door, on television or on a website.

Proposal to public
Although all jurisdictions concur that in case of such a *proposal to the public* the rule also applies that it only amounts to an offer if the offeree could rea-

sonably believe that an offer was made, the outcome of this test differs from one jurisdiction to another. Some jurisdictions regard an advertisement as an offer, others only as an invitation to treat.

French and Dutch law

In French and Dutch law, an offer to the public is binding in the same way as if it had been made to a particular person. In one of the leading French cases (*Maltzkorn v Braquet* of 1969), a Mr. Braquet placed an advertisement in a local newspaper advertising a plot of land for sale for FF250,000 (€ 38,000). Mr. Maltzkorn saw the advert and accepted the 'offer', as he said. Mr. Braquet denied that he was bound, arguing that an advertisement can never be a binding offer. However, the *Cour de Cassation* could not find any legal basis for this rule and considered it possible that an advertisement is a binding offer to the public that binds the offeror to the first person who accepts it. This does not mean that any advertisement is an offer. If the personal qualities of the other party are of interest to the offeror, as is undoubtedly the case in employment contracts and credit agreements, but also in case one wants to rent out an apartment or buy a house (or indeed a plot of land, as in the French case), these are usually contracts *intuitu personae*. An illustration of this is provided by the Dutch case of *Hofland v Hennis* (1981), in which a house in the Dutch town of Bussum was put up for sale in a local newspaper. The advertisement contained the address, the price and details of the layout of the house. When Mr. Hennis had visited the house, he told the seller that he accepted his offer. However, when the sale had to be closed, the seller refused to cooperate with the transfer of the house, arguing that no contract had come into being. The Netherlands *Hoge Raad* denied that an offer had been made:

> An advertisement offering to sell a specific property at a certain price does in principle not qualify to be interpreted by potential offerees as anything else than an invitation to enter into negotiations, whereby matters such as the price, additional conditions of the purchase and the prospective buyer may be of importance.

English and German law

Contrary to French and Dutch law, English and German law do not accept that an advertisement to bring about a bilateral contract can amount to an offer. It merely invites potential customers to make an offer to the seller to buy the good. In the curious case of *Partridge v Crittenden* (1968), Lord Parker of the High Court put it like this: 'I think when one is dealing with advertisements and circulars (...) there is business sense in their being construed as invitations to treat and not offers for sale.' This conclusion was beneficial to the advertiser Mr. Partridge, who had put on sale in a magazine 'Bramblefinch cocks, Bramblefinch hens, 25 s. each.' As it happened, these birds were protected by law and Mr. Partridge was charged by the Royal Society for the Prevention of Cruelty to Animals (RSPCA) with unlawfully offering the cocks and hens. However, as the advertisement was only seen as an invitation to treat, he could not be convicted. German law adopts the same position.

More interesting than describing this difference between the French-Dutch and the English-German approach is *why* it exists. What are the policy reasons behind treating an advertisement as a mere invitation to treat instead of as an offer? The rule is clearly to the advantage of the seller, who can still decide after the advertisement was published whether he wants to deal with the interested party or not. This may even lead to further negotiations to the seller's benefit who by contrast in French law is in principle bound by the stated price – something that French supermarkets take pride in, using slogans such as 'Un prix affiché est un prix tenu' ('We stick to the price we published'). What the French and Dutch could contend against this view is that their rule at least protects customers against a seller who advertises at a low price to lure people into his shop or onto his website, and then makes up some excuse for not selling to them. In addition, it is argued in Germany and England that, as an advertisement can be read by anyone, the advertiser cannot be expected to sell to all interested parties as stocks are always limited. This last argument, in turn, does not convince the French and the Dutch as they assume that an offer will automatically lapse when the stock is finished. This is again a matter of the reasonable person: the offeree cannot reasonably expect that the offeror is still willing to sell if the products are sold out. This is also the position taken by Art. 2:201 (3) PECL:

> A proposal to supply goods or services at stated prices made by a professional supplier in a public advertisement or a catalogue, or by a display of goods, is presumed to be an offer to sell or supply at that price until the stock of goods, or the supplier's capacity to supply the service, is exhausted.

No matter how one appreciates these different policy arguments, there is one important practical difficulty with the English-German approach. In some cases the advertiser simply wants to be bound to its proposal by the mere acceptance of somebody else without the need to negotiate. The police may wish to offer a reward for information that can lead to the arrest of a criminal, or a driver may wish to park her car in car park with a ticket machine. Buying a Coca-Cola can from a vending machine falls in the same category of cases. In such cases French and Dutch law have no trouble finding an offer that is accepted when the other party performs the act for which the reward, service or product was offered. If these were only invitations, a binding contract

would not emerge from providing information, parking one's car or quenching one's thirst. It lies in the very nature of these announcements that the advertiser demonstrates a serious intention to be bound to potential respondents. This is why English law regards these as offers for a unilateral contract. In the case of parking one's car, the Court of Appeal held in the case *Thornton v Shoe Lane Parking* (1971), per Lord Denning:

> The customer pays his money and gets a ticket. He cannot refuse it. He cannot get his money back. He may protest to the machine, even swear at it. But it will remain unmoved. He is committed beyond recall. He was committed at the very moment when he put his money into the machine. The contract was concluded at that time. It can be translated into offer and acceptance in this way: the offer is made when the proprietor of the machine holds it out as being ready to receive the money. The acceptance takes place when the customer puts his money into the slot.

Another classic illustration of regarding an advertisement for a unilateral contract as an offer under English law is provided by the *Carbolic Smoke Ball* case (see Box 3.2).

Meanwhile, German law provides another solution in case of an advertisement for a reward (*Auslobung*). § 657 BGB states:

> Anyone offering by means of public announcement a reward for undertaking an act, including without limitation for producing an outcome, is obliged to pay the reward to the person who has undertaken the act, even if that person did not act with a view to the promise of a reward.

This provision places the reward outside contract law. It regards the announcement of a reward as an independent juridical act that out of itself creates the legal effect that whoever undertakes what is necessary is entitled to the reward. Interestingly, this means that even if the finder of a lost laptop was not aware of the €1,000 reward announced by the owner, she can still claim the money. However, the advertiser may withdraw the offer for the reward before the necessary act is performed (§ 658 (1) BGB).

Website The above rules are not any different in cases where goods are offered for sale on a website. Although European directives require online sellers to supply the consumer with extensive information on the product, giving them the possibility to withdraw from the contract within 14 days after delivery (see Chapter 6), the offer and acceptance question is governed by the respective national laws. German and English law therefore regard advertising goods on a website as non-binding invitations to treat. This proved convenient when in 1999 Argos accidentally put Sony televisions up for sale at a price of £2.99 instead of £299: orders of customers were not acceptances but offers to buy that could easily be rejected by the UK retailer.

BOX 3.2

FROM THE CARBOLIC SMOKE BALL TO THE HOOVER FLIGHTS FIASCO

One of the best-known English contract law cases is *Carlill v Carbolic Smoke Ball Co*, decided by the Court of Appeal in 1893. The background to the case is formed by the flu pandemic that killed one million people worldwide between 1889–94. During this period, a business called the Carbolic Smoke Ball Company produced and sold a product called the 'Carbolic Smoke Ball', filled with phenol and aimed at providing protection against the potentially lethal influenza virus. The company placed several advertisements in newspapers to market the product. One such advertisement, published in the Pall Mall Gazette in November 1891, read as follows: '£100 reward will be paid by the Carbolic Smoke Ball Company to any person who contracts the increasing epidemic influenza colds, or any disease caused by taking cold, after having used the ball three times daily for two weeks, according to the printed directions supplied with each ball. £1000 is deposited with the Alliance Bank, Regent Street, showing our sincerity in the matter. (…).' A Mrs. Carlill bought one of the balls and used it as instructed. Unfortunately, she still contracted influenza and decided to claim the £100. The company refused to pay, arguing that the ad was not meant as an offer, but was a mere advertising hype that was not to be taken seriously.

The company's argument was rejected by the court. Bowen LJ reasoned in the following way:

> It was also said that the contract is made with all the world – that is, with everybody; and that you cannot contract with everybody. It is not a contract made with all the world. There is the fallacy of the argument. It is an offer made to all the world; and why should not an offer be made to all the world which is to ripen into a contract with anybody who comes forward and performs the condition? It is an offer to become liable to any one who, before it is retracted, performs the condition, and, although the offer is made to the world, the contract is made with that limited portion of the public who come forward and perform the condition on the faith of the advertisement. It is not like cases in which you offer to negotiate, or you issue advertisements that you have got a stock of books to sell, or houses to let, in which case there is no offer to be bound by any contract. Such advertisements are offers to negotiate – offers to receive offers (…). If this is an offer to be bound, then it is a contract the moment the person fulfils the condition. That seems to me to be sense (…).

Mrs. Carlill was therefore entitled to the £100 reward. She died (not of influenza) in 1942 at the age of 96.

The main lesson a good lawyer would learn from this case is that marketing efforts should go hand in hand with measures to limit liability. If advertising for free trips to exotic places, T-shirts, or dinners in expensive restaurants is seen as an offer that becomes a binding unilateral contract as soon as people satisfy the requirements, it is necessary to limit the time during which the promotion is valid, or to add to the offer that it only lasts until the stock is exhausted. No doubt the biggest marketing disaster

➡

in UK history was caused by forgetting to consult the in-house lawyer on this important point. When in 1992 the British division of electronics manufacturer Hoover wanted to get rid of its surplus stock of washing machines and vacuum cleaners, it promised free airline tickets to continental Europe and the US to anyone buying more than £100 worth of their products. The action was a big success: Hoover had 200,000 extra customers (with not surprisingly a high interest in the Turbopower Total System vacuum cleaner, priced just over £100). However, the collateral damage consisted of Hoover Britain having to pay £50 million on air tickets, leading to such financial difficulties that the company had to be taken over by a competitor in order to survive.

Products offered on websites are considered as offers under French and Dutch law. In a case similar to Argos (*Stichting Postwanorder v Otto BV*, 2008) the Dutch court therefore had to find a different way of dealing with a clear mistake in the advertisement. In this case online retailer Otto had offered for sale a Philips HD Ready LCD TV for €99.99. This proved to be an attractive offer: in six days, 11,000 customers ordered 14,000 televisions through the Otto website. All customers received an automatic e-mail confirming their order. When Otto refused to deliver, claiming that there was an obvious mistake in the pricing of the product, dissatisfied customers took Otto to court. The Court of Appeal in Den Bosch made clear that an offer was made by Otto, but denied that a valid contract had come into being:

> The question is whether the consumers at the moment they accepted the offer – thus at the moment they ordered over the internet – could reasonably assume in the circumstances of the case that this offer was correct. (…) The answer to this question is dependent on what an average consumer, i.e. a consumer who is as informed as the average person, can expect. One can expect from a consumer who is planning to buy an LCD TV that they prepare themselves generally on the prices of LCD TVs. If this consumer subsequently sees that the Otto website offers for sale:
>
> a) an HD ready widescreen LCD television
> b) of A-brand Philips
> c) with a screen diameter of 80 cm
> d) for a price of €99.90 or €99.00
> e) with in red capitals the qualification 'NEW'
> f) while there is no indication that this is a one time stunt offer, a blockbuster or in any other way a 'special' offer,
>
> then this consumer must understand that there is an inaccuracy. An average informed consumer knows, or at least should know, that the prices of comparable LCD televisions vary between €700.00 to approximately €1,300.00.

> Even if the consumer does not immediately recognise the error, the difference in price is so considerable that in any case there must have been doubt. In case of doubt about the correct price, the consumer should have further investigated the matter. (…)

In order to address this problem, many websites provide specific rules to the consumer on how to order, avoiding the situation where the online seller is bound too soon. A website could for example state that the prospective buyer only becomes bound if he submits a form and that the seller is to confirm the order. A common clause is that 'By completing and submitting the following electronic order form you are making an offer to purchase goods which, if accepted by us, will result in a binding contract.' It follows from European law that in cases where the online seller makes use of such a special procedure, it must communicate to the consumer the technical steps to follow in a clear, comprehensible and unambiguous way prior to the order being placed (Art. 10 of EU Directive 2000/31 on electronic commerce). This explains why many websites require the consumer to click his way through several 'I agree'-boxes before the contract is finally formed.

C.   Offers to the public: goods on display in shops

Not only advertisements can qualify as offers to the public: if goods are put on display in a shop or a window, the question also arises whether the customer can claim that the good is to be sold to him at the indicated price. If the law says he can, this means that the shopkeeper is obliged to sell to anyone who is willing to pay the price. The contrary view implies that bargaining is still needed, giving the seller the freedom to select whom he wants to serve. In the latter case a shop does not have to stick to the price tag it put on the product, nor does it have to sell the item at all: the shopkeeper can simply tell the customer to go somewhere else.

Policy arguments The policy arguments behind the choice that the various jurisdictions make are identical to those in case of a public offer by way of an advertisement. It therefore does not come as a surprise that French and Dutch law consider the display of goods in a shop as an offer, while English and German law in principle do not. The customer at a Tesco in Bath actually makes an offer to buy to the cashier (acting on behalf of the shop) at the checkout and it is up to the cashier whether or not to accept this offer. The cashier's colleague at the Casino supermarket in Bourg d'Oisans, however, cannot but conclude that the customer has accepted the offer by the time the latter has reached the till.

The leading case *Pharmaceutical Society v Boots* (1953) provides an interesting reason for the English approach. Display of goods in a shop could never qualify as an offer for a bilateral contract because, in the words of Somervell LJ, 'once an article has been placed in the receptacle [basket, shopping cart] the customer himself is bound and would have no right, without paying for the first article, to substitute an article which he saw later of a similar kind and which he perhaps preferred'. But this is a false reason. It can also be argued that the acceptance of the buyer takes place at the till at the moment of check out – even though French law did indeed adopt the peculiar position that Somervell criticises in the case of the *Exploding lemonade bottle* of 1964. In this case, a bottle of Vittel lemonade that had just been taken out of the basket at the checkout exploded and injured the customer. The French court held that the customer could claim damages in contract (which was easier for her to do than file a tort claim) as, in the words of the Court of Appeal:

> the sale takes place as soon as the customer, seeing an item marked with a price the client is prepared to accept, places the item in the basket or bag made available to her and which she is required to use until the goods are checked out by the employee at the till.

This leaves as the main policy reason for the English position – as we saw before with the advertisement – that it reserves to the shop the right to do business with whom it wants, possibly putting it in a better position to negotiate. But while this may be true for the bespoke tailor, the antiques shop and the art dealer, it is difficult to see the argument in a world dominated by Sainsbury's, Kaufhof and H&M. In addition, the freedom of a business not to accept a customer is limited by anti-discrimination rules, not only in the UK but in any other European country.

Can an offer be revoked?

Once it is established that a binding offer was made, a second question emerges: is it possible for the offeror to revoke his offer before the offeree has brought about the contract by acceptance? Revocation (*révocation, Widerruf, herroeping*) of an offer means that the offeror is no longer bound by his offer. Allowing revocation is clearly in the interest of the offeror, who may have discovered that he is able to sell the goods at a much better price to somebody else and therefore wants to end his dependency on the offeree. The offeree on the other hand relies on the offer and may have taken action as a result before formally accepting (for example by negotiating a loan from a bank, or trying to find potential customers to whom he can resell the products). Different jurisdictions weigh these two interests in different ways.

Germany German law is at one end of the scale (and the same is true for other countries in the German legal tradition such as Austria, Switzerland and Greece). § 145 BGB reads as follows: 'One who has offered to conclude a contract with another is bound by that offer unless he states that he is not bound.' This provision leaves no doubt that the offeror cannot revoke his offer. If Jonas offers for sale to *Bild* some private pictures of Sylvie van der Vaart and receives a better offer from *Express* a few days later, he cannot run away from the offer he made; the only thing he can hope for is that *Bild* will reject his offer. But Jonas is bound if it is accepted. Of course, he does not have to wait indefinitely: if a reasonable period has expired during which he does not hear anything from the offeree, Jonas is again free to offer the pictures to anyone else (see below). To avoid this uncomfortable position, he can of course limit the validity of the offer by telling *Bild* that it is only made *freibleibend* (subject to change) or that he reserves the right to revoke it. This follows from the fact that the rules on offer and acceptance are only default rules and can be set aside by the parties if they wish (see Chapter 2).

It is important to note that there is one self-evident case in which an offer need not be revoked. This is not only true in German law, but also in any other jurisdiction. An offer is a declaration of intention that naturally needs to reach another person before it can become effective. If the offeree does not know of the offer – which can only happen if some means of distance communication such as e-mail or post were used – no harm is done if the offer is withdrawn by the offeror. It is therefore generally accepted that an offer may be retracted if the withdrawal (*rétractation, Widerruf, intrekking*) reaches the offeree before or at the same time as the offer. The withdrawal then simply 'overhauls' the offer; the result is as if it was never made. Art. 1115 CC, Art. 3:37 (5) Dutch Civil Code and § 130 (1) BGB explicitly provide so, as does Art. 1:303 (5) PECL.

England English law is at the opposite end of the scale. Revocation is always allowed: an offer can be revoked at any time before it has been accepted, even if the offeror included a deadline for acceptance in the offer. If Adele offers her veterinary practice for sale to James and tells him that 'a definite answer needs to be given within six weeks', she can still revoke it regardless of the time limit. The reason for this extreme view lies in a peculiar requirement of English contract law called the doctrine of *consideration*. Consideration will be explained in detail in Chapter 4, but at its core lies the idea that a promise can only be enforced if the other party does or promises something in return. In the case of an offer, the offeree does not provide any consideration and therefore the offer is not binding. This sounds harsh on the offeree and indeed English law is exceptional in adopting this position in the common law world. The Uniform

Commercial Code (UCC), the uniform law that governs commercial transactions in almost the entire US, has for example abandoned the English view and provides that 'firm offers' are not revocable 'during the time stated or if no time is stated for a reasonable time' (Section 2-205). If an English offeror is determined to give the other party the right to accept the offer within a set time, it can always make an 'option contract', for which consideration does exist, but this may be too complicated in normal day-to-day transactions.

France French law and most other jurisdictions that stand in the French legal tradition such as Belgium adopt an intermediate position. It is settled case law of the *Cour de Cassation* since 1919 that any offer is revocable before acceptance, but that this revocation is abusive (and therefore a tort under Art. 1240 *Code Civil*) if it frustrates the legitimate expectations of the offeree. This is the case if the offer contains a time period within which it is to be accepted (*offre avec délai*), or if the offeree could reasonably believe that the offer would remain open for a reasonable time (*offre avec délai raisonnable*). This does not mean that revocation does not have effect in these two cases, but the offeror must compensate the damage the offeree suffers as a result (for example the costs of travel to inspect the goods or the lost profits on other deals the offeree turned down). The new Art. 1116 CC contains a rule to this effect.

Despite the different approaches of these three jurisdictions, there is unanimity among the drafters of international texts such as the CISG (Art. 16), PECL PICC (Art. 2.1.4), PECL (Art. 2:202) and DCFR (Art. II-4:202). Art. 6:219 of the Dutch Civil Code also adheres to this position. Art. 2:202 PECL speaks for all others:

> (1) An offer may be revoked if the revocation reaches the offeree before it has dispatched its acceptance (…).
> (2) An offer made to the public can be revoked by the same means as were used to make the offer.
> (3) However, a revocation of an offer is ineffective if:
> (a) the offer indicates that it is irrevocable; or
> (b) it states a fixed time for its acceptance; or
> (c) it was reasonable for the offeree to rely on the offer as being irrevocable and the offeree has acted in reliance on the offer.

How long does the offer last?

It was seen above that, except in German law, an offer can in principle be Lapse revoked, after which it is no longer in existence. If the offer is accepted, the contract comes into being. But what if the offeror does not revoke the offer, or is not allowed to do so, and the offeree does not accept it either? Does this mean that the offer stays open forever? It is clear that this would be too great a burden on the offeror. Commercial intercourse would come to a near standstill if an offer remains open until the offeree is so good to give a definitive answer. The law therefore provides rules on when an offer ceases to exist. This so-called *lapse* (*caducité, Erlöschung, verval*) of an offer exists in the following circumstances.

A.   The offer is rejected

If Ahmed offers to lease his Audi A6 to Caroline for €200 per month and she says no, she is not able to come back the next day and still accept the offer. She will have to make a fresh offer to Ahmed, who is subsequently free to accept or reject it. The PECL put this succinctly in Art. 2:203: 'When a rejection of an offer reaches the offerer, the offer lapses.'

Counter-offer   In case Caroline's initial reaction were that she was willing to lease the car for €100, this is seen as a *counter-offer* that also terminates Ahmed's original offer. It does not make a difference whether the time fixed for acceptance has expired or not. In the English case of *Hyde v Wrench* (1840), Wrench offered to sell his farm to Hyde for £1,000 and two days later Hyde offered £950, which was rejected by the seller. When Hyde then told the seller that on second thought he agreed to buy for £1,000, the seller was no longer bound to his offer: the offeree's counter-offer had terminated it.

B.   The time for acceptance expires

§§ 146–148 of the German BGB read as follows:

> § 146 An offer expires if a refusal is made to the offeror, or if no acceptance is made to this person in good time in accordance with § 147 to 149.

> § 147 (1) An offer made to a person who is present may only be accepted immediately. This also applies to an offer made by one person to another using a telephone or another technical facility.
> (2) An offer made to a person who is absent may be accepted only until the time when the offeror may expect to receive the answer under ordinary circumstances.

> § 148 If the offeror has determined a period of time for the acceptance of an offer, the acceptance may only take place within this period.

Circumstances   These provisions reflect what any jurisdiction would accept (see also Art. 2:206 PECL). The offer lapses if the time that the offeror has set for acceptance expires. An offer 'valid until 30 April 2014' can no longer be accepted on 1 May. If no time has been fixed, acceptance must take place within a reasonable time. How long this is will depend on the circumstances of the case. As the German Code implies, an answer can be expected in the very same conversation if the offer was made face-to-face or in any other type of real time (instantaneous) communication (such as telephone, Skype and online chat). If the offer is made *inter absentes* (for example by post, e-mail or WhatsApp), much depends on the speed of the means of communication (someone who sends his offer by regular mail cannot expect an answer on the next day: the offeree can generally be expected to make use of the same means of communication for transmitting his answer) and on the subject matter. An offer to buy fresh fish, or any other perishable good, will usually last for a shorter period than an offer to buy a painting. If the price of the product is susceptible to market fluctuation (as in case of shares on the stock market), a reasonable period may even be a matter of seconds.

What are the requirements that the acceptance must meet?

The contract is concluded when the offer is accepted. This acceptance (*acceptation, Annahme, aanvaarding*) will usually take place in writing or orally. It does not have to meet any specific requirements as long as it makes clear to the offeror that the offeree unconditionally agrees with the terms of the offer (English law speaks of the 'mirror image' rule: the offer must be mirrored by an acceptance). If it does not, it is at best a counter-offer that 'kills' the original offer. Art. 2:204 PECL reflects this:

(1) Any form of statement or conduct by the offeree is an acceptance if it indicates assent to the offer.
(2) Silence or inactivity does not in itself amount to acceptance.

Prescribed method

It is not uncommon that the offer specifies the method of acceptance. This means that it indicates, for example, in what form the acceptance must be sent and to whom it must be addressed. For example, the offer could prescribe: 'Acceptance must take place by returning the attached form', or indicate that any replies are 'to be sent by registered delivery'. This raises the important practical question what happens if a disobedient offeree simply sends an e-mail containing his acceptance. Does this mean that the contract is not concluded? In other words: is the specified method of acceptance exclusive or not? The answer naturally depends on how the offer should be interpreted. Normally, the offeree will have to comply with the specified method of acceptance. But if the only reason why the offeror prescribed a certain method is to ensure a speedy reaction, the offeree's use of another method that achieves the same purpose also forms a valid acceptance. English law seems to get this right. Thus, in *Tinn v Hoffman* (1873), it was held that that if 'post' is described, a quicker method is fine as well. And if 'registered or recorded delivery' is required, an ordinary letter is also acceptable (*Yates Building Co Ltd v R.J. Pulleyn & Sons (York) Ltd*, 1975).

Silence
An important question is whether silence can count as acceptance of the offer. Article 2:204 (2) PECL reflects the view of any jurisdiction that silence 'in itself' does not suffice. There is good reason for this. If Anna writes an email to Agustin in which she offers to buy his Aquariva Super for €100, adding 'If I do not hear from you before next Monday at noon, you have accepted my offer', Agustin's mere silence cannot be seen as evidence of his intention to sell the boat. It may be that he did not receive the e-mail or thought this was a joke. The true reason, however, is that the law is generally suspicious of such surprise tactics. This is also why so-called inertia selling is prohibited by the EU Directive on Consumer rights, which states in Art. 27:

> The consumer shall be exempted from the obligation to provide any consideration in cases of unsolicited supply of goods, water, gas, electricity, district heating or digital content or unsolicited provision of services (…). In such cases, the absence of a response from the consumer following such an unsolicited supply or provision shall not constitute consent.

Despite the law's general aversion to considering silence as an acceptance of an offer, it is not impossible. Most examples deal with commercial relationships. Thus, in a case decided by the French *Cour de Cassation* in 1988, the parties had agreed that the buyer could exercise an option to buy an amusement park attraction from the seller by proposing a price and that the seller would then reply within 14 days. After the offeree had exercised the option by offering FF100,000 (€15,000), he did not hear anything from the seller. The court found that the silence amounted to acceptance. It is clear that, in cases like this, silence never comes alone: it is usually accompanied by a whole range of surrounding circumstances such as previous negotiations between the parties, a long-standing business relationship and thereby a course of business that parties are used to, the need for a speedy reply, etc. The French speak of a *silence circonstancié* ('circum-
Confirmatory note
stantial silence'), now codified in the new Art. 1120 CC. Another example is the commercial practice of so-called confirmatory notes (*Bestätigungsschreiben* in German). If parties have been in negotiations and are almost ready to enter into a contract, one of them is likely to send a 'confirmation' of what they orally agreed upon, summarising the main points and possibly adding its general con-

BOX 3.3

BATTLE OF THE FORMS

It is not always easy to apply the offer and acceptance model. A notoriously difficult question is what happens if each party uses its own general conditions. A commercial buyer of goods will usually send a written purchase order with reference to the general conditions it uses on the back or in the attachment. These conditions are obviously designed to be the most beneficial from the buyer's perspective. The seller is then likely to confirm the receipt of the order with reference to his conditions, naturally drafted with a view to *his* interests. This does not pose a problem if the standard forms are not in conflict with each other, but this is rarely the case. The question then is how to solve this 'battle of the forms'. A strict application of contract law rules results in the conclusion that no contract at all has come into being for lack of agreement. But this would be an absurd outcome: parties were agreed on the main points, have often already started to perform, and only find out about the differing standard forms at a later stage. Another

solution is to apply the 'first shot' rule: the conditions of the offeror prevail unless they were explicitly rejected in the acceptance (a rule adopted by Art. 6:225 (3) Dutch Civil Code). English law adopts a different solution. It considers each new reference to general conditions as a counter-offer; if this offer is accepted by performance of the obligation (such as delivery of the goods), the offeree is presumed to have accepted the general conditions referred to in the latest offer (the 'last shot' prevails). But the criticism of both solutions is that it is often mere coincidence who fired the first or the last shot. This is why German law adopts yet another solution, the so-called 'knock out' rule. This rule entails that general conditions only become part of the contract in so far as they are common in substance. If they are different, they 'knock out' each other, leaving the resulting gap to be filled by default rules (called 'terms implied in law' in England, as we shall see in Chapter 7). This is also the solution adopted by Art. 2:209 PECL and Art. 2.22 PICC.

ditions. German case law firmly states that if the other party does not agree with the document, it must quickly reject it at the risk of being bound.

Another phenomenon that is not uncommon in practice is that the offeree does not formally accept the offer, but *acts* as if it has accepted it. Sometimes, Conduct we do not even realise that there is such *acceptance by conduct*: only an eccentric would tell a taxi driver that he accepts his offer when opening the door of the car. Another example is an offeree who refrains from sending back the order form, but simply starts to deliver the goods to the offeror who willingly accepts them. And if KLM offers to buy ten A380 airliners and Airbus already starts to paint the planes in white and blue, this may also amount to acceptance. The criterion in each of these cases is whether there is a need to communicate the acceptance to the offeror or whether the latter can already reasonably infer from the circumstances that his offer was accepted.

What is the time of conclusion of the contract?

The final question to be addressed in this chapter is at which moment in time the contract is concluded. The obvious answer is 'upon acceptance of the offer', but the truth is that one can have different views of when exactly the acceptance has to take effect. There is no need to think about this if the contract is concluded while both parties are present (as in a shop), or make use of an instantaneous means of communication such as the telephone or FaceTime). But this is different if time passes between the various moments necessary to form the acceptance. Consider the following example:

> On 1 May, Brad offers for sale to Amélie the Golden Bear he won at last year's Berlin film festival. On 2 May, Amélie saves in her 'drafts' folder a draft e-mail in which she accepts Brad's offer. On 3 May at 23.58, she sends the message to Brad, who receives it in his mailbox on 4 May at 00.03. On 5 May, Brad checks his e-mail and reads Amélie's acceptance.

In this example there are four possible moments at which the acceptance takes effect:

Four theories
(a) the moment the message containing the acceptance is written (2 May), known as the externalisation theory;
(b) the moment the message is sent or posted (3 May), the expedition or dispatch theory;
(c) the moment the message is received by the offeror (4 May), the receipt theory;
(d) the moment the offeror reads the message (5 May), the actual notice theory.

Before we discuss which of these theories is applied in practice, it is important to realise why the question is relevant at all. One reason is, of course – as we saw before – that from this moment onwards the offeror can no longer revoke his offer. Another is that the parties need to know as of when they have to perform the contract. In addition, many jurisdictions (including France, Belgium, England and Poland) make the transfer of property dependent on the conclusion of the contract: once the contract of sale is formed, the buyer becomes the owner of the good, even if the actual delivery did not yet take place (as is required in for example German and Dutch law).

Shortlist Only two of the four mentioned theories are serious candidates to be short-listed in an economically viable jurisdiction. Both the externalisation theory and the actual notice theory suffer from a lack of practicability. In the above example, it will be difficult to establish when Amélie wrote the e-mail or when Brad actually read it. If the actual notice theory was applied, it would also open the door to unscrupulous manipulation by the offeror. All he needs to do to prevent the contract from being concluded is to leave his mail unopened.

It is therefore not surprising that all jurisdictions adopt either the expedition or the receipt theory. The clearest proponents of the latter are German, French and Dutch law, all three followed by the PECL.

> § 130 (1) BGB: 'A declaration of intention to another, if it is made to another in his absence, is effective at the moment when it reaches him. (…)'

> Art. 1121 CC: 'A contract is concluded as soon as the acceptance reaches the offeror. (…)'

> Art. 3:37 (3) BW: 'A declaration addressed to a specific person must have reached ('bereikt') this person in order to have the sought legal effect. Nevertheless, if such a statement has not reached this person or it did not reach him in time, and this is merely a result of his own actions, of the actions of other persons for whom he is responsible, or the result of other circumstances which justify that he is accountable for any disadvantage caused by it, then this statement will still have its originally intended legal effect.'

> Art. 2:205 (1) PECL: 'If an acceptance has been dispatched by the offeree the contract is concluded when the acceptance reaches the offeror.'

This is a sensible approach: the acceptance (or any other declaration) takes effect when it reaches (*zugeht, bereikt*) the addressee, meaning that it has entered into his sphere of influence. This puts the risk of the message getting lost *before* arrival in the hands of the sender (which seems right because he has chosen the medium and route of communication), while the risk of the message not being read *after* arrival lies with the recipient. This is also what the clumsily formulated second sentence of Art. 3:37 (3) Dutch Civil Code aims to express. The example mentioned in the well-known textbook by Zweigert and Kötz is that of the bird lover who chooses not to empty the letterbox in his garden for fear of scaring the birds within: then, the declaration is treated as having arrived. Other examples are not regularly checking one's e-mail or simply deleting unread e-mails out of fear that the sender has indeed accepted the offer.

Is the receipt theory so sensible that all jurisdictions accept it? The outlier in Europe is English law (other common law-jurisdictions, including the US, adopt the same position). English law makes a sharp distinction between instantaneous and non-instantaneous communication. In the former case, if parties sit opposite each other or speak to each other over the phone, the receipt theory is applied. The famous example given by Lord Denning is the following:

> Suppose, for instance, that I shout an offer to a man across a river or a courtyard but I do not hear his reply because it is drowned by an aircraft flying overhead. There is no contract at that moment. If he wishes to make a contract, he must wait till the aircraft is gone and then shout back his acceptance so that I can hear what he says. Not until I have his answer am I bound.' (*Entores Ltd v Miles Far East Corporation*, 1955)

The motivation for this is that the offeree will know when his acceptance was not communicated to the other party, and can try again. This reasoning can also be applied to other instant methods of communication, such as the use of telex (as the Court of Appeal held in the *Entores* case), and probably also fax and online chatting. In all these cases, the acceptor is likely to know whether its communication has reached the other party or not: fax machines and chat services tend to indicate a failure in sending the message. An interesting question is whether communication by e-mail must also be seen as instantaneous. The problem with e-mail is that the moment the 'send' button is pressed is not always the same moment the message is received at the other end (as in the above example). During busy times e-mail servers tend to store the message and deliver it later without the sender necessarily noting this. Sometimes, e-mail even gets lost in cyberspace. Although the English courts have yet to decide on the question, it seems likely that they will not treat e-mail as a form of instantaneous communication.

The relevance of all this is that in case of non-instantaneous communication, such as sending a letter by regular post, English law does not accept the receipt theory. Instead, it adopts the expedition theory, usually referred to in England as the *postal rule* or *mailbox rule*. This follows from a decision made in 1818 in the case of *Adams v Lindsell*, at a time when the use of postal services was becoming increasingly popular. The postal rule entails that the acceptance becomes effective at the moment of posting and not when it is received by the offeror. This means that in the above example the contract is formed on 3 May. It is good to consider the implications of this view.

First, the postal rule implies that the contract is formed even in cases where the letter containing the acceptance never arrives at its destination, for example because it gets lost in the post. Contrary to the receipt theory the Policy reasons postal rule thus favours the offeree by putting the risk of a late or lost acceptance on the party that made the offer. The historical reason for this is that the rule was formulated in a time when the post was not too reliable and it was easier to prove that one posted a letter than it is to prove that it was received by the other party.

Second, the practical effect of the postal rule is that it limits the possibility of revocation by the offeror. It was seen above that under English law revocation is always allowed before acceptance. If the acceptance has already taken effect when it is posted, the effective time left to revoke the offer is restricted. This is even more so as the revocation of an offer must reach the offeree before it becomes effective. The classic illustration of this rule is provided by the High Court case *Byrne & Co v Leon van Tienhoven & Co* (1880). Van Tienhoven posted a letter in Cardiff on 1 October, offering tinplates for sale to Byrne in New York. Byrne received the letter on 11 October and immediately telegraphed acceptance. But on 8 October Van Tienhoven had posted a letter revoking its offer because of the fact that tinplate prices had risen by 25 per cent. The court found that the postal rule should not be applied to a revocation, leading to the result that a contract had in fact been formed. Lindley J considered that any other conclusion would lead to extreme injustice and inconvenience:

> If [Van Tienhoven's] contention were to prevail no person who had received an offer by post and had accepted it would know his position until he had waited such a time as to be quite sure that a letter withdrawing the offer had not been posted before his acceptance of it.

The practical relevance of the now almost 200 years old postal rule is sometimes questioned. In today's world less and less communication takes place by regular mail, and even where it does postal services tend to be more reliable than they were in the nineteenth century. However, the postal rule is still applied and has even found new applications with the rise of modern technology. Telemessaging (which has replaced the use of telegrams), e-mail and texting through mobile phones are also likely to qualify as non-instantaneous forms of communication and are therefore governed by the postal rule – even though the highest courts of England have not yet had the opportunity to decide as much.

TOPICS FOR REVIEW

Consensus ad idem
Offeror and offeree
The importance of the offer and acceptance model
Offer and invitation to enter into negotiations
Offers to the public
Rewards
Goods on display in shops
Revocation of an offer
Withdrawal of an offer
Rejection and counter-offer
Lapse of an offer
Acceptance
Battle of the forms
Time of conclusion of the contract
Acceptance theories
Postal rule

 FURTHER READING

– John H. Baker, 'From Sanctity of Contract to Reasonable Expectation?,' 32 *Current Legal Problems* (1979), 17.
– Hugh Beale et al, *Cases, Materials and Text on Contract Law, Ius Commune Casebooks for the Common Law of Europe*, 2nd ed., Oxford (Hart Publishing) 2010, Chapter 6.
– Catherine Elliott and Frances Quinn, *Contract Law*, 10th ed., Harlow (Pearson) 2015, Chapter 1.
– Hein Kötz, *European Contract Law Vol. 1* (translated by Tony Weir), Oxford (Oxford University Press) 1997, Chapter 2.
– Peter Nayler, *Business Law in the Global Marketplace: The Effects on International Business*, Oxford (Elsevier) 2006, Chapter 2.
– G.H. Treitel, *The Law of Contract*, 14th ed. by Edwin Peel, London (Sweet & Maxwell) 2015.
– Ewan McKendrick, *Contract Law: Text, Cases and Materials*, 7th ed, Oxford (Oxford University Press) 2016.
– Arthur Von Mehren, *The Formation of Contracts*, IECL VII-9, 1992.
– Rodolfo Sacco, 'Formation of contracts', in: Arthur Hartkamp et al (eds.), *Towards a European Civil Code*, 4th ed. Nijmegen (Ars Aequi) 2011, Chapter 20.
– Rudolf B. Schlesinger, *Formation of Contracts: A Study of the Common Core of Legal Systems*, Dobbs Ferry (Oceana) 1968.
– Francois Terré, Philippe Simler and Yves Lequette, *Droit civil: les obligations*, 11th ed., Paris (Dalloz) 2013, Book 1, Title 1.
– Konrad Zweigert and Hein Kötz, *An Introduction to Comparative Law* (translated by Tony Weir), 3rd ed., Oxford (Oxford University Press) 1998, Chapter 26.

4

The intention to create legal relations

CHAPTER OVERVIEW

An essential element of a contract is that parties have the **intention to be legally bound** to their agreement. This chapter discusses:

- **when** the intention to be legally bound exists;
- **how** the test of earnestness is applied in different types of agreements (commercial, gratuitous and disadvantageous as well as social and domestic agreements).

In addition to the intention to create legal relations, English law requires that the contractual promise be supported by **consideration**. This means that a party must give, do or promise something in return for what it obtains from the other party. Jurisdictions in the French legal tradition, though no longer French law itself, require that the contract have a **causa**. This chapter also explains these extra requirements.

Consensus ad idem

A legally binding contract must, in addition to meeting the requirement that the parties have the intention to create legal relations between themselves, also ensure that the agreement of the parties consists of an offer and a corresponding acceptance. This means that parties not only need to agree on the same thing (a meeting of minds, or *consensus ad idem*), but they also need to agree that what they agree upon is binding in law, meaning that each of them can go to court and enforce the agreement if necessary. The difference between a mere agreement and an agreement with intended legal consequences becomes clear if one thinks of a person who promises his fiancée to take her to dinner tomorrow evening. If he does not show up, no sensible person would claim that she can go to court and force her partner to feed her. Of the vast majority of promises that people make in their lives, we can say at best that it would be *morally* wrong not to keep them. Breaking a promise may have many negative consequences for the friends that we keep, for the people we love and for the reputation we have – but none of this is the law's business. A contrary view would make society unliveable and would flood the courts with futile cases.

All modern jurisdictions accept the intention to create legally binding relations as the criterion to distinguish binding promises or agreements from statements that do not qualify as such. The PECL put this succinctly in Art. 2:101 (1) by stating that a contract is concluded 'if the parties intend to be legally bound' and 'reach a sufficient agreement'. As we saw before (Chapter 1), this provision is the end result of a long historical process in which the law of contract moved from accepting the binding nature of only certain contracts towards the general principle of *pacta sunt servanda*. Of course, the exact formulation may differ from one legal system to another, but they all adhere to the same thought. While the Dutch Art. 3:33 BW plainly states that 'a juridical act requires an intention to create legal relations, which intention becomes manifest in a declaration', the well-known English textbook of Treitel on *The Law of Contract* requires a similar 'intention of creating legal relations.' In *K Speditionsgesellschaft* (1956), the German *Bundesgerichtshof* spoke of the 'intention to create a legal commitment' ('Rechtsbindungswille') while the French analyse a contract as a 'meeting of intentions' ('rencontre des volontés').

Despite this common core of the world's legal systems on how to separate binding from non-binding agreements, one cannot say that the criterion is without its problems. This chapter looks into three main questions that can be asked about the intention to create legal relations:

Three questions

- What is the intention of the parties and when does it lead to agreement?
- What test of earnestness is to be applied in problematic cases in which there is doubt about a party's intention?
- How does the legal intention relate to another requirement that some jurisdictions pose for the valid formation of a contract, namely the common law requirement of *consideration* and the French requirement of *cause*?

What is the intention of the parties? The objective approach to agreement

All communication has two parts: a sender and a receiver. While the sender aims to convey a certain message by putting it into words, the receiver interprets the message in a certain way. Luckily, in the great majority of cases sender and receiver understand each other perfectly well, but these are not the cases that lawyers are interested in. Many things can prevent the intended message from being received accurately. If you rent 'the first floor' of my house and I understand this to refer to the rooms on the first level above the ground, while you believe to have rented the ground floor, our intentions differ. Likewise, if we agree that you will 'clean my house' for €50 and you believe this only means to clean the inside, while I meant you would also wash the windows on the exterior, what have we agreed upon, if anything?

These examples show that it is not always clear what the intention of the parties is when making a contract. But there are not the only cases in which a *Dissensus* so-called *dissensus* of intention and declaration exists. Next to the misunderstandings mentioned above (parties disagree as a result of their use of vague terms), parties can also fall prey to a slip of the pen or the tongue (they say '40' in their offer but they mean '4') or send their message to the wrong person (your e-mail to book a room in a B&B is not sent to zimmer@gmail.com as intended, but to its more expensive competitor zimmer@hotmail.com). It can also happen that someone declares he wants to conclude a contract while being under the influence of stress, alcohol or drugs, or being hypnotised or mentally ill, and later argues this is not what he intended.

The law has to deal with this problem of diverging intention and declaration in various stages of the life of the contract. In the stage of formation, different intentions may stand in the way of the parties actually having reached an agreement (discussed in this chapter). Once this hurdle is overcome, and the *consensus ad idem* is present, it may be that the parties still quarrel about what they could expect as to the qualities or the value of the good that they bought possibly leading to avoidance of the contract (a question of *mistake*, discussed in Chapter 9), or about what it is that they actually agreed upon in their contract (a question of interpretation, discussed in Chapter 7).

As a matter of legal technique, the problem of *dissensus* is treated differently in different jurisdictions (see Box 4.1). However, the criterion that is used and the results that are reached do not fundamentally differ. Contract law is *Objective* *approach* not interested in the parties' mental state of mind: all legal systems accept that it is impossible to look into the mind of man. The approach is instead to look for an objective meaning of the used words rather than to try to discover what the 'real' intention of the parties was. In the law, intention is always imputed. Decisive is what the words or actions of the other party suggest to a reasonable person in the position of the promisee. This is a sound view because a person making a statement must always realise that the addressee is likely to rely on what he thinks it means. This puts a responsibility on the person expressing himself. It is useful to look at some different formulations of this objective approach.

BOX 4.1

DISSENSUS: DIFFERENT WAYS TOWARDS A SIMILAR RESULT

A contract is not concluded if there is no meeting of the minds. This means that *dissensus* (the intention and declaration of a party differ) prevents the formation of a contract, albeit that the reasonable reliance of the other party is protected. While this objective approach to contract formation is accepted in all European jurisdictions, the doctrinal technique used to reach this result differs from one legal system to another.

In French law, any *dissensus* is regarded as standing in the way of the valid formation of a contract (cf. Art. 1101, 1128 CC), but if the other party could reasonably believe the first party intended to say what it did, the latter is to compensate the other party for the damages on basis of tort (Art. 1240 CC). German law regards a 'mistake in the declaration' (*Erklärungsirrtum*) as a ground to avoid the contract on basis of § 119 I BGB (cited in Chapter 9). However, as

in French law, a party's reasonable reliance is protected by way of a damages claim: § 122 BGB prescribes that 'the person declaring must (...) pay damages (...) for the damage that the other (...) party suffers as a result of his relying on the validity of the declaration.' The Dutch Art. 3:35 BW provides a third alternative by prohibiting a party from invoking the discrepancy between intention and declaration against someone who could reasonably rely on this party's declaration. The effect of this is that the juridical act is concluded as if there is consensus. The English solution, finally, is a highly practical one. Again, the absence of a meeting of the minds prevents the contract from coming into being. But whether or not there is a meeting of the minds is assessed objectively: reasonable reliance on a party's declaration will bring the contract about.

The classic English case is *Smith v Hughes* (1871), in which Blackburn J held: 'If, whatever a man's real intention may be, he so conducts himself that a reasonable man would believe that he was assenting to the terms proposed by the other party, and that other party upon that belief enters into the contract with him, the man thus conducting himself would be equally bound as if he had intended to agree to the other party's terms.'

In *K Speditionsgesellschaft* (1956), the German *Bundesgerichtshof* considered: 'The question of whether there is an intention to be legally bound should not be decided according to some inward intention of the person giving the service which has not been made apparent. It should be determined by whether the recipient of the service should have concluded from the actions of the person providing the service that there was such an intention in the given circumstances according to the principle of good faith and having regard to business custom. It is therefore a question of how the actions of the person providing the service appear to the objective observer.'

Art. 3:35 BW: 'The absence of intention in a declaration cannot be invoked against a person who has interpreted another's declaration or conduct in conformity with the sense which he could reasonably attribute to it in the given circumstances, as a declaration of a particular meaning made to him by that other person.'

Art. 2:102 PECL: 'The intention of a party to be legally bound by contract is to be determined from the party's statements or conduct as they were reasonably understood by the other party.'

The French textbook of Terré, Simler and Lequette on *Les obligations* states: 'Since the consent of the parties is a psychological phenomenon, it can only lead to a contract if it is externalised in order for the other party to be understood.'

Factors

What this means in practice only becomes clear in the circumstances of each individual case. Courts apply the objective approach by looking at factors such as:

- How easy it is for the addressee to investigate whether the declaration was really intended to mean what it says. If a shop offers to sell the latest state-of-the-art television at a price of €99 only, it is fairly easy for the customer to ask if this is a stunt offer or if perhaps a mistake was made (as in the case of *Stichting Postwanorder v Otto* (2008), discussed in Chapter 3). In such a case, a reasonable consumer should doubt the intention of the seller and without further investigation by the buyer a contract has not come into existence. This is different in cases where the other party has no reason to doubt what is said. If someone orders a curtain at Kwantum of four metres, while he actually means five, the salesperson normally does not have any reason to believe this was not what the buyer intended. This is simply a mistake that is the fault of the buyer (an example of what is called *culpa in contrahendo*, fault in contracting).
- Whether the transaction would be beneficial for one of the parties. A promise to provide free services or to sell a house far below its value should make the other party doubt about the true intentions of the promisor. In the Dutch case of *Hajjout v IJmah* (1983) the foreign employee Mr. Hajjout, who only knew a few words of Dutch ('such as bread, milk and holidays', as the court observed), was dismissed on the spot and asked by his employer to sign a piece of paper waiving all rights following from the termination of the contract. The *Hoge Raad* held that 'the employer will have to investigate with reasonable care whether the

employee understood that he was asked to agree with ending the employment contract' because of the severe consequences this can have for the employee (such as losing one's job without any claim to social security).

- What is customary in a certain branch or location. The stock example is someone who visits an auction and waves to a friend sitting at the other end of the room. It is customary at auctions that raising one's hand means that one bids on the object. If the auctioneer could reasonably believe that the visitor was making a bid, a contract has come about.

- The meaning of the disputed term in everyday speech. This meaning will prevail unless special circumstances dictate that the term should be understood differently by a reasonable person in the position of the addressee. If a person, when talking to friends, constantly refers to her old Lada as her 'Mercedes', and then decides to sell this 'Mercedes' to one of these friends, the buyer cannot claim that the contract does not exist arguing that he did not intend to buy a Lada. In contract law, the literal meaning of words as contained in the dictionary is never decisive. So if a party uses a technical term, it is relevant whether this party could expect the other party to know of its meaning. If parties are in the same line of business, the meaning a term has in that context prevails.

- The place of contracting. If the seller intended to get paid in US dollars, but the buyer had in mind Canadian dollars, the place where the contract was made or the location of the bank may reveal to a reasonable person what was agreed upon.

- The expertise and experience of the parties. A more sophisticated party, or one that is assisted by experts, should make greater effort to make sure that the other party understands what its intention is than a layperson. A municipality buying land from an individual will have a hard time invoking the technical meaning of terms in the contract if it has not made any effort to inform the seller about these terms at the time the contract was made.

The effect of the objective approach to agreement is that the party who justifiably relies on the contents of the other party's unintended declaration can claim that the contract has come into being. Only in cases where it is impossible to find one meaning of an ambiguous term on an essential point of the agreement (meaning that a reasonable person would find more than one meaning plausible), is there no agreement. A nice example of this is provided by the French case of *Société Tirat et Cie v Société Orazzi et Fils* (1961). Orazzi intended to buy 2,000 hectolitres of wine to be transported to Algiers. Tirat offered to sell the wine at FF60 per hectolitre. Orazzi found this too much and sent a telegram that it was willing to buy for FF30, but due to a mistake the text read 'FF300'. The seller naturally accepted and delivered the wine.

BOX 4.2

THE BASIS OF CONTRACTUAL LIABILITY: WILL, EXPRESSION AND RELIANCE

One of the most discussed questions in the European legal literature of the late nineteenth and early twentieth century was why exactly a contract is binding. The debate received impetus from the German case *Oppenheim v Weiller*, decided in 1856 by the local court in Cologne. Oppenheim intended to send his broker Weiller a written message to *buy* shares on the stock market, but due to a mistake made by the telegraph operator, Weiller received a message to *sell* shares. Weiller now had to deliver the shares, which he first had to buy himself at great loss because they had risen in value. The court found that Oppenheim was liable in damages. In cases like this, three theories compete to be applied. In the *will theory* (in line with the emphasis on the autonomy of parties as discussed in Chapter 1), the internal will of a party is decisive. However, even if it were possible to discover in hindsight what this internal intention must have been (something that future neuroscience will perhaps be able to discern with the help of brain scans), this cannot be decisive. The other party is not able to read the person's mind at the time of contracting. In addition, if the will were indeed decisive, a party could always claim after having declared something that it has changed its mind and now no longer wants to be bound. Adopting

this view would clearly disrupt society. The other extreme is the *expression theory*. It looks at what a party has declared, regardless of what its intention was. This favours too much the interest of the addressee, who could then even claim a contract was concluded if it knew, or had to know, that the declaration was not in conformity with what the other party intended (perhaps Weiller knew that Oppenheim did not have any shares in the company to sell). The third theory is the *reliance theory*. In its original version, this theory applies the criterion that a party is bound if it could reasonably rely on the other party *performing* in line with the declaration that it made. A more viable version is the one that finds decisive whether there is reliance on the *will* of the other party to be bound (the *will-reliance theory*, as for example adopted by the Arts. 3:33 and 3:35 of the Dutch Civil Code). This debate on the foundations of contractual liability still continues today. Next to the just-mentioned theories, numerous other views have been proposed to explain why one is bound to a contract. Well-known theories explain the contract as a *Geltungserklärung* (Karl Larenz), as a *speech act* (John Austin), as a *promise* (Charles Fried), or as a means to advance the objective of economic efficiency (Richard Posner).

When the contract was later disputed by Orazzi on the ground that he did not intend to buy the wine for a price five times as high as the original offer, the court held that no contract had come into being as the parties' intentions differed. This so-called *erreur-obstacle* ('mistake-obstacle') literally expresses that the mistake a party has made prevents the meeting of the minds.

Some comparative lawyers assert that French law gives more weight to the
subjective intention of the parties than other jurisdictions. If a party can

Difference?

prove that it did not intend to declare as it did, the internal will would prevail
and the contract is not seen as validly concluded. It is true that legal doctrine
in France puts more emphasis on the will of the parties, but it is hard to say if
this is also reflected in court practice. If it is, it would mean that French courts
would be less willing to uphold a contract in cases where a party's intention
and declaration diverge. If this were so, it would not mean that the reasonable
expectations (*confiance légitime*) of the other party are not protected. It only
may take place in a different way, for example by forcing the party that reck-
lessly made a declaration that did not accord with his intention to pay
damages in tort for the losses suffered by the relying party.

The test of earnestness in problematic cases

Now that the intention of the parties as a requirement for the valid formation
of a contract has been considered, a second question must be asked: when is

Legal question

this intention directed towards the creation of legal relations? The first thing
to say is that this is a *legal* question: the law decides when such an intention
exists. It is usually not a problem to 'find' this intention in cases where the
respective promises of the parties are more or less of the same value, or if the
parties are sophisticated businesspeople who can take care of their own interests (as in commercial agreements). However, the law is much more reluctant
to enforce purely gratuitous promises or promises among family members or
friends (domestic and social agreements). This is because it finds it much
less likely that someone would wish to be legally bound in these situations.
The law, suspicious as it is of altruism, presumes that a party will only bind
itself *legally* if it is to gain from the transaction.

In the following, these various types of situations will be discussed in some
detail. Next to commercial agreements (A) and gratuitous and disadvanta-

Four categories

geous transactions (B), we will look at agreements in the social sphere (C)
and at promises in a domestic (usually family) context (D). In each of these
situations, the question is how to apply the test of earnestness. We will find
that the distinction between promises serious enough to be enforced in the
courts and non-binding promises is primarily a matter of what society finds
appropriate.

A.   Commercial agreements

Parties to commercial contracts are assumed to have the intention of being
legally bound. The reason for this is that it lies in the very nature of com-

mercial parties that they make contracts, and that if they do not wish to be bound, they should take appropriate measures to prevent this from happening (for example by agreeing on a 'subject to contract' clause: see below). This assumption exists in all jurisdictions, but it is perhaps the strongest in English law in which there is even a legal presumption that a commercial agreement is legally binding. Such a presumption means that it is for the other party to prove that it did *not* intend to be bound, which is difficult in practice. In the English case of *Bear Stearns Bank plc v Forum Global Equity Ltd* (2007), Forum Global was one of the creditors of the insolvent Italian dairy company Parmalat. When it became clear that Forum Global would receive back some of the money it had lent to Parmalat, it sold the title to this loan to investment bank Bear Stearns in New York for almost €3 million. This agreement was made over the phone and the parties decided that the details would be worked out later by their lawyers. When Forum Global refused to finalise the transaction, Bear Stearns brought a successful claim in the High Court. Smith, J held:

> If the parties have shown an intention to be contractually committed, albeit while deferring discussion of some aspect or aspects of the deal, then the court will recognise a contract unless what remains outstanding is not merely important but essential in the sense that without it the contract is too uncertain or incomplete to be enforced.

Forum Global was not able to rebut the presumption that it intended to be bound.

The main exception to the bindingness of commercial agreements is when parties explicitly say that they do *not* intend to be bound. They are able to do so because it is also part of the freedom of contract *not* to conclude a contract. They can do so by making their negotiations 'subject to contract', which means that any agreement the parties reach orally or by way of a written summary or 'heads of agreement' is not binding: only a signed formal contract will then count as such. It is clear why the parties would make such an agreement: first, it allows them to negotiate in all freedom and second, once the contract is put into writing, to have it checked by lawyers and approved by whoever needs to approve of it before it is formally signed.

'Subject to contract'

The deliberate intention not to be bound can also be put in different wording. Parties could for example agree to be bound only 'in honour' (a so-called *honour clause*) or conclude a 'gentlemen's agreement'. The result is the same: there are no legally enforceable rights if the other party does not do what it promised. This led an English judge to define a gentlemen's agreement as 'an agreement entered into between two persons, neither of whom is a gentleman, with each expecting the other to be strictly bound, while he himself has no intention of being bound at all' (*Bloom v Kinder*, 1958).

B.   Gratuitous and disadvantageous transactions

In a second category of cases the intention to be legally bound is not assumed.

Donation

If a party enters into a gratuitous transaction, the law raises suspicions about the earnestness of the intention. The first type of a gratuitous transaction is the promise to make a gift (*donation*) – usually viewed with so much suspicion that most civil law jurisdictions require this promise to be put in the form of a notarial deed. This forces the donor to think through his act of benevolence and allows an independent notary (in most civil law countries a trained lawyer) to warn the donor of the consequences of his act and to check if he really intends to give something away.

Under English law, a gratuitous promise is equally unenforceable, but for the reason that it does not have any consideration. Consideration requires that there is a *quid pro quo* ('something for something'): as we shall see later in this chapter, a promise must always be given in return for a counter performance by the other party, or at least the promise thereof. This requirement is clearly not met in case of a gratuitous promise. If businessman and owner of the New England Patriots Robert Kraft promises to donate his Super Bowl-ring to Vladimir Putin, this is not a binding promise as Putin does nothing in return. In the absence of a notary as exists on the European continent, English law therefore requires the donative promise to be put in a *deed*. This written and signed document that is attested by a witness may not offer the same security as a notarial deed on the continent, but it does make the donor reflect upon his plan to perform an act of altruism and forces him to put his promise into precise writing. One could say that the law's suspicion about an intention being present in case of a donation is made good by satisfying the formality.

Other gratuitous transactions

This is more difficult in a second type of gratuitous transactions. My neighbour can allow me to live in her house for free, I can give someone a loan of €1,000 without interest, or I can allow the owner of my favourite delicatessen to use my car on Mondays. These transactions are not formal gifts, and yet they concern cases in which a party does something without asking anything in return (the French would say '*par complaisance*'). English law normally does not find these promises enforceable as they lack consideration, but in the civil law they can be enforced even without a notarial deed. Decisive is whether the promisee could reasonably expect from the words and the conduct of the promisor that the latter intended to be bound, which is probably dependent on what the reasons for making the promise were and what the consequences would be for the promisee if the promise were to be held unenforceable. If the promisee has acted to its detriment in reliance upon the promise, the presumption against an intention may be rebutted. Thus, in the examples above, if I immediately gave notice to my landlord after hearing my neighbour's generous offer, thereby leaving me without a home if she should renege on her promise, or if the deli owner had already sold her own car in reasonable reliance on my promise, these are strong arguments to claim that there is a binding contract.

This is not any different in a third category of cases. A promise need not be purely gratuitous for it to raise suspicions about the earnestness of the intention. I can sell my Tesla X for €10 or agree to provide legal services to coffee shop Easy Going on the sole condition that its owner regularly comes over to my house to water my plants. Neither civil law nor English law requires these

Disadvantageous transactions

disadvantageous transactions to be put in any particular form, but whether or not they are enforceable depends again on how likely it is that the court will find an intention to be legally bound on the part of the promisor. As these transactions are not particularly beneficial to the promisor, there must be clear evidence that he was really willing to commit himself beyond the boundaries of the ordinary. The same factors as just mentioned will play a role here.

C.   Social agreements

The third type of situation concerns promises in the social sphere, usually among friends or people who know each other well enough to enter into an agreement without realising the consequences. Again, such an agreement is not assumed to be legally binding, unless clear and unequivocal evidence exists for the contrary. Particularly in the social sphere the law tends to protect the 'freedom from contract': in their private lives, citizens should be protected from unnecessary interference by the courts.

No money value

Social agreements often lack any money value. The understanding of two friends to go on holiday together, to organise a barbecue next week, or that one of them will be the designated driver on a night out are in principle not relevant to the law. Even if parties explicitly want to make this promise legally binding by putting it in writing, it would be difficult to find a court willing to enforce it. So it is highly unlikely that the dinner host will be able to force her friend to come over or claim back the costs she incurred in preparing the meal.

Babysitting

There is more doubt in cases where someone provides services without remuneration if these services have money value and would normally be paid for, but parties deliberately refrain from making them paid. One can think of a professor who promises to give a speech for a student society, the promise to help a friend move house and the reassurance that one will come over this Thursday to babysit a friend's son. These cases do not tend to end up in the courts – and rightly so, most people would say.

Cost-sharing

A type of promise that lies even more in the economic sphere is the agreement to share costs. Car-pooling in particular is a fertile ground for court cases. If parties agree that one of them will drive one day and the other the other day, no problems occur. But this is different if one of them pays the other. Courts concur that a cost-sharing agreement can be enforced, but it is not likely that the parties' intention is also directed at the duty of the driver to ensure the safety of the passenger, or at a contract of carriage to give lifts in the future. As Upjohn LJ held in the English case of *Coward v Motor Insurers Bureau* (1963):

> The hazards of everyday life, such as temporary indisposition, the incidence of holidays, the possibility of a change of shift or different hours of overtime, or incompatibility arising, make it most unlikely that either contemplated that the one was legally bound to carry and the other to be carried to work.

Lottery

An interesting question arises if a group of friends or colleagues buys tickets for the lottery or play bingo and the person who actually bought the ticket wins a prize. Can the others claim their part? It must be assumed that the answer is affirmative if the parties all contributed to the competition and could reasonably expect that any prize money would be shared. This was also the outcome in the English case of *Simpkins v Pays* (1955), in which the defendant had told her fellow-bettor 'You're lucky, May, and if we win we will go shares.' This must be distinguished from the situation in which people club together to make a bet and the person who promised to place it forgets to do so or puts the money on the wrong numbers or on the wrong horse. What happens if the bet would have won? Under English law, there is not likely to be any consideration for the promise to place the bet. In the *Lotteriefall* case decided in 1974 the German *Bundesgerichtshof* also denied a legal obligation to correctly hand in the lottery ticket. It weighed the interest of the parties and found that against the economic interest of the bettors to cash the prize stands the interest of the 'agent' not to be held liable for the damage in the very unlikely case that the bet would have won. This would lead to the 'elimination of his economic existence'. The court thus reasoned that 'the person placing the bet would be affected incomparably more severely than his fellow-bettors would be affected by losing the chance of winning, something that they could not seriously count upon'. So the court found that the only thing he had agreed to do was to share the winnings if the ticket had been placed in the right way. We must keep in mind that the parties were individuals and that no money was paid to the unlucky agent to place the bet. If they had paid a betting company to place the bet, or if they had been businessmen who systematically engaged in betting with large amounts of money, things would have been different.

D.   Domestic agreements

A lesson to be drawn from the above is that the context in which a promise is made makes a lot of difference. The situation in which I promise to put away your car when you come over to my house for dinner, differs fundamentally from the one in which you trust a fancy restaurant's valet service to park your car. The importance of context is also clearly visible in the final group of cases discussed here. These concern domestic or family agreements. A father can promise his daughter to pay for her driving lessons if she does not smoke until she is 18 years old and a husband can promise his wife that he will no longer visit the local bars. No sensible lawyer would advise these promisees to take their relative to court for not keeping their word. The law is reluctant to deal with what people agree upon in a family context. Most legal systems assume that people in one household are not legally bound to their promises unless the contrary is proved. The emphasis must here of course be on the word 'legally': socially and morally close relatives are arguably more obliged towards each other than anyone else.

Prenups

Most court cases on domestic agreements are about (former) spouses or cohabitants. Civil law courts across Europe have come to accept these agreements as valid if they deal with the financial consequences of living together (cohabitation agreements) or of future divorce or separation. These latter so-called premarital or prenuptial agreements ('prenups') are contracts entered into prior to the marriage or civil union and provide for what happens to the property of the partners in case of divorce or separation. In most civil law countries, including Germany and the Netherlands, they are a matter of routine and usually come with the matrimonial regime ('marriage contract') that the spouses can choose with the help of a notary.

In the United Kingdom, however, prenuptial agreements have long not been enforceable for being against public policy, leading to the qualification of London as the wife-friendly 'divorce capital of the world'. English courts have been willing to set aside prenuptial agreements, even if these were made

BOX 4.3

BALFOUR V BALFOUR: A VICTORIAN VIEW OF MARRIAGE AND A FEMINIST CRITIQUE

In the seminal decision in *Balfour v Balfour* (1919), which is still regarded as a precedent under English law, Lord Atkin gave the traditional reason for the reluctance to enforce domestic agreements. He wrote: 'The common law does not regulate the form of agreements between spouses. Their promises are not sealed with seals and sealing wax. The consideration that really obtains for them is that natural love and affection which counts for so little in these cold Courts.' In this case a civil engineer, who was stationed in Ceylon, (the present Sri Lanka) had to leave behind his wife in England because her arthritis did not react well to the jungle climate at her husband's workplace. Before leaving, he promised to pay her £30 per month until she came back to Ceylon. When the couple decided to separate, she claimed that he should continue to pay the monthly allowance. The court denied the claim on basis of the above reasoning.

This case – that would probably be decided differently today – was later heavily criticised by legal feminists. Feminist jurisprudence is a field of law that originated in the 1960s. It adopts the view that the law is mainly written from a male perspective. Legal rules would therefore be biased and reinforce male values. This shows for example by presenting things that men value as the norm, considering female preferences as a deviation from what is 'normal.' The decision in *Balfour v Balfour* and the general presumption that domestic agreements are not enforceable are in this view prime examples of a masculine society. It favours market relations over things like love, care and community. The author Steve Hedley has argued that the role of the intention to create legal relations is then nothing but a veil for the policy decision to keep contract in its masculine environment, namely 'to keep it in the commercial sphere and out of domestic cases'. Lord Atkin's focus on 'natural love and affection' may seem impartial, but is in reality a subjective view of what should be the nature of the relationship between husband and wife and the roles and duties they have.

Regardless of what one thinks of this feminist analysis, one cannot deny that the decision in *Balfour v Balfour* is particularly harsh on the ill Mrs. Balfour. The message her husband – supported by the court – sends her is that after 16 years of marriage it is in his power not to honour his promise to financially assist her. She will not have had many possibilities to find suitable employment and earn a living for herself. Is it proper reasoning to give Mr. Balfour's promise to support his (ex-) wife the same legal status as the promise to a friend to join him for a walk in the park? Lord Atkin had no difficulty in saying so.

under a foreign law that does recognise the agreement. Famous cases include ex-Beatle Paul McCartney who had to pay £24 million to Heather Mills and Formula I boss Bernie Ecclestone who is supposed to have settled with his ex-wife for £750 million. However, the English position may have changed with the decision in *Radmacher v Granatino* (2010), in which the UK Supreme Court held that 'in the right case' a prenup can have decisive weight in a divorce settlement. This was to the benefit of Ms. Radmacher who, in a German marriage contract, had stipulated that her (at that time future) husband would not make any claims on her fortune of (supposedly) £100 million. The Supreme Court upheld the clause, reversing a previous decision of a High Court judge that she had to pay almost £6 million to her ex-partner. Meanwhile, although it was hailed by some as a legal revolution, the decision does not mean that any prenup will from now on be enforced: it still allows the court to refuse to do so, in particular if this is found to be unfair to any children born out of the marriage. In 2014 the English Law Commission drafted a Nuptial Agreements Bill that, upon enactment, should end the uncertain state of the present law and accept prenups, provided certain safe-guards are met.

Domestic agreements can also relate to matters that the law does not see as
Public policy   suitable for contracting because they violate public policy (see Chapter 10). When an 18-year-old woman agreed with her boyfriend that she would use the pill, but stopped taking it without his 'consent' and gave birth to a child, the court did not allow the father to claim for breach of contract or to be relieved of the duty to pay alimony for the child. In the *pill case* (1986) the German *Bundesgerichtshof* did not consider her promise legally binding because of a lack of intention. The policy argument behind this somewhat clinical reason-ing was of course that the law regards it as a violation of one's personal freedom if one could make binding contracts about having a child or not.

Consideration and *causa*

It was seen in the above that both agreement and intention to create legal relations are required for the formation of a valid contract. Art. 2:101 (1) PECL provides the concise summary of this:

> A contract is concluded if:
>
> (a) the parties intend to be legally bound, and
> (b) they reach a sufficient agreement
>   without any further requirement.

The law of many jurisdictions, including those of Germany, the Netherlands, the Nordic countries and the CISG, is accurately described by this provi-sion. But this is not true for all. In English law, an agreement also needs to be supported by so-called *consideration*. In French-based legal systems (such as Italy, Spain, Belgium, Romania and Bulgaria) on the other hand, the civil code requires the contract to have a so-called *causa*. Interestingly, France itself decided to abolish the causa requirement with the grand reform of 2016. The new Art. 1128 CC no longer mentions causa as a requirement for the valid formation of a contract. The reasons for this bold decision are discussed below (sub-section C). Both consideration and causa are complicated legal devices and it is not always clear what their exact role in the process of contract formation is. The following will first consider the common historical roots of consideration and causa (A) and then continue to describe consideration in English law (B) and causa in the French legal tradition (C).

A. Common historical roots: finding the reason for being bound

Although the requirement of consideration is a unique feature of the common law family and causa makes French-based legal systems stand apart from the rest of the world, both doctrines have very similar origins. It was explained in Box 1-4 that on the European continent the Roman system of recognising only a limited number of enforceable types of contract had, by the seventeenth century, made way for the general principle of *pacta sunt servanda*. But this raised the question of whether or not this was too wide a principle: that to hold *all* agreements made by consent enforceable was too broad. There was, therefore, a need for a criterion to distinguish binding from non-binding agreements. This badge of enforceability was found in the requirement of causa: a *naked* agreement (*nudum pactum* in Latin, the legal language of that time) was not enforceable for lack of causa, whereby 'causa' simply stood for a proper reason to be bound. This allowed courts to consider if the parties' motives for contracting were legitimate. If one asks which elements played a role in answering this question, it is likely that these were the same as when we analysed the intention to enter into legal relations: the value of the counter performance, the context in which the contracting took place (commercial or social/domestic) and the interests of the parties.

Pacta sunt servanda

A similar development took place in the common law. The actions a party could bring in case of non-performance of a contract were at first limited, but by the sixteenth century a claim for damages (as we shall see in Part 5 the main action in common law in case of breach of contract) could be brought on basis of *assumpsit* in any case in which the promisor did not perform. But in England too this was seen as a principle too wide to be accepted across the board. The English courts therefore also developed a device to keep the expansion of binding contracts under control. This was found in a sufficiently adequate 'consideration' for the promise, a good enough motive for why a promisor was bound.

The observant reader will comment that on this account causa and consideration must have become superfluous when the criterion of the intention to create legal relations rose to prominence in the nineteenth century. As was seen earlier in this chapter, it is after all this intention that now fulfils the role of separating binding from non-binding agreements. Put differently: the only good reason (causa, consideration) why a party is bound to its promise is because it seriously and deliberately intended to be bound. This is a sharp comment that has a lot of merit. It is exactly the reason why the Dutch decided to abandon causa when they introduced their new Civil Code in 1992 and it also played a role for the French lawmaker when it decided to get rid of causa. However, the law does not always develop in a logical way and sometimes suffers from historical accidents. We already encountered the saying of the great American judge Oliver Wendell Holmes (1841–1935) that 'The life of the law has not been logic: it has been experience.' The explanation for why causa and consideration are still requirements for the formation of a valid contract is therefore mostly historical. This helps us to understand why both have an uneasy relationship with the intention to create legal relations and why in jurisdictions that require causa or consideration, constant pleas are made – sometimes successful – to abolish the requirement.

B. Consideration in English law

English law requires that an agreement is supported by consideration. This means that each party to the agreement must give, do or promise something in return. If you pay me £100 and I give you my bike, our agreement is supported by consideration. To be more precise, English law will dissect our agreement into two separate acts. My payment is consideration for your delivery of the bike whereas your delivery is consideration for me paying the price. The consideration often only consists of a promise without the other party acting. If you promise to paint my house, there is no consideration if I do or promise nothing in return. But if I give you, or promise to give you, £2,000 in return, this is consideration for your promise and I will be able to enforce the agreement. This makes clear that in the terminology of English lawyers, the consideration is the thing, service or promise that is given in return. This is confirmed in a recent restatement of the English law of contract, where it says: '"Consideration" means that, in exchange for a promise by one party, a counter-promise or performance is given by the other party.' In cases where there is only an exchange of promises to perform acts in the future (for example if A and

B conclude a bilateral sales contract with delivery and payment seven days from now), this is called *executory consideration*. In contrast, *executed consideration* exists when a promise is made in exchange for an act and the act is performed (the moment A delivers the goods to B, A's consideration becomes executed).

Reciprocity

The above makes clear that the core of consideration lies in a bargain, an element of reciprocity. This comes out in the classic definition in the case *Currie v Misa* (1875): 'a valuable consideration in the sense of the law may consist either in some right, interest, profit or benefit accruing to one party, or some forbearance, detriment, loss or responsibility given, suffered or undertaken by the other'. It does not require much imagination to see the link with consideration as a good reason for being bound: the badge of enforceability is given only if there is a *quid pro quo* and not in case of a gratuitous promise. However, things are not that straightforward. Over the course of centuries, English courts have developed a complex body of rules not all of which easily match the picture of 'only enforcement in case of counter performance or a promise thereof': sometimes courts simply find or 'invent' consideration only to reach a just result. It is impossible to give a full overview of the whole consideration doctrine (its treatment in *Chitty on Contracts*, the leading English contract law textbook, takes 150 pages), but it is useful to have a closer look at some main points. These can be summarised in four rules.

1.   Consideration must be sufficient but it need not be adequate

It was seen above that in a simple sales contract the price paid by the buyer is the consideration for the seller's promise to deliver, while delivery by the seller is the consideration for the buyer's promise to pay. The question is whether it makes any difference that the buyer pays 'too little', for example only £1 for a house worth £190,000. The answer is that this is irrelevant to the law. Consideration must be 'sufficient', meaning that it must consist of 'something of value in the eye of the law', but this something does not have to be 'adequate': its economic value is not taken into account. That a party pays too much or too little is not relevant as long as something is given in return for the promise. This view that a nominal consideration is enough is some-

Peppercorn

times referred to as the 'peppercorn theory', after the case *Chappell v Nestlé* (1960), in which it was held that: 'A peppercorn does not cease to be good consideration if it is established that the promisee does not like pepper and will throw away the corn.' A peppercorn worth less than a penny is just as good consideration as £1 million.

2.   *Past consideration is not good consideration*

As consideration needs to be given in return for a promise or performance by the other party, so-called *past consideration* is not good consideration. If Ranomi saves Pieter from drowning and Pieter promises to pay her £1,000 as a reward to show his gratitude, Ranomi cannot claim the money from Pieter. Pieter's promise was not made in return for anything, but was subsequent and independent of him being rescued. So any act carried out before a promise is given is not given in exchange for the promise and does therefore not qualify as consideration to support it.

3.   *An existing duty does not amount to valid consideration*

An important rule, although controversial in practice, is that if a promisee is already under an obligation to perform (the promise), to perform this duty does not amount to valid consideration. This seems logical: if the promisee does something that he is already obliged to do he suffers no detriment, while the promisor only obtains what he was already entitled to and therefore obtains no benefit from the 'extra' promise.

Existing public duty

The rule applies both to cases in which there is an existing public duty and to cases in which there is a contractual duty. A case in which a public duty existed is *Glasbrook Brothers v Glamorgan County Council* (1925). When the employees of a coal mine went on strike, the owners of the mine asked the authorities for protection by quartering police officers on the premises of the mine. When the police refused and said that visiting patrols were sufficient, the coal mine owners offered to pay the police £2,200, which they accepted. When the strike was over the police requested payment. The owners, however, refused to pay arguing that there was no consideration for the promise to pay for the police protection as there was already an existing duty to protect the mine. The House of Lords reasoned that the police had provided an extra service that went beyond the normal public duty to maintain law and order. The police was therefore able to claim the £2,200 from the mine owners.

More modern applications of the 'existing duty' rule are to be found in cases in which the courts have to decide who has to pay for the costs of police services in and around football stadiums. In line with the *Glasbrook Brothers* case the courts then ask whether these are special police services provided to football clubs, or mere existing duties to maintain law and order. Thus, in *Harris v Sheffield United Football Club Ltd* (1988), it was found that the police officers had to attend inside the stadium itself, clearly a special service at the request of the club. But law and order sometimes also need to be maintained in the direct vicinity of the stadium. In *Leeds United Football Club v The Chief Constable of West Yorkshire Police* (2013), the Court of Appeal held that police authorities can only charge for the costs of policing in areas owned, leased or controlled by the football club. In public areas the policing also benefits local residents whose properties may otherwise be vandalised: the existing duty of the police towards the general public to keep the peace prevents the police from claiming back the costs from the club.

Existing contractual duty

An existing duty does not necessarily follow from public law. Consideration is also absent if the duty already follows from a pre-existing contract. The classic case is *Stilk v Myrick* (1809). On a trip from London to the Baltic and back, two sailors deserted their ship in Kronstadt. The captain failed to find replacements for them and promised the eight remaining seamen that the wages of their two disappeared colleagues would be divided between them if they worked the ship back to London. However, after the ship had safely arrived in England the captain refused to pay the sailors the extra salary. The court agreed, arguing that the sailors had not provided any consideration for the promise the captain had made: they had only done what they had already promised to do in the initial contract, namely sail back the ship. There is much to be said in favour of this outcome. A different decision would open the door for 'contractual blackmail': a party could threaten not to perform the contract, and make unreasonable demands, in every case in which the other party is in distress (which could be a reason for invalidation of the contract on basis of *threat*). On the other hand, it is debated whether this outcome should be reached on basis of the consideration doctrine. This seems misplaced as in fact there was a benefit to the promisor (it allowed Myrick to have the ship sailed home) and a detriment to the promisees (who had to work a bit harder than otherwise). This explains why the 'existing duty' rule has been under heavy attack.

Williams v Roffey Bros

The most important inroad on it was made in the landmark case *Williams v Roffey Bros & Nicholls (Contractors) Ltd*, decided by the Court of Appeal in 1990. Building contractors Roffey entered into a contract with a housing association to refurbish a block of 27 flats. The contract contained a so-called *damages clause* (see Chapter 12): if Roffey did not complete the work on time, they were liable to pay a fixed amount in damages. Roffey sub-contracted the carpentry work to Williams for a price of £20,000. When Williams ran into financial difficulties because he had under-priced the job and had trouble supervising his employees, a meeting was held with Roffey, who was obviously concerned about completing the contract on time. Roffey agreed to pay Williams an additional £575 per completed flat. Williams managed to finish eight more flats, but was then refused the promised extra money by Roffey who argued that he had not provided consideration for the promise of extra payment. However, the Court of Appeal did find good consideration for Roffey's promise in a decision that is generally seen as pragmatic and aimed at reaching a just result, rather than being a proper application of the 'existing duty' rule. The court found that Roffey had obtained a practical extra benefit by Williams's promise to complete the work on time against extra pay. This practical benefit consisted of Roffey avoiding having to pay a penalty in their contract with the housing association *and* of having to go through the trouble of finding an alternative carpenter to finish the job. English contract layers have spilt much ink on how to reconcile this case with *Stilk v Myrick*, but it seems now clear that an additional practical benefit makes good consideration. This is generally seen as a clear example of the 'watering-down' of the consideration doctrine.

4.   *There is no good consideration for the promise to accept part payment of a debt as discharge of the entire debt*

If someone owes another person money, it often happens that the debtor offers to pay a smaller sum than the entire debt in return for the creditor accepting this as full discharge. Based on the very old *Pinnel's case* (1602) English law does not regard the creditor's promise to accept this part payment as valid consideration. If you agree to discharge me of the £250 I owe you in return for me paying you £200, you can always go back on your promise as I have not provided you with consideration for it: I am already obliged to repay the entire debt. However, this is different if I add some extra element. What I could promise, for example, is to pay back the debt at an earlier date, providing you with a clear benefit and therefore with consideration for your promise.

Circumventing consideration

Having set out the main rules of the consideration doctrine, a further question arises: is consideration always needed as a requirement for the valid formation of a contract? English law indeed recognises two techniques to set consideration aside. One method is to put the agreement in a deed, something that is possible with any agreement. The other method is to invoke the doctrine of promissory estoppel, which is only available in a limited number of cases.

1.   *Agreement by deed*

Parties can escape from the requirement of consideration by putting their agreement in a so-called *deed*. Unlike a 'simple' contract, a contract made up in the form of a deed is a formal contract. The requirements a deed must meet are laid down in section 1 of the *Law of Property (Miscellaneous Provisions) Act 1989*. The written document must indicate that it is a 'deed', be signed by the maker, and the signing must be attested by a witness (which means that the witness watches the maker sign the document and signs his own name as a witness of this). Although since 1989 a deed no longer needs to be sealed (which originally took place with real wax and later by simply adding the letters LS for *loco sigilli*, 'place of the seal'), it will in practice often still contain the traditional words 'signed, sealed and delivered'. A deed provides an easy way for a party to make a gratuitous promise enforceable. If Bill wishes to donate £10 million to the London Wildlife Trust, the law must make this possible even in the absence of consideration. One way to realise this would of course be to make a binding contract by having the charity do or give something in return (such as create a 'Bill Fund' or give Bill £1 in return for his promise), but to make a deed would be another possibility.

2. *Promissory estoppel*

A principle accepted in any legal system is that no one is allowed to act in a manner contrary to one's own previous conduct, particularly not when another person has acted in reliance on this. German law calls this the prohibition of *venire contra factum proprium* (literally 'to go against one's own behaviour'). In English law, the principle is reflected in the doctrine of *estoppel* that is often described as providing a legal bar to alleging or denying a fact in contradiction of one's own previous conduct. If a municipality enters into a contract and tells the other party that the contract is approved of by the city council, the city is usually 'estopped' from claiming that the contract is invalid if it turns out that the council made all kinds of reservations. Estoppel thus prevents a party from going back on what it said or did. However, English law lacks one uniform principle of estoppel: its exact conditions are dependent on the field to which it is applied (property law, procedural law, etc.). In the context of contract law we must examine the doctrine of *promissory estoppel* that was developed in equity (see Chapter 2).

High Trees case

The question to be answered here is whether promissory estoppel can make a promise binding even if there is no consideration for it. The seminal case on this question, and one of the most famous English court decisions of the last century, is *Central London Property Trust Ltd v High Trees House Ltd* (1947). In 1937 Central London leased a block of flats in Clapham, London, to High Trees for a period of 99 years at a rent of £2,500 per year. The outbreak of World War II, and people leaving London as a result thereof, made it impossible for High Trees to sublet the flats to individual tenants who would actually occupy the building. In 1940 Central London therefore agreed to reduce the rent to £1,250. In 1945 the London property market was again in full swing and Central London demanded that High Trees resume payment of the full rent. This was not a problem for the period from 1945 onwards as the waiver by Central London was assumed to only cover the period in which the flats were unlettable as a result of the war. But it was not clear that the same was true for the period between 1940 and 1945. A sound application of the consideration doctrine (more in particular of *Pinnel*'s case) would have meant that the claim by Central London to be paid the full rent had to succeed: its promise to accept a lower yearly amount was not supported by consideration. Nevertheless Denning J made clear that if Central London had claimed the rent for 1940–45 its claim would have been rejected. After a survey of old judicial decisions that most lawyers had long forgotten about, he stated:

> They are cases in which a promise was made which was intended to create legal relations and which, to the knowledge of the person making the promise, was going to be acted on by the person to whom it was made and which was in fact so acted on. In such cases, the courts have said that the promise must be honoured. (...) The courts have not gone so far as to give a cause of action in damages for the breach of such a promise, but they have refused to allow the party making it to act inconsistently with it. It is in that sense, and that sense only, that such a promise gives rise to an estoppel. (...) In my opinion, the time has now come for the validity of such a promise to be recognized. The logical consequence, no doubt is that a promise to accept a smaller sum in discharge of a larger sum, if acted upon, is binding notwithstanding the absence of consideration (...).

The revolutionary aspect of this High Court decision is that it recognises that a promise lacking consideration (and not laid down in a deed) can still be binding on basis of promissory estoppel. The doctrine can only be applied if strict requirements are met:

- There must be a pre-existing contractual relationship between the parties. This was clearly the case in *High Trees* as the parties had already concluded a lease contract before Central London made its promise;
- A clear promise must have been made that the promisor will not enforce his legal rights against the promisee. In *High Trees* Central London's promise to reduce the rent was not contested: it had even been put in writing;
- The promisee must have acted in reliance on the promise, preferably to its own detriment (sometimes called *detrimental reliance*). High Trees continued to let the flats to its tenants and lowered the rent the tenants had to pay in order to attract more tenants to the building;

- It must be inequitable for the promisor to go back on its promise. If the promisee has acted in reliance on it, this requirement is usually met;
- Promissory estoppel is 'a shield but not a sword'. This important limitation of promissory estoppel means that it can only prevent the enforcement of an *existing* right and cannot create a new right. High Trees did not claim it had acquired a new contractual right (using its reliance as a 'sword'), it only defended itself against the claim by Central London to pay the full rent (as a 'shield'). One must realise that this severely restricts the field of application of promissory estoppel. If detrimental reliance could be used to create a new right for the promisee (as a so-called 'cause of action'), much of the doctrine of consideration would be abolished through the backdoor. This is the course that for example American and Australian law have taken: there, any promise without consideration can be binding if the promisee reasonably relied on that promise.

That English law refuses to follow the example of other common law jurisdictions became even more clear in the case of *Baird Textile Holdings Ltd v Marks & Spencer plc* (2001). When in the 1990s Marks & Spencer decided to trade in its traditional English suppliers for cheaper manufacturers abroad, one of these suppliers (Baird) brought a court action. Baird had been making clothes for M&S for over 70 years and claimed that M&S should be estopped from ending their business relationship (that was not based on a formal contract) without reasonable notice. To substantiate this claim (so not a defence against any claim from M&S, but a new action) Baird argued that M&S had made them believe they had a long-term relationship with them and that over the years they had invested heavily to meet the needs of M&S. However, the Court of Appeal confirmed that promissory estoppel cannot be used to create a legal right and the claim of Baird therefore had to be rejected.

Abolitionism

The difficulties caused by the complexity of consideration and the inroads that have been made on it in *Williams v Roffey Bros* and through the doctrine of promissory estoppel have led some English authors to argue that the doctrine is a confusing element of English law. Others have said that the absence of consideration in the CISG, PECL, PICC and DCFR shows that a legal system can very well do without it. This is not a recent view. In the 1936 volume of the Harvard Law Review Lord Wright wrote:

> [Consideration has no] place in the laws of France, Italy, Spain, Germany, Switzerland and Japan. These are all civilised countries with a highly developed system of law; how then is it possible to regard the common law of consideration as axiomatic or as an inevitable element in any code of law? (. . .) I cannot resist the

conclusion that the doctrine is a mere incumbrance. A scientific or logical theory of contract would in my opinion take as the test of contractual intention the answer to the overriding question whether there was a deliberate and serious intention, free from illegality, immorality, mistake, fraud or duress, to make a binding contract.

Despite these forceful attacks it is not very likely that the English courts will be willing to eradicate an age-old doctrine like consideration. But the conclusion that probably anyone can agree with is that in the course of the last three centuries, the consideration requirement has moved away from its original function of providing a good enough motive for why a promisor must be bound.

C.   *Causa* in French law

As explained in subsection A above, not only consideration in English law but also the requirement of 'causa' initially stood for a proper reason to be bound to a promise (well expressed by the Latin term *causa obligationis*). Although in the French-based legal systems this function of causa is now mostly taken over by the requirement of the intention to be legally bound, its historical origins can still be recognised in the two functions that causa has today. Before we get to these two functions, we need to define what causa means in French-based jurisdictions such as Italy, Spain, Romania and Belgium and, outside of the EU, Quebec. They usually define causa as the goal (*cause finale*) that the parties pursue with the contract. This in itself is not a clear definition as the goal of a contract can be defined at both an abstract level and at a more concrete one. At the abstract level (the so-called objective causa) the goal of the parties with a certain type of contract is always identical. In a sales contract it is for the seller to obtain a price and for the buyer to be delivered a good, in a contract of employment for the employer to pay a salary and for the employee to carry out the work. So in bilateral contracts the objective causa is the counter performance (or promise thereof) by the other party, similar to consideration under English law. At the concrete level (subjective causa) the goal differs from one party to another. The seller is perhaps in need of cash to play in the nearby casino while the buyer intends to give the good as a present to her lover. The subjective causa is therefore the individual motive of a party to bind itself. Both meanings can be found in the case law.

Two types of 'causa'

The first function of causa is that it allows courts to prevent contracts from taking effect if the goal that the parties pursue cannot be realised. A textbook example of a missing (objective) causa in a sales contract is if the good in reality does not exist: the contract then misses the essential element of the counter performance. At a time when causa was still a cornerstone of French

Objective causa

law, the *Cour de Cassation* applied this reasoning for example in the *Chronopost* cases (1996 and 2006). Here, the courier service Chronopost failed to deliver on time an important letter containing a bid in a tender procedure, despite Chronopost marketing itself as a specialist in swift transport and guaranteeing the reliability of its service to customers. The courier tried to escape from liability by invoking an exemption clause in the contract, but to no avail. The court saw a speedy and reliable service as a fundamental obligation (*une obligation essentielle*) under the contract and therefore the exemption clause could not be invoked as this would have deprived the contract of causa. Put differently: in a contract like this the counter performance of paying the price lies in a quick and reliable delivery of a letter. A clause limiting liability would obstruct this and leave the contract without causa.

Subjective causa A contract could also lack the subjective causa. In the case *Vidéo-club* (1996), a couple rented 200 videocassettes at a price of FF40,000 (€6,100) for a period of eight months with a view to starting a videoshop in their little village of only 1,300 inhabitants. When the rental company asked for payment the couple invoked the nullity of the contract for lack of causa. Interestingly, the *Cour de Cassation* agreed and held that 'the performance of the contract on the economic scale envisioned by the parties was impossible'. This is a clear example of a search for the subjective goals that the parties envisioned with their contract – even though the outcome can be criticised for being at odds with legal certainty. The only way to rationalise the decision is to assume that the rental company knew about the plans of the couple, but failed to warn them as a professional and experienced party that exploitation was not economically viable. A final example of a missing causa is where a party believes it has a debt towards another person, which turns out to be untrue. In the case *Manuela* (1985) someone maintained a child on the assumption that he was the father; when he found out that the statements made to this effect by the child's mother were incorrect, the court held that his payments were made without causa.

The field of application of causa does not end with these types of cases. In reality French courts applied causa in very diverse circumstances. Unfortunately, this did not help in finding a proper place for the doctrine. Despite fierce resistance of French lawyers who hailed causa as a unique characteristic of the French legal tradition, it was abolished with the grand reform of French contract law in 2016. The argument for this was that the exact function of causa was not very clear and overlapped with other doctrines, such as formation and mistake. Indeed, in all the cases mentioned above, it would have been possible for the court to decide the case in the same way using other rules. In addition, the French lawmaker reasoned that causa is absent in the Principles of European Contract Law (PECL) and the Draft Common Frame of Reference (DCFR).

Prohibited contracts

The second function of causa in French-based jurisdictions is that it prevents contracts against public policy or good morals from being valid. To this end, the old Art. 1133 *Code Civil* stated: 'A cause is unlawful when it is prohibited by law, when it is contrary to good morals or to public policy.' The new French law no longer needs causa to realise this; Art. 1162 CC now simply states that a contract cannot derogate from public policy. Prohibited contracts are discussed in Chapter 10.

 TOPICS FOR REVIEW

Intention to create legal relations
Types of *dissensus* of intention and declaration
Objective approach to agreement
Factors relevant in applying the objective approach
Theories of contractual liability
Intention in commercial agreements
Intention in social and domestic agreements
Intention in gratuitous and disadvantageous transactions
Agreements subject to contract
The politics behind *Balfour v Balfour*
The common roots of consideration and *causa*
Consideration in English law
Adequacy of consideration
Past consideration
The current state of the 'existing duty' rule
Part payment of debts
Deed
Promissory estoppel
Functions of *causa* in the French legal tradition
Objective and subjective *causa*

 FURTHER READING

– Atiyah's, *An Introduction to the Law of Contract*, 6th ed. by Stephen Smith, Oxford (Oxford University Press) 2006, Chapter VI.
– John Austin, *How to do Things with Words?*, Cambridge Mass. (Harvard University Press) 1962.
– Hugh Beale et al, *Cases, Materials and Text on Contract Law, Ius Commune Casebooks for the Common Law of Europe*, 32nd ed., Oxford (Hart Publishing) 2010, Chapter 8.
– Hugh Beale (ed.), *Chitty on Contracts*, 2nd ed., London (Sweet & Maxwell) 2015, Chapter 3.
– Andrew Burrows, *A Restatement of the English Law of Contract*, Oxford (Oxford University Press) 2016, Art. 8.
– Catherine Elliott and Frances Quinn, *Contract Law*, 10th ed., Harlow (Pearson) 2015, Chapter 6.
– Charles Fried, *Contract as Promise: A Theory of Contractual Obligation*, Cambridge Mass. (Harvard University Press) 1981.

– James Gordley, *The Philosophical Origins of Modern Contract Doctrine*, Oxford (Oxford University Press) 1991.
– James Gordley (ed.), *The Enforceability of Promises in European Contract Law*, Cambridge (Cambridge University Press) 2001.
– Steve Hedley, 'Keeping Contract in its place', *Oxford Journal of Legal Studies* 5 (1985), 391.
– Hein Kötz, *European Contract Law Vol. 1* (translated by Tony Weir), Oxford (Oxford University Press) 1997, Chapter 4.
– Karl Larenz and Jörg Neuner, *Allgemeiner Teil des bürgerlichen rechts*, 11th ed., München (Beck) 2016.
– Law Commission, *Matrimonial Property, Needs and Agreements*, 26 February 2014, Law Com No. 343.
– Ewan McKendrick, *Contract Law*, 11th ed., Basingstoke (Palgrave Macmillan) 2015.
– Richard A. Posner, *Economic Analysis of Law*, 9th ed. (Wolters Kluwer) 2014.
– Francois Terré, Philippe Simler and Yves Lequette, *Droit civil: les obligations*, 11th ed., Paris (Dalloz) 2013, Book 1, Title 1
– G.H. Treitel, *The Law of Contract*, 14th ed. by Edwin Peel, London (Sweet & Maxwell) 2015.
– Robert Wright, 'Ought the Doctrine of Consideration to be Abolished from the Common Law?', *Harvard Law Review* 49 (1936), 1125 ff.
– Reinhard Zimmermann, *The Law of Obligations: Roman Foundations of the Civilian Tradition*, Cape Town (Juta) 1990 (paperback edition with Oxford University Press, Oxford 1996), Chapter 18.

5

Legal capacity of the parties

CHAPTER OVERVIEW

A contract (or any other juridical act) can only be validly concluded by someone who has the **legal capacity** to do so. The law does not consider everyone fit to have this capacity. Two categories of people qualify for not being legally capable: certain **minors** (in particular young children) and **people with mental disorders**. This chapter examines both categories.

It was seen in Chapter 4 that a party can only be bound to a contract if it has expressed its (apparent) intention to enter into a legal relationship with somebody else. This assumes that people have control over what they intend and are able to assess what is in their best interest. If someone buys a house, opens a restaurant or decides to participate in the local Beauty Queen election, everyone will assume that these are rational decisions taken by people having full cognitive ability. Luckily the great majority of people indeed have this so-called *legal capacity* (the ability of a natural person to enter into a valid legal transaction), but this is not true for everyone. In the eye of the law some people lack the necessary understanding, judgement or experience to enter into juridical acts, including the ability to bind themselves by contract. Two categories of people qualify for this: certain minors (in particular young children) and people with mental disorders. If these persons conclude a contract with somebody else, most jurisdictions allow the legal representative of the incapacitated person (such as a parent in case of a child) to have this contract invalidated.

Protection

It is important to realise which conflicting interests are at stake here. Legal incapacity (*incapacité de contracter, Geschäftsunfähigkeit, handelingsonbe-kwaamheid*) is an instrument to protect parties who are presumed not to be able to take care of their own interests. It could cause a psychiatric patient, unable to oversee the consequences of his actions, great trouble if he were able to validly buy anything being offered for sale. And a nine-year old would have a bad start in life if its parents were not able to invalidate the €25,000 online loan it obtained from BNP Paribas. But this interest to receive legal protection may conflict with two other interests.

Policy reasons

First, it would be odd if *all* transactions of a minor or a mentally ill person could be invalidated. Nothing seems to be wrong with a 15-year old buying a copy of Richard Dawkins' book *The God Delusion*, which is clearly in the interest of the child's upbringing. This argument is even more acute for adults: to declare them incapable means that they are no longer allowed to be responsible for their own acts, presenting a grave violation of their right to determine which life they want to lead.

Second, the law has to balance the interests of the incapacitated person with those with whom they deal. In particular in the case of mentally ill persons, it is not always apparent to the outside world that a party is not capable of making a rational decision. If Mac, on his weekly trip to the town close to the mental institution in which he lives, buys a new car, it may not be clear to the local Mercedes dealer that he is dealing with a patient suffering from a psychiatric disorder. The question then is whether the dealer's reliance that Mac was perfectly able to form his own will should prevail over the need to protect Mac against himself. As we saw before, the law tends to protect the objective reliance of a party: should this reliance be made subordinate to the protection of the mentally weak?

Each jurisdiction balances these interests in its own way, but the starting point is the same everywhere: every natural person has the legal capacity to perform legal transactions. Article 1145 of the French *Code Civil*, a provision practically unchanged since 1804, well reflects this universal principle by saying: 'Any person may enter into a contract, unless he has been declared incapable of it by law.' It is also generally accepted that the two categories of persons mentioned before may lack legal capacity for their incapability of rational decision-making. But the extent to which minors and adults in need of protection are indeed unable to enter into valid transactions differs from one country to another. This chapter looks at these different approaches.

Minors

All European jurisdictions set the age of legal capacity at 18. But this does not mean that a transaction entered into by someone below that age is necessarily invalid. Although in principle the contract of a minor is not binding upon him (meaning that the adult other party cannot claim enforcement), each jurisdiction allows exceptions to this rule.

English law

English law allows a minor to validly enter into a 'contract for necessaries.' According to section 3 (3) of the Sale of Goods Act 1979, which reproduces the case law on this issue, necessaries are 'goods suitable to the condition in life of the minor or other person concerned and to his actual requirements at the time of the sale and delivery'. This includes food, clothing, accommodation and anything else that the minor requires at the relevant certain point in time *and* that is reasonable to acquire in view of his 'condition in life'. The latter means that this particular minor's income and position need to be taken into account. If a 17-year-old student orders ten pairs of Jimmy Choo handmade shoes, this may be suitable to her position in life (as she is the daughter of a Lincoln's Inn barrister), but it is not in conformity with her actual requirements as she already has 25 pairs of shoes in her wardrobe. In case the contract for necessaries would be binding, the minor is only bound to pay a reasonable price (Sale of Goods Act 1979, s. 3 (2)).

English law also considers employment, apprenticeship and training contracts as binding on the minor provided that they are on the whole to the minor's benefit. Football player Wayne Rooney therefore concluded a valid training contract with Everton FC at age 17, but the 'representation contract' he made with a sports management company at age 15 was not binding upon him as Proform did not give any training to Rooney and it was not compulsory for a football player to enter into such a contract (*Proform Sports Management Ltd v Proactive Sports Management Ltd*, 2006).

English law lacks the institution of a statutory representative who can represent a minor when making a contract. The only relevant question is whether the contract meets the requirements that were just discussed. In so far as an English parent does act in the name of his or her children (for example in litigation), this is usually not because a statute says so, but because the court has appointed the parent for this specific purpose (while it could also have appointed another person as a so-called 'next friend'). In civil law jurisdictions on the other hand, parents do have the general power to represent their children, which also means that they are able to 'consent' to the contract that a minor entered into. This clearly influences the way civil law countries deal with contracts made by minors.

French law   French law does not differ from English law in accepting as a main principle that contracts entered into by minors can be invalidated (Arts. 388, 1145 and 1146 *Code Civil*). However, instead of the minor themself, it is the *administrateur légal* (usually a parent) who acts on behalf of the minor. Article 388-1-1 *Code Civil* states: 'The statutory administrator acts as an agent for the minor in all civil transactions, except cases where the law or usage authorises minors to act for themselves. (…)'

There are two important exceptions to the main rule that contracts by minors are invalid. First, as Art. 1148 CC indicates, minors do have capacity if law or usage says so (*capacité usuelle*). This is the case in normal transactions of which it is customary that a minor of a certain age performs them alone. One must think of contracts of daily life that pose no risk to the minor's financial position and are in line with the lifestyle the minor is used to. Purchasing a car surely does not qualify, but buying a CD surely does. This is confirmed in Art. 1149: even a day-to-day act can be annulled in case it brings an economic disadvantage (*lésion*) to the minor. Second, in the nineteenth century the *Cour de Cassation* had already decided that the ratio behind legal incapacity is not that the minor is not allowed to contract, but that he is not allowed to damage his own position. The minor (or his statutory representative) can therefore only invalidate the contract if he proves that he would otherwise suffer an economic disadvantage (*lésion*). This rule can now also be found in Art. 1151 *Code Civil*, which states that: 'A contract cannot be invalidated if it was useful to the minor and he did not suffer any economic disadvantage from it, or profit from it.' As a result of this French courts will have to ask themselves the same question as their English colleagues when they have to decide about a minor's demand to invalidate the contract: is it beneficial to the minor or not?

German law

Unlike English and French law, which ultimately attach great importance to how beneficial the contract is for the minor of whatever age, German law (and the same is true for other countries in the German legal tradition such as Austria and Greece) adopts a different approach. It puts much greater emphasis on the consent of the parents as a necessary requirement for a valid contract. In addition, it distinguishes between two different age categories. These are the relevant provisions of the German BGB:

§ 104: 'A person is incapable of contracting if:
1. he is not yet seven years old,
2. he is in a state of pathological mental disturbance, which prevents the free exercise of will, unless the state by its nature is a temporary one.'

§ 105: '(1) The declaration of intent of a person incapable of contracting is void. (2) Also void is a declaration of intent that is made in a state of unconsciousness or temporary mental disturbance.'

§ 106: 'A minor (*Minderjähriger*) who has reached the age of seven has limited capacity to contract under §§ 107 to 113.'

§ 107: 'For a declaration of intent as a result of which he does not receive only a legal benefit, a minor requires the consent (*Einwilligung*) of his legal representative.'

§ **108** (1): 'If the minor enters into a contract without the necessary consent of the legal representative, the effectiveness of the contract is subject to the ratification (*Genehmigung*) by the legal representative.'

§ **110**: 'A contract entered into by the minor without the approval of the legal representative is deemed effective from the beginning if the minor effects performance under the contract with means that were given to him for this purpose or for free disposal by the legal representative, or by a third party with the ratification of the representative.'

§ **113**(1): 'If the legal representative authorises the minor to enter service or employment, the minor has unlimited capacity to enter into juridical acts that relate to entering or leaving service or employment of the permitted nature or performing the duties arising from such a relationship. (...)'

The German code here distinguishes between minors below seven years old (§ 104 (1)), who are deemed wholly incapable of making rational decisions (§ 105 (1)), and minors from the age of seven to the age of 18 who still have some possibilities to enter into a valid contract by themselves (§ 106–113). But these possibilities are limited. The first is mentioned, somewhat hidden in § 107: if the minor obtains 'only a legal benefit' from the contract it is valid without consent of a parent. However, German law applies this exception in a very strict way: the minor must not incur any obligation. This severely limits the scope of application of the provision. Even if a plot of land is donated to a minor, German courts tend to hold that this is a void contract because obligations will follow from this (such as the duty to pay property tax). The second possibility is provided by § 110. A contract entered into thanks to the money that a minor has received from a parent for a specific purpose or for free disposal (for example weekly pocket money, or money to buy a return ticket to Lloret de Mar) is also valid.

This means that German law puts much emphasis on the consent of a parent or other legal representative. Without this consent, either given before (*Einwilligung*: § 107) or after (*Genehmigung*: § 108), the transaction can be invalidated.

Dutch law — Article 1:234 of the Dutch Civil Code combines the English-French and the German approach. It states:

> 1. In so far as the law does not provide otherwise, minors have the legal capacity to perform juridical acts, provided they are acting with the consent of their legal representative.

2. Consent may be granted only permission for a specific juridical act or for a specific purpose.
3. Consent is presumed to have been granted to a minor if it relates to a juridical act of which it is generally accepted practice that it is performed independently by minors of his age.

On the one hand, Dutch law adopts the German approach that a minor needs parental consent in order to perform a valid juridical act. It even goes further than German law by requiring consent under all circumstances (sections 1 and 2). On the other hand, consent is presumed to have been granted (a presumption that cannot be rebutted by the parents) if a minor performs a juridical act 'of which it is generally accepted practice that it is performed independently by minors of his age'. This is reminiscent of the French-English approach because the potential benefits of the juridical act will be an important factor in assessing what the societal norms ('accepted practice') bring with them. The innovative aspect of the Dutch approach is that the Code explicitly allows for taking into account what is customary for minors of the same age as the minor who performed the juridical act. One can very well argue that a six-year old who buys the latest issue of *Donald Duck* at a nearby store is presumed to have been granted consent by his parents. This is because it is generally accepted in Dutch society that children of this age can buy a €2 comic book. There is even less doubt in case a 15-year old buys books to be used at school or clothing at H&M. But the younger the child, the bigger the financial burden, and the less the contract facilitates necessaries, the less likely it is that societal norms allow a minor to act independently. A 17-year old living 20 km from school buying a second-hand scooter is different from a 15-year old ordering a road bike to be handmade by Pegoretti.

Adults in need of protection

A. Legally incapacitated adults

In several countries, including France and the Netherlands, the second category of people lacking legal capacity are adults in need of protection. They usually suffer from a mental disability (either because of a psychiatric illness or because of a mental handicap) and are therefore formally declared incapable of entering into valid legal transactions. This so-called *curatelle* (*curatele*, sometimes translated as *wardship*) is clearly a far-reaching measure: although there may be a need to protect the vulnerable against exploitation by malicious others, it does prevent full participation in legal life and is thereby a grave intrusion on someone's personal autonomy. This explains why the decision to declare someone incapable (Art. 428, 440 CC and Art. 1:378

Curatelle

BW) can only be taken by an independent court and must meet strict require-ments in order not to violate the right to respect for private and family life as protected by Art. 8 of the European Convention on Human Rights (ECHR). In civil law jurisdictions the court will also appoint a legal representative who is able to perform juridical acts for the protected person (*curateur, curator*).

Betreuung

The severe consequences of legal incapacity of adults have led several coun-tries to develop less intrusive regimes to protect the vulnerable. German law does so by way of *Betreuung* (§ 1896 BGB), meaning that a custodian (*Betreuer*) is appointed by the court to take care of the affairs of the person in so far as this is necessary. The court can decide that a person can validly perform certain types of juridical acts with the consent of the custodian (the so-called *Einwilligungsvorbehalt*, reservation of consent). But if the person binds himself to a transaction that only confers a legal advantage or concerns a trivial matter, he is bound anyway. § 1903 BGB states to this effect:

> (1) To the extent that this is necessary to prevent a substantial danger for the person or the property of the person under custodianship, the custodianship court orders that the person under custodianship requires the consent of the custodian for a declaration of intention that relates to the group of tasks of the custodian (reservation of consent). (...)
>
> (3) Where a reservation of consent is ordered, the person under custodianship nevertheless does not require the consent of his custodian if the declaration of intention merely confers a legal advantage on the person under custodianship. To the extent that the court does not order otherwise, this also applies if the declaration of intention relates to a trivial matter of everyday life.

English law also shies away from declaring someone completely incapable of participating in legal life and has adopted special legislation (in particular the Mental Health Act 1983 and the Mental Capacity Act 2005) to reflect this. Next to the regime of legal incapacity France also developed less intrusive

Sauvegarde de justice

protective measures to safeguard the interests of adults (such as the tempo-rary measure of *sauvegarde de justice* that has existed since the 1960s: it does not take away the legal capacity, but it allows a court to invalidate lesionary transactions).

Legal incapacity of an adult in France and the Netherlands and custodianship in Germany in principle lead to the same result as incapacity of a minor: the contract entered into can be avoided (set aside) by the legal representative or is even regarded as void. There are certain exceptions to this rule in cases where the transaction is beneficial to the adult or concerns contracts of daily life (as we just saw with § 1903 BGB; see also Art. 1148 CC and Art. 1:381

(3) BW), but usually the other party is bound: the rationale behind the protection of an incapacitated person means that only he can avoid the contract. The argument of the other party that it had no reason to doubt its counterpart's age ('he had a beard and drove a car') or medical condition ('she looked as healthy as Sophie Dahl') plays no role. In case of legal incapacity, the law sacrifices legal certainty and the objective approach in order to protect people not able to exercise their free will. The shop owner who is close to selling a BeoSound 5 audio system to a young looking customer can always ask for an ID. Court decisions incapacitating adults are usually published in a national public register that in some countries is even available online for a quick and easy check.

B.   Other adults

Contracts can obviously also be concluded by people who are not formally declared incapable or in need of a custodian by a court decision, but who *Interests* do suffer from some mental disorder. In particular if this disorder is only of a temporary nature (depression) or not yet diagnosed (Alzheimer), it is not likely that the patient is formally incapacitated. In addition, people can also be prevented from making a rational decision as a result of a psychosis or blackout, using too much alcohol or drugs, or simply by being stressed or tired. An important question is whether they deserve the same protection as their legally incapacitated partners in misfortune discussed in section A above. A positive answer is clearly not as self-evident as in case of formal legal capacity: in the cases dealt with here, the other party is not able to check a public register. This implies that the interest of the other party relying 'in good faith' on the valid formation of a contract and the interest of the disordered person in need of protection may have to be weighed in a different way.

The German solution is clearly stated in § 105 (2) BGB: 'Also void is a decla-*Germany* ration of intent that is made in a state of unconsciousness or temporary mental disturbance.' The text implies that any reliance of the other party is not relevant: German law protects any person who suffers from a disorder against the other party even if they have no reason to doubt that person's mental abilities. But there is a strict requirement, developed in case law, that the disorder must be so serious that it fully negates the ability to form one's will. Court practice is that the adult, who has to prove that his will was affected by a mental disorder, will provide the judge with expert opinions on his state of mind at the time of contracting. If the person of unsound mind can indeed prove he was prevented from rational decision-making, he can choose whether or not to keep the contract in place. But there is a similar exception as in cases of *Betreuung*, making an everyday transaction perfectly valid:

§ 105a BGB: 'If a person of full age incapable of contracting enters into an everyday transaction that can be effected with funds of low value, the contract he enters into is regarded as effective with regard to performance and, if agreed, counter performance, as soon as performance has been effected and counter performance rendered. Sentence 1 above does not apply in the case of considerable danger to the person or the property of the person incapable of contracting.'

France

French law starts from a similar assumption as the German § 105(2) BGB. Article 414-1 *Code Civil* states:

In order to enter into a valid transaction, it is necessary to be of sound mind. But it is for those who seek annulment on that ground to prove the existence of a mental disorder at the time of the transaction.

The French courts take this provision quite literally and usually do not find a valid transaction in case of a mental disorder (*trouble mental*). Again, as in German law, it is not relevant if the other party relied on any intention: the proof of mental disorder is enough to invalidate the contract.

England

English law is more generous in protecting the other party 'in good faith'. Only if the other party knew that its counterpart was not able to appreciate the nature and effect of the transaction (she saw him drink ten malt whiskies in one hour), the latter can decide not to be bound by it (*Hart v O'Connor*, 1985). This is clearly different from how minors are treated: they can escape the contract even if the other party was not aware of the young age. This may sound harsh on the mentally disabled – who as a result are left unprotected in most cases – but this can be explained from the overall desire of English law to protect reasonable reliance in a contractual relationship. In addition, the rule mentioned before on necessaries is not only applicable to a minor, but also to a person who by reason of mental incapacity (in English law the term is used for anyone having a disturbance in the mind or brain) or drunkenness is incompetent to contract: irrespective of whether the other party knew of the disability, a contract for necessaries is valid and will be converted into a contract for a reasonable price – if needed (Sale of Goods Act 1979, s. 3 and Mental Capacity Act 2005, s. 7).

Netherlands

This generosity on the other party 'in good faith' in case of a not formally incapacitated person can also be found in Dutch law. On the one hand, the Dutch legislator has made it easy on a person of unsound mind to prove that he did not intend to be bound. To this end, Art. 3:34 of the Dutch Civil Code states that in cases where the juridical act is disadvantageous for the mentally disturbed person, he is presumed to have acted under the influence of the mental disturbance. On the other hand, the other party can always invoke his reasonable reliance on basis of Art. 3:35 BW. If A feels haunted by demons that tell him to sell his mansion as soon as possible and B accepts A's offer to buy the house for €300,000, A cannot invalidate the contract if B did not know, nor had to know, about A's mental inability.

 TOPICS FOR REVIEW

The ratio behind legal incapacity
Contracts binding on a minor in English, French, German and Dutch law
The role of age in legal incapacity of minors
Contracts binding on adults with a mental disability
The role of reliance of the other party
The role of statutory representatives of incapacitated persons

 FURTHER READING

– Hein Kötz, *European Contract Law Vol. 1* (translated by Tony Weir), Oxford (Oxford University Press) 1997, Chapter 6.
– Ewan McKendrick, *Contract Law*, 11th ed., Basingstoke (Palgrave Macmillan) 2015, Chapter 16.
– Basil S. Markesinis, Hannes Unberath and Angus Johnston, *The German Law of Contract: A Comparative Treatise*, 2nd ed., Oxford (Hart) 2006.
– Francois Terré, Philippe Simler and Yves Lequette, *Droit civil: les obligations*, 11th ed., Paris (Dalloz) 2013, Book 1, Title 1.

6

Formalities

 CHAPTER OVERVIEW

One of the four main principles of contract law is the **principle of infor-mality**: contracts can be concluded in any form. However, some contracts do require a certain form in order to be valid or to prove their existence. In other contracts there is a duty on the professional party to give the consumer all kinds of information before entering into the contract. This chapter discusses:

- **reasons** for formalities;
- **types** of formalities (notarial deed and common law deed, contracts to be made in writing and contracts to be evidenced in writing, contracts requiring pre-contractual information duties);
- the **sanction** if a contract lacks the required form.

Informality

Chapter 1 showed that one of the main principles of contract law is that con-tracts do not require any form. It was explained that this principle of infor-mality is the end result of a long historical process. By the nineteenth century the principle had become so self-evident that the French *Code Civil* and German BGB have not even codified the principle. The Dutch Civil Code put it in Art. 3:37 (1), which states: 'Unless provided otherwise, declarations, including communications, can be made in any form and can be inferred from conduct.' However, this does not mean that contracts, or certain parts thereof, can always do without formalities. It has always been the case that some contracts need to be put in writing (such as gratuitous contracts in the common law), need to be laid down in a notarial deed (such as donation in the civil law), or are to be preceded by giving notice to the outside world, fol-lowed by speaking solemn words in the presence of witnesses and of a public official (marriage). What is more, formalities are on the rise again as a result of the wish of legislators to balance unequal bargaining strength between parties by requiring one of them (the professional party) to provide informa-tion to the other (the consumer).

Reasons for formalities

There is a very good reason for the principle of informality: it makes it easy to conclude a contract. It would be extremely cumbersome if I were to sign, or even draft, a form every time I buy a cup of coffee or my company wants to do business. This means that there must be a very good reason for the law to introduce a formality. In the field of contract law formalities can be grounded on three different rationales. A specific formal requirement is usually based on a combination of these.

First, requiring some kind of formality can be useful to warn a party (or both parties) that it is entering into an important or financially dangerous transaction. This can be called the *cautionary (or warning) function*.It aims to prevent a party from inconsiderate action: mere consensus of the parties is not seen as sufficient because this would bind them too easily. Good examples are consumer credit and consumer suretyship, in most jurisdictions both require a written contract before they become binding on the consumer. Consumer credit is seen as dangerous because the usually high interest rate could burden the debtor and his family for a long period of time. In case of suretyship, also known as 'guarantee' or 'personal security', a party promises to pay a creditor if somebody else does not meet its obligations, for example a mother can stand surety for the debts of her child against a bank. Here too, the debtor is inclined to overestimate its own solvency and what is more, it is often difficult for the debtor to refuse a family member to stand surety. The obligation to put things on paper will offer a party a final chance to reflect on the transaction.

Warning function

Second, a formality can be motivated by the wish to provide a party with legal advice or information before it is bound. This is the *information function*. A good example is the notarial deed that a civil law notary must draft in case of transfer of immovable property. The notary must warn the parties of the legal consequences of their action. Other examples are the extensive information duties on professional parties that follow from European directives. In cases of consumer credit and distance contracts, for example, the credit supplier and the seller must give extensive information to the consumer at various stages of the contracting process.

Information function

Third, a form can be required to secure evidence of the contract. This is called the *evidentiary function*. In particular by putting the contract into writing certainty is provided about the existence and the contents of the parties' obligations. This may avoid future disputes about what the parties actually intended (even though in practice the words of a written contract

Evidentiary function

can still be interpreted differently by the parties; see Chapter 7). An example from English law is suretyship (in England usually called 'guarantee'). Under the English Statute of Frauds 1677 a guarantee must be 'evidenced in writing', meaning that the contract itself does not have to be written but the claimant must be able to prove the existence of the contract through written evidence (such as a letter signed by the defendant or an e-mail in which the suretyship is mentioned). This means that in the absence of written material even a CEO of a large company, who promises over lunch to guarantee another's debt, will not be bound despite the availability of three witnesses present at the restaurant table. As we will see, German, French and Dutch law do not require the written form for the validity or proof of a commercial suretyship.

Another example of the need to put things into writing is the so-called 'holographic testament'. In civil law countries (see e.g. Art. 970 CC, 2247 BGB, Art. 4:94 ff. BW) the testator is able to dispose of at least some of his goods (which goods exactly differs from one country to another) by way of a completely handwritten document. This 'do it yourself' testament is only valid if handwritten to ensure that it is really the testator's well-considered last will. The Guinness Book of World Records reports as the shortest will ever written: 'Vse zene' (Czech for 'all to my wife'), written on the bedroom wall of a man realising his imminent death. English law regards such a holographic will as invalid if not made in the presence of two witnesses who have signed the document.

Even if the written form is not legally required, many parties will still put their contract into writing. This forces them to think through the consequences of the contract and will make it easier to provide evidence of the binding agreement if necessary. In the English case of *Hadley v Kemp* (1999), three members of the pop group Spandau Ballet took the band's songwriter Gary Kemp to court claiming that they should receive part of the royalties on the band's music. Their claim was that they had orally agreed upon sharing these royalties, but were not able to prove the existence of such a contract in the absence of any written agreement.

Types of formalities

A.   Contracts to be made by notarial deed

French, German and Dutch law require certain contracts to be made by notarial deed (*acte authentique, Beurkundung, authentieke akte*). This can be seen as the most strict formality available in the civil law. It requires not only that a deed is drafted by the notary and signed by the parties, but also that the

notary establishes that the parties indeed intend to be bound after having been warned about the legal consequences of their action (see Box 6.1). Civil law countries typically require intervention of a notary in case of donation (also known as the promise to make a gift: Art. 931 CC, § 518 BGB), creating
Gift a mortgage (Art. 2416 CC, § 873 BGB, Art. 3:260 BW), matrimonial contracts (Art. 1394 CC, § 1410, Art. 1:115 BW), the making of a public testament (Art. 971 CC, § 2232 BGB) and the establishing of a corporation (§ 23 *Aktiengesetz*, Art. 2:64 (2) BW).

But the requirement of a notarial deed should not frustrate daily life. One can readily see the importance of notarial intervention in the types of transactions mentioned above: they almost all concern complicated acts that people tend to make only once or twice in their life and therefore require careful consideration and advice. There is one possible exception to this: giving something away on the spot. If one presents someone with a birthday present or hands over goods with the intention to benefit the donee, this is a binding contract despite the absence of a notarial deed. This is after all not a *promise* to make a gift, but the actual *giving* (Art. H.-1:104 DCFR speaks of an 'immediate donation', French law of a *don manuel*, German law of *Handschenkung* and Dutch law of a *gift van hand tot hand*). § 518 BGB makes this explicitly clear in section 2:

> (1) For a contract by which performance is promised as a donation to be valid, notarial recording of the promise is required. (...)
> (2) A defect of form is cured by rendering the performance promised.

There is a good reason for this relaxation of the notarial requirement: it is much easier to promise to give something away than to actually carry out this promise. The law recognises this by equating a party's seriousness apparent from a notarial act to a party's seriousness apparent from actually handing over a good.

Immovables The sale and transfer of land and immovables are often also subject to notarial requirements. For most people these are the most expensive transactions they ever enter into during their life. Thus, German law requires that both the sale of a plot of land (§ 311b BGB) and the later separate transfer of ownership (§ 925 BGB) take place through intervention of a notary. Dutch law on the other hand only requires the actual transfer of ownership in immovables to be made by a notarial deed (Art. 3:89 BW). Only the previous purchase of a residential house or apartment is to be made in writing (see subsection B below). French law in this respect offers the least protection to the buyer. In Chapter 3 the point was made that under French law (Art. 1583 CC) ownership of a good passes as

BOX 6.1

CIVIL LAW NOTARY AND NOTARY PUBLIC: A WORLD OF DIFFERENCE

The civil law or 'Latin' notary (in short: notary) is a typical product of the civil law tradition. He or she is a full-time legal professional with (usually) a law degree and licensed by the State to draft and record legal documents. The main activity of a notary as a public (and therefore independent) official lies in conveyancing (such as transferring property and creating servitudes and mortgages) and in drafting matrimonial contracts, testaments and corporate charters. Their public function comes out in their task of not only facilitating parties, but also protecting them against the consequences of their acts. § 17 of the German *Beurkundungsgesetz* 1969 nicely illustrates this. If the notary is to draft an authentic act (as in case of transfer of immovable property or donation), he is required 'to ascertain the intention of the parties, explain the content of the transaction, inform the parties about the legal consequences of the transaction, and record their statements in a clear and unequivocal way'.

Although notaries are public officials, they do work in private practice and are paid by the parties on a fee basis. The access to the notarial profession (and in some countries also the fee system) is regulated by the State. In practice most notaries do not only carry out the public tasks assigned to them by law, but also provide specialist legal advice, in particular in the field of family law and estate planning. They are normally not allowed to litigate. Civil law notaries can naturally be found on the European continent, but also in South and Central America, most French-speaking countries in Africa (including Morocco and

Congo) and Asia (for example in China, Indonesia and Japan). Most countries that have a civil law notary are members of the International Union of Notaries (UINL).

The common law lacks an official assigned with the tasks of a civil law notary. This explains why the common law does not require notarial documents to make a valid donation or transfer immovable property. However, England does have a group of legal professionals called notaries public (or public notaries). These are qualified lawyers who certify documents and transactions for use outside the UK. While a solicitor attests and authenticates normal documents for use within the UK, a notary is addressed if one needs a document drafted or authenticated for use in a foreign country. This can range from birth certificates to taking evidence for use by a foreign court. A notary public typically has strong foreign language skills and knowledge of foreign laws. There are about 1,000 of such notaries, most of whom work as a solicitor as well. They are organised in the Notaries Society.

The American legal system also recognises a profession called notary public. There are no less than 4,5 million of such notaries. They are typically lay people without legal training and are not allowed to give any legal advice. Their main task is to act as an impartial witness, to record sworn statements and to certify signatures. There are several organisations of notaries that aim to serve the interests of their members (including the National Notary Association). The 'notarius publicus' in Nordic countries plays a similar role as the American notary public.

soon as the contract is concluded. The making of a notary deed and the subsequent registration of this deed in the land register is therefore no requirement for the contract to be valid or for the transfer of the property. The reason why a notary deed is made in French law is therefore a different one: only after registration of such a deed is it apparent to third parties who is the owner of the immovable. If registration did not take place, the owner could therefore not enforce his rights against a third party who, not in bad faith, also bought the land from the seller and filed for registration first. So if the seller decides to sell the house a second time to somebody else, or mortgages the property, the first buyer needs to have registered his notarial deed in order to prevail against the second buyer or moneylender. This effect of registration is so important that in French practice notarial deeds for the sale of immovables are always made and registered, but the rationale of protection of the seller and purchaser against their own inconsiderate action does not apply: between seller and buyer the property of the immovable is transferred even without a notarial deed.

B.   Contracts to be made in writing

EU law

There is a whole range of contracts (or clauses therein) that need to be made in writing in order to be valid (usually meaning that the obligor's signature must be put on the document). It is mostly the cautionary function of formalities that makes legislatures adopt this requirement: it should make a party think twice before agreeing to the contract. This motive is particularly clear in European directives that aim to protect the consumer by requiring a contract to be in writing. The two best examples of this are the contract of consumer credit and of timeshare. Thus, Art. 10 (1) of the Directive on Credit Agreements for Consumers states that: 'Credit agreements shall be drawn up on paper or on another durable medium. (…)', while Art. 5 (1) of Directive 2008/122 on Timeshare declares: 'Member States shall ensure that the contract is in writing, on paper or on another durable medium (…).'

But many national laws also require a contract to be in writing. When exactly this is the case differs from one country to another and anyone who aims to give a complete list will rapidly lose its readers. Examples include the following:

English law

- It was seen in Chapter 4 that under *English law* a gratuitous promise can be made binding by way of a deed (a document signed by the maker and attested by a witness). English law also requires a deed in case of a lease for three years or more (Law of Property Act 1925, ss 52, 54). Contracts for the sale of land (or other dispositions of an interest in land) do not require a deed (as in case of a gift), but they must be made in writing and signed by each party (Law of Property (Miscellaneous Provisions) Act 1989, s. 2). The contract is void if the document does not state all the terms to which the parties have explicitly agreed. As in many other jurisdictions English law also requires the written form in case of a so-called hire purchase contract (Consumer Credit Act 1974, s. 60). If a buyer cannot afford to pay the asked price for a product at the moment of concluding the contract, but can afford to pay a monthly percentage, hire purchase allows the buyer to still conclude the contract. The hirer purchaser becomes the owner of the good when the monthly instalments equal the total price (naturally plus interest). This type of contract is often used to buy ('lease') a new car.

- *German law* requires the written form (*Schriftform*) for example in case of consumer suretyship (*Bürgschaft*: § 766 BGB and § 350 *Handelsgesetzbuch*), lease (*Mietvertrag*) for a specified period of more than one year (§ 550 BGB) and in case of ending an employment contract (§ 623 BGB) or lease (§ 568 BGB).

German law

- In *French law* writing (*écrit ordinaire*) is not only required in cases of an employment contract for a definite period (Art. L 1242-12 Code du Travail), but also – to give just a few examples – in case of a contract to build a residential house (Art. L 231-1/2 and 232-1 *Code de la construction et de l'habitation*), to obtain life insurance (Art. L 132-5 *Code des assurances*) and to engage a real estate agent (Act of 2 January 1970, Art. 6) or a marriage agency (Art. L224-90 Consumer Code). Interestingly neither French nor Dutch law requires the written form for the validity of a contract of consumer suretyship. French courts consider the relevant Arts 1376 and 2292 of the *Code Civil* only as rules of proof, while Art. 7:859 Dutch Civil Code explicitly says that suretyship can only be proved against the guarantor by a document signed by him, unless the guarantor already performed (part of) his obligations.

French law

- The *Dutch* Civil Code requires the written form (*akte*) for a range of potentially 'dangerous' transactions, including hire purchase (*huurkoop*: Art. 7A:1576i BW), ending a residential lease (Art. 7:271 (3) BW), the contract to build a residential house (Art. 7:766 BW) and several clauses that can be part of an employment contract, such as the non-compete ('restraint of trade') clause (Art. 7:653 BW), on which, more in Chapter 10. In 2003 the Dutch legislator also introduced protection for the buyer of a residential house by requiring the contract to be made in writing and giving the consumer-buyer a three-day period within which he can withdraw from the contract without giving any reason. Article 7:2 BW states to this effect:

Dutch law

1. The purchase of an immovable good or a part thereof that is intended to be used as a residence, has to be concluded in writing if the buyer is a natural person who,

when entering into the agreement, does not act in the course of his professional practice or business.

2. The document, drawn up for this purpose between the parties, or a copy of it must be handed over to the buyer against issuance, if the seller desires so, of a dated receipt. During three days after the document or its copy has been handed over to the buyer, the buyer has the right to terminate the purchase. When within six months after the buyer has used this right, the same parties enter again into a new sale agreement related to the same immovable thing or part of it, then this right of termination does not arise again.'

Taking stock of these contracts to be made in writing, one may be inclined to say that for most of these contracts legislative intervention is superfluous as they would normally be made in writing anyway. But this overlooks that the law has an interest in general rules that can be uniformly applied by the courts – in particular if these rules have the function of preventing a party against inconsiderate action.

C. Contracts to be evidenced in writing

A formality is not always a requirement for the validity of the contract. It could also be that the legislator introduces a formality (in particular the written form) as a form of *evidence*. One speaks of contracts that need to be evidenced in writing, or of a form that is required *probationis causa* (with an eye to proof), as contrary to forms that are required in order to make the contract valid (*solemnitatis causa*). The main category of contracts that need to be evidenced in writing under English law has already been encountered above: a suretyship (personal security) does not have to be made in writing, but the claimant must be able to prove the existence of the contract by referring to written evidence. The still applicable section 4 of the Statute of Frauds 1677 puts it like this:

> Noe Action shall be brought (…) whereby to charge the Defendant upon any speciall promise to answere for the debt default or miscarriages of another person (…) unless the Agreement upon which such Action shall be brought or some Memorandum or Note thereof shall be in Writeing and signed by the partie to be charged therewith or some other person thereunto by him lawfully authorized.

This evidence can be derived from any written document, for example from a correspondence (including e-mails) that mentions the oral agreement, even if only in passing. It is essential, however, that the writing is clearly from the party against whom the claim is brought (which is easy in cases where its name is on the document).

It is not only English law that requires certain contracts to be evidenced in writing. Although both German and Dutch law allow the court the freedom to decide about proof and therefore about whether a binding contract exists or not, there are exceptions to this rule (consumer suretyship in Dutch law is one, as was seen above).

French law is in theory much more restrictive in allowing the parties to prove the existence of a contract. Some even speak of 'evidentiary formalism'. This is because the French civil code clearly prioritises written evidence over any other type (such as proof by witnesses or experts). The two main provisions of the *Code Civil* are the following:

Evidentiary formalism

> **Art. 1359 CC**: 'A juridical act relating to a sum of money or value in excess of an amount fixed by decree [€1500] must be proved by evidence in writing, whether privately signed or authenticated.
>
> No proof may be brought beyond or contrary to evidence in writing establishing a juridical act, even if the sum of money or value does not exceed this amount, except by other written evidence which is signed or contained in privately signed or authenticated writing.
>
> A person whose contractual right exceeds the threshold mentioned in the previous paragraph may not be dispensed from proving it by evidence in writing by reducing his claim.
>
> The same rule applies to a person whose claim, even if lower than this amount, concerns the balance of a sum or a part of a right higher than this amount.'

> **Art. 1361 CC**: 'Evidence in writing may be supplemented by an admission in court, by a decisive oath, or by a beginning of proof by writing which is supported by another means of proof.'

Although perhaps difficult to read for non-specialists, Art. 1359 simply states that all transactions exceeding the value of €800 and not made in writing (by a notary or by the parties themselves) cannot be proved by witnesses, but only in writing. This is a far-reaching provision that would seriously restrict the binding force of contracts if it were strictly applied. However, two important restrictions exist. First, the provision does not apply to commercial transactions (Art. L 110-3 *Code de Commerce*). And second, Art. 1361 allows that proof by witnesses is allowed if there is so-called 'prima facie' written evidence. This means that if some document can be produced (not the contract itself, but – as in English law – for example an e-mail or a document from which it can be inferred that an oral contract was concluded), further evidence by witnesses is possible. The courts easily find this '*commencement de preuve*', almost turning Art. 1359 into a dead letter. This does of course not keep knowledgeable parties from writing down their agreement – as they will also do in any other jurisdiction.

D. Contracts requiring pre-contractual information duties

In particular as a result of European directives still one other type of 'formality' must be mentioned: the duty of a professional seller or service provider to supply information to the consumer. The classic picture of two equal parties who are able to collect all necessary information themselves in order to conclude a contract based on informed consent has long ceased to be reality. It must, at least when it comes to B2C-contracts, be replaced by a view of contract that requires compliance with pre-contractual information duties in order to restore the balance of power among the parties. Such duties exist for timeshare, package travel, doorstep sales, distance selling and consumer credit. These are usually accompanied by a withdrawal right, allowing the consumer to withdraw from the contract within a set period of usually seven or 14 days.

EU law

The information to be provided typically relates to the characteristics of the goods or services, the characteristics of the trader and the rights of the consumer under the contract. There are clear indications that with each new European directive the number of information duties grows. A good example of this is Directive 2008/48 on Consumer Credit. It requires the creditor to include six items in the advertising, to mention 19 items in the written offer it makes to the consumer, and to inform the consumer about no less than 22 items in the credit agreement itself. The European legislator justifies the need to give information in the stage of advertising in the following way in the preamble to the directive:

> In order to enable consumers to make their decisions in full knowledge of the facts, they should receive adequate information, which the consumer may take away and consider, prior to the conclusion of the credit agreement, on the conditions and cost of the credit and on their obligations. To ensure the fullest possible transparency and comparability of offers, such information should, in particular, include the annual percentage rate of charge applicable to the credit, determined in the same way throughout the Union. As the annual percentage rate of charge can at this stage be indicated only through an example, such example should be representative.

Sanctions

It is important to ask what is the sanction for breach of an information duty following from a European directive. Interestingly, European directives typically leave this to the Member States and only require that the imposed sanction is effective, proportionate and dissuasive. The sanctions therefore differ widely from one Member State to another. The Directive on Consumer Credit again offers a good example. Even though this is one of the rare examples of a maximum-harmonisation directive (meaning that the Member States cannot offer more protection than the directive does), Art. 23 states:

> Member States shall lay down the rules on penalties applicable to infringements of the national provisions adopted pursuant to this Directive and shall take all measures necessary to ensure that they are implemented. The penalties provided for must be effective, proportionate and dissuasive.

The highly diverse consequences of infringing an information duty under the consumer credit directive can be illustrated in the following way. In Austria not mentioning the interest rate leads to the applicability of the statutory interest (no doubt lower than the rate the lender envisaged). In Greece not giving the necessary information gives the consumer the right to terminate the contract. In Germany § 494 BGB provides a whole list of different sanctions, including that the contract is void unless the borrower in fact receives the loan. In the latter case, the interest rate is reduced to the statutory rate. In Poland and France (Art. L 341-3 Consumer Code) not complying with the information duties leads to a free loan (meaning: an interest rate of 0 per cent). Under Polish law failing to inform the consumer can even be a criminal offence, while in Italy administrative sanctions can be taken (such as suspending the license of the credit institution). Section 127 of the UK Consumer Credit Act allows the court to enforce the disclosure of information if it considers this reasonable on the facts of the case. In Dutch law, finally, non-compliance with the information requirement is regarded as an unfair commercial practice (Art. 7:60 (3) BW), creating a liability in tort. Although this varied picture surely has the charm that each European Member State can decide how to fit in the directive with its own preferences of how to enforce it, it is difficult to see how this varied picture can contribute to one, harmonised, level playing field for European business.

Meanwhile, a crucial question is to what extent extensive information requirements are effective: do they really put consumers at a higher level of information or do they lead to information overload?

Effective?

What type of writing is required? On internet shopping

Many of the laws that require a contract to be in writing were made at a time when it was clear what 'writing' meant. This has changed with the rise of the internet. Most of today's non-oral communication no longer takes place by writing letters, sending faxes or signing forms, but by e-mail and instant messaging services such as WhatsApp. The question relevant to the law is whether these means of communication in electronic form also satisfy the need for 'writing'. There seem to be two problems with this. The first is that the warning function of having to sign a piece of paper may be watered down if it is just as easy to obtain consumer credit by clicking a few buttons on a website, or text one's grandmother with the question if she could stand surety for your debt against a friend. The second problem is that a paper signature is still seen as more reliable than an e-mail containing one's name. While a written signature is unique to a person, a typed name is not.

Online
contracts

It will come as no surprise that the EU has a great interest in this matter. It regards contracts concluded over the internet as the jewel in the crown of cross-border shopping, and therefore of the European internal market. Electronic contracts are not hampered by physical borders: presumably it is just as easy for an e-trader in Hungary to sell to his fellow countrymen as it is to sell to any other European. This explains why the European legislature issued two directives particularly aimed at facilitating online contracts. Directive 2000/31 on Electronic Commerce states in Art. 9 (1):

> Member States shall ensure that their legal system allows contracts to be concluded by electronic means. Member States shall in particular ensure that the legal requirements applicable to the contractual process neither create obstacles for the use of electronic contracts nor result in such contracts being deprived of legal effectiveness and validity on account of their having been made by electronic means.

Article 5 (1) of Directive 1999/31 on Electronic Signatures states:

> 1. Member States shall ensure that advanced electronic signatures which are based on a qualified certificate and which are created by a secure-signature-creation device:
> (a) satisfy the legal requirements of a signature in relation to data in electronic form in the same manner as a handwritten signature satisfies those requirements in relation to paper-based data; and
> (b) are admissible as evidence in legal proceedings.

Article 9 (2)–(3) of the Directive on Electronic Commerce allows an exception for contracts that create or transfer rights in real estate, notary deeds, consumer suretyship and contracts in the field of family law and succession, but Art. 9 (1) makes clear that the validity of any other contract cannot be affected only because it was made through electronic means.

The Member States have implemented these provisions in their national laws (see e.g. Arts. 1125 ff. CC, § 126 ff. BGB and the UK Electronic Commerce (EC Directive) Regulations 2002). When doing so, some countries took the opportunity to further clarify which requirements internet shopping should meet, just to make it even more reliable for the consumer. An interesting provision in this respect is Art. 6:227a Dutch Civil Code; it mentions four advantages of putting a contract on paper and then goes on to state that if these four points are also met by electronic communication the contract is just as valid:

> 1. If a statutory provision implies that a contract can only be formed validly in writing, then this formal requirement is also met if the contract is entered into by electronic means and:
> a. the contract is and remains accessible for the parties;
> b. the authenticity of the contract is sufficiently guaranteed;
> c. the moment at which the contract was formed, can be determined with sufficient certainty; and
> d. the identity of the parties can be established with sufficient certainty.
> 2. Paragraph 1 does not apply to contracts for which the law requires the intervention of a court, a public authority or a person whose profession it is to exercise a public responsibility.

There is one important aspect of electronic contracts that has not yet been mentioned. As said before, the quoted provisions do not solve the problem that electronic communication may not 'warn' an interested party of the dangers of the transaction. This is exactly the reason why, as a counterweight to facilitating e-commerce, the European legislature requires e-sellers to give information to the consumer. Directive 2011/83 on Consumer Rights states that in case of 'distance contracts' (such as contracts concluded over the internet) the trader must provide information, for example on the main characteristics of the goods or services, the identity and address of the trader, the price and the mode of delivery (Art. 6). In addition, the trader must provide the consumer with a confirmation of the contract on a durable medium (according to the preamble of the directive not only paper, but also 'USB sticks, CD-ROMs, DVDs, memory cards or the hard disks of computers as well as e-mails') at the latest at the time of delivery of the goods (Art. 8 (7)). After delivery the consumer has 14 days to withdraw from the contract without giving any reason (Art. 9 (1)). The directive contains a model withdrawal form that can be used by the consumer. The combination of these requirements probably provides the consumer with better protection than the old-fashioned written form.

Information duties

BOX 6.2

RIGHTS OF WITHDRAWAL

The right of a consumer to withdraw from a contract has become a prominent feature of European contract law. The most important contracts in which the right exists are distance contracts (such as those concluded over the internet), off-premises contracts (such as doorstep selling), consumer credit and timeshare. In each of these contracts the consumer has 14 days after delivery or the day of conclusion to end the contract without giving any reason. In case the trader failed to inform the consumer about the right of withdrawal, the period expires 14 days after the consumer was informed.

Two different motives exist to allow the consumer this 'cooling off-period' in which she can reconsider her assent to the contract. The first is that a consumer sometimes needs to be protected against a lack of psychological strength. This is a good reason for a withdrawal right if the other party makes use of aggressive sales techniques, takes the consumer by surprise or intrudes into the privacy of her home (as in case of doorstep sales and timeshare). The second possible motive is when a lack of informational strength prevents the consumer from forming an accurate picture of the product being sold or of the nature of the transaction (which is typically the case in distance contracts and consumer credit). A withdrawal right can then be used to remedy the information asymmetry: it allows the consumer to acquire the information she needs by inspecting the product before being definitively bound or by assessing the risks involved in the transaction (as in consumer credit). To see a photo on a website is different from being able to actually touch and feel the product. Withdrawal rights thus help consumers to better exercise their freedom of contract: their consent is presumably more free and informed.

These statutory rights of withdrawal must be distinguished from so-called *rights to return*. Many retail shops throughout the world have adopted the policy that customers can return goods at will and receive back the contract price or at least a credit note with which they can buy a different product in the same shop. This return policy is often laid down in the general conditions of the retailer. These contractual rights are even so common that the general public sometimes thinks that there is a 'general right to return goods'. But this is not the case: the existence of these contractual rights is entirely dependent on the retailer's willingness to provide these to its customers, thus allowing it to distinguish itself from its competitors. This explains why different shops use different return periods: while some shops offer 14 days, others allow 90 days, 180 days or even an indefinite period.

Sanctions if a contract lacks the required form

A.   Voidness and avoidability of the contract

An important question is what are the consequences of the failure to comply with a formality. We have already seen that when it comes to a violation of a European information requirement each Member State decides for itself how it wants to sanction this. It is also clear that this question does not arise for contracts to be evidenced in writing: these are normally valid, albeit that it is up to the claimant to prove the existence of the contract by reference to written documents. But if the written form (either a notarial deed, a deed under English law or the requirement of a contract being 'in writing') is not met, does this mean that the contract is not valid? This indeed seems to be the starting point of both the German and the Dutch Civil Code:

> **§ 125 BGB**: 'A juridical act that lacks the form prescribed by statute is void. In case of doubt, lack of the form specified by juridical act also results in voidness.'

> **Art. 3:39 BW**: 'Unless the law provides otherwise, a juridical act that is not performed in accordance with formal requirements, is null and void.'

Aim of the rule

English law adopts practically the same approach by holding the contract 'unenforceable'. But things are not that straightforward. In practice much depends on the ratio of the formality. It is indeed justified to hold the contract void if the formality not complied with serves the interest of both parties, or some general interest such as the legal certainty that third parties must be able to rely on. If for example no notarial deed was made for the transfer of immovable property in German or Dutch law, it is wholly reasonable to hold the transfer void. The court must note this out of its own motion. This is different in cases where the formality only aims to protect one party to the contract. So in case of suretyship, residential lease, employment and consumer contracts – all contracts where the formality exists only to protect one party against the other, or against itself – it is often sufficient to hold the contract only avoidable. This means that the protected party can decide if it wants to keep the contract in place or not. This approach of making it dependent on the purpose of the formality whether the contract should be void or avoidable is not only adopted in France, but also in any other jurisdiction – even though the text of § 125 BGB seems to suggest otherwise.

B.   Curing a lack of form

But this is not the end of the story. Even in cases where a formality was not observed one could think of circumstances under which the defect is cured. There are three basic situations in which this can be the case.

First, it could be that the statute itself indicates that an invalid contract is converted into a valid one in the interest of the party for whose protection the formality was introduced. If a residential lease concluded for a period of more than one year is not made in writing, § 550 BGB simply converts it into a contract for an indeterminate time. The formal requirement solely exists in the interest of the lessee and this justifies that the defect of form is cured to his benefit.

Second, it may happen that one party or both parties actually carry out the intended contract without worrying about any formalities. In such a case the performance itself could cure the defect. Sometimes the law explicitly states this. If the guarantor in a consumer suretyship simply performs (meaning that he pays the creditor) the contract is valid, despite the fact that the guarantee was only made orally (Art. 7:859 BW and § 766 BGB explicitly say so). The 'immediate donation' as discussed above is another example: the gift is valid despite the absence of a notarial deed.

Third, one party could make its counterpart intentionally or negligently believe that no formalities are needed while in fact this is not true. If the other party justifiedly relies on such statements by acting upon them, courts are inclined to disallow the first party claiming that the contract is invalid for lack of formalities. In Germany and the Netherlands the basis for this is usually found in the principle of good faith (reasonableness and fairness, discussed in detail in Chapter 8), in England in the doctrine of proprietary estoppel, while in France such behaviour could amount to *abus de droit* (abuse of right). Most case law is about the practically important promise to transfer land or a house without satisfying the requirement of a notarial deed (in Germany) or of writing (in England).

An example of reliance making good the defect of form in such a case is provided by a decision of the *Bundesgerichtshof* in 1967 (*Kaufmannsehrenwort*). The buyer of a plot of land was given a document signed by the director of the selling company containing the details of the sale. The buyer was a former employee of the seller. In response to the buyer's request to have a notary make a deed (as required by § 311b BGB) the seller said that he was 'used to respect his obligations, no matter whether they were made orally, in writing or in notarial form'. When the buyer insisted, the seller replied that 'the contract was equivalent to a notarial contract'. When the seller later argued that no valid contract had been formed for lack of a notarial deed, the court found that he could not invoke this defect, in particular not now that the buyer had acted in reliance on the seller's promises. This is another application of the principle that one is not allowed to go against one's own previous behaviour, as encountered before in Chapter 4. This can also be seen in the English case *Pascoe v Turner* (1979). Mr. Pascoe owned a house in Cornwall and Mrs. Turner moved in as his housekeeper, later his mistress. Mr. Pascoe repeatedly told Mrs. Turner that the house was hers. When he started seeing another woman, he asked her to leave the house, in which she had invested all her savings to repair and redecorate it. Despite the absence of consideration or the promise being put in a deed, the court found that the house should be conveyed to Mrs. Turner. His assurances, her detriment in reliance thereon, and the fact that he saw her spend her money on the house without protesting against this, were sufficient to estop Mr. Pascoe from claiming the house was his. This so-called proprietary estoppel was thus used to found a cause of action (unlike promissory estoppel discussed in Chapter 4).

 TOPICS FOR REVIEW

The principle of informality
Different reasons for formalities
Contracts to be made by notarial deed
Civil law notary and Notary Public
Contracts to be made by deed
Contracts to be made in writing
Contracts to be evidenced in writing
Donation
Consumer credit
Suretyship
Contracts requiring pre-contractual information duties
Form in electronic contracts
Withdrawal rights in distance contracts
Sanctions for lack of form
Curing a lack of form

 FURTHER READING

– Hugh Beale et al, *Cases, Materials and Text on Contract Law, Ius Commune Casebooks for the Common Law of Europe*, 2nd ed., Oxford (Hart Publishing) 2010, Chapter 5.
– Sjef van Erp and Bram Akkermans (eds), *Cases, Materials and Text on Property Law, Ius Commune Casebooks for the Common Law of Europe*, Oxford (Hart) 2012, Chapter 8.
– Lon Fuller, 'Consideration and Form', 41 *Columbia Law Review* (1941), 799.
– Hein Kötz, *European Contract Law Vol. 1* (translated by Tony Weir), Oxford (Oxford University Press) 1997, Chapter 5.

– Peter Rott, 'Information obligations and withdrawal rights', in: Christian Twigg-Flesner (ed.), *The Cambridge Companion to European Union Private Law*, Cambridge (Cambridge University Press) 2010, 187–200.
– Francois Terré, Philippe Simler and Yves Lequette, *Droit civil: les obligations*, 11th ed., Paris (Dalloz) 2013, Book 1, Title 1.

Part Three

The contents of the contract

Once the contract is validly concluded, the second stage of its life begins: the parties have to perform in conformity with what they promised. Fortunately, this does not pose a problem in the great majority of cases. However, sometimes problems do arise. It could happen that the parties quarrel about what they actually agreed upon, prompting the need for **interpretation** of the party agreement. In addition, more often than not the parties have not spoken about all the eventualities that might occur. This calls for **gap filling (supplementation)** of the agreement. Both interpretation and gap filling are discussed in Chapter 7. Finally, it could happen that a party claims that one or more terms of the contract are unfair. Although this is not a claim that is likely to succeed, the law does control some types of **unfair terms** (Chapter 8).

7

The party agreement: Interpretation and gap filling

CHAPTER OVERVIEW

The **party agreement** consists of the contractual terms that the parties have explicitly agreed upon. This agreement can be unclear, which calls for **interpretation** in order to give one meaning to the used terms. The agreement can also be incomplete, calling for **gap filling** (also known as supplementation of the party agreement). This chapter examines:

- interpretation of the party agreement;
- the various methods that legislators and courts use to fill gaps in the party agreement.

Interpretation

A validly concluded contract obliges the parties to perform their contractual obligations. This is not as straightforward as it may sound. Practice shows that parties frequently dispute what it is that they actually agreed upon. The most important reason for this is that words are never clear in and of themselves. They are acts of communication that require both a sender and a receiver who, given their different background, knowledge and experience, may not understand each other in the way they think they do. The law therefore shares with literature and theology the characteristic that it is an *interpretative discipline*: just like poetry, the Bible and the Quran, statutes, treaties and contracts need to be given a meaning by the reader or listener. This often takes place implicitly, without the interpreter realising it. However, it may also happen that parties differ explicitly about the contents of their agreement. If Newcom Ltd agrees that its customer Agri Gmbh is allowed to 'give back' the machine it purchased within three months after delivery, it could well be that seller Newcom intended Agri to be allowed to terminate the contract only in the event of a defect with the machine, while buyer Agri understood the term as allowing it to simply end the contract at its own will. This process of establishing one single meaning to the words explicity used in the party agreement is called *interpretation* (*interprétation, Auslegung, uitleg*). Its aim is to establish one meaning for all parties affected by the contract.

Three reasonsThe mere interpretation of the party agreement is almost never enough to establish what the parties need to do under the contract. Parties often only agree on a few main points ('eight sofas as seen by the buyer, €300 each, payment upon delivery on 20 May') and do not bother about agreeing on anything else (such as the place of delivery and the rights of buyer and seller in case of non-performance). This is perfectly sensible behaviour. First, because the great majority of parties cannot conceive of all possible contingencies that could happen during the course of the contract. This is particularly true if the contract is intended to last for a long time, as for example in case of residential lease or franchise. Second, because in most cases it is not efficient to negotiate and draft contracts that aim to foresee all possible contingencies. The contract would have to represent a high value to invest the time and money to make this worthwhile (although it may be cost-effective if the terms are to become applicable to many future contracts, as in case of general conditions). Third, because the law provides solutions to deal with incomplete contracts. In each jurisdiction this so-called *gap filling* or *supplementation of the party agreement* takes place in two different ways.

Ad hoc gap
fillingFirst, it can happen that parties did not provide for a certain contingency because it is such an obvious part of the contract that they did not believe it necessary to spell it out. If I rent a car from Hertz, the rental company will have to provide me with the car keys, even though one will not find anything on this in the contract or in Hertz's general conditions. If necessary the court fills this gap in the party agreement by speaking for the parties: although they did not consider the matter, the court construes what they would have said. In several jurisdictions this is regarded as a type of interpretation, called *supplementary* or *constructive interpretation*. This is true for Germany (where it is called *ergänzende Vertragsauslegung*) and France (*interprétation créatrice*). English law is a bit more candid by speaking of *terms implied in fact*. The overall term used in this book for these techniques is *ad hoc gap filling*: the party agreement is supplemented with terms that follow from the hypothetical will of the parties in the circumstances of the case.

Gap filling
through default
rulesSecond, it frequently happens that interpretation of the party agreement and supplementation by way of ad hoc gap filling are not sufficient to establish all the rights and obligations of the contracting parties. If Mika has his car repaired by Sophie, they usually do not provide for inspection by Mika of the material to be used, for return of the car before the repair is finished, or for who carries the risk of the car being destroyed by fire in Sophie's garage. This is where the second type of gap filling comes in, namely *gap filling through default rules*. As was already hinted at in Chapter 2, the gaps in the contract left by the parties are filled by the default (or 'facilitative') rules that are automatically applicable in so far as the parties did not deviate from them. These default rules (*règles supplétives, dispositives Recht, aanvullend recht*) provide standard solutions for problems that typically arise in certain types of contracts. In civil law jurisdictions they can be found in the national civil code. In English law they are called *terms implied in law* and are more frequently developed by the courts.

This chapter discusses all three aspects of establishing the contents of the contract: interpretation of the party agreement, ad hoc gap filling, and gap filling through default rules.

Interpretation of the party agreement

A.   Subjective and objective interpretation

Interpretation, aimed at establishing the meaning of the words used by the parties, is not an exercise that takes place in a vacuum. The core of a contract as an act of exercising party autonomy is that it is *made* by the parties. This means that interpretation must be directed at ascertaining what parties have intended with it, not at what the court or anyone else finds the most 'fair', suitable or efficient interpretation. In other words, interpretation of a contract is to search for the *common intention of the parties*. This search can take

Subjective place starting from two fundamentally different positions. One method (*subjective interpretation*) is to give preference to the 'real' intention of the parties. Since the words the parties used are only an expression of their intention, it is this intention that should prevail. The obvious difficulty with this approach, as we saw before in Chapter 4 when the consensus of parties was discussed, is that the 'actual' intention of a party can never be established: even a psychological or neuroscientific investigation into a party's mind is not likely to uncover the historical intention as it existed at the time of concluding the contract. The opposite view is to give priority to the declaration and therefore to the external expression of the intention, this being the only thing that

Objective can be apparent to the other party. This *objective interpretation* thus protects a party's reliance on the words actually used. The most famous formulation of the objective approach was given by the American judge Learned Hand. In *Hotchkiss v National City Bank of New York* (1911), he states:

> A contract has, strictly speaking, nothing to do with the personal, or individual, intent of the parties. A contract is an obligation attached by the mere force of law to

certain acts of the parties, usually words, which ordinarily accompany and represent a known intent. If, however, it were proved by twenty bishops that either party when he used the words intended something else than the usual meaning which the law imposes on them, he would still be held (…).

The tension between giving priority to a party's (subjective) intention and to its (objective) declaration is clearly visible in the great codifications of private law. Article 1188 of the French *Code Civil* requires the court to find the 'common intention of the parties', but it also prescribes that if the intention cannot be discerned, the contract must be interpreted in the sense which a reasonable person placed in the same situation would give to it. The German BGB states in §133 that the aim of interpretation must be 'to ascertain the real intention', but continues in §157 with the rule that interpretation should take place 'in accordance with fairness and reasonableness taking into account general practice'.

The same tension between *verba* (words) and *voluntas* (intention) can be found in English law. The traditional starting point of English law in case of doubt about the meaning of contractual terms was not to look for the common intention of the parties, but an extreme version of the objective approach, namely to interpret a contract according to its literal meaning. In the case of *Lovell & Christmas Ltd v Wall* (1911), for example, it was held that 'it is the duty of the court (…) to construe the document according to the ordinary grammatical meaning of the words used therein'. This approach has been abandoned. According to the authoritative formulation of Lord Hoffmann in *Investors Compensation Scheme Ltd v West Bromwich Building Society* (1998), interpretation is 'the ascertainment of the meaning which the document would convey to a reasonable person having all the background knowledge which would reasonably have been available to the parties in the situation which they were at the time of the contract'.

This makes clear that all European jurisdictions adopt a compromise between attaching importance to the intention and the expression thereof. This compromise does not fundamentally differ in civil law and common law. Interpretation is always directed at finding the common intention of the parties; if parties differ about what their common intention is, the reasonable meaning to be given to the words in the circumstances of the case prevails. The only practical difference is that in civil law jurisdictions this reasonable meaning is primarily found by taking the understanding of the *contracting parties* as the starting point, while English law adopts the perspective of a *reasonable person* in the position of the contracting parties. These traces of respectively the subjective and objective approach come out nicely in the following

Reasonable meaning

two quotes. The first is taken from the seminal case *Haviltex* (1981) in which the *Hoge Raad* formulated the main rule for interpretation in Dutch law:

> The question how a written contract regulates the relationship between parties, and whether this contract leaves a gap that must be supplemented, cannot be answered on basis of only a purely literal interpretation of the provisions of the contract. To answer that question, it is decisive what is the meaning that parties in the circumstances of the case could mutually reasonably attach to these provisions and what they could in that respect reasonably expect from each other. In this process, it is inter alia of relevance what the parties societal position is and what knowledge of the law can be expected of such parties.

The second quote is from Lord Steyn in the English case *Lord Napier and Ettrick v R F Kershaw Ltd* (1999). It explains further why Lord Hoffmann (see above) put so much emphasis on interpretation by a reasonable person:

> Loyalty to the text of a commercial contract, instrument, or document read in its contextual setting is the paramount principle of interpretation. But in the process of interpreting the meaning of the language of a commercial document the court ought generally to favour a commercially sensible construction. The reason for this approach is that a commercial construction is likely to give effect to the intention of the parties. Words ought therefore to be interpreted in the way in which a reasonable commercial person would construe them.

It must be emphasised that this difference is one of perspective. It is merely a matter of in which position the court places itself to interpret the words of the contract: that of the reasonable parties or that of a reasonable third person in a similar position as the parties. Different practical results are not likely to follow from this difference. This is why all international instruments were able to draft a convincing provision on interpretation that both civil law and common law lawyers are eager to accept. Thus, Arts 8 CISG, 4.1 PICC and II-8:101 DCFR convey the same message as Art. 5:101 PECL:

> (1) A contract is to be interpreted according to the common intention of the parties even if this differs from the literal meaning of the words.
> (2) If it is established that one party intended the contract to have a particular meaning, and at the time of the conclusion of the contract the other party could not have been unaware of the first party's intention, the contract is to be interpreted in the way intended by the first party.
> (3) If an intention cannot be established according to (1) or (2), the contract is to be interpreted according to the meaning that reasonable persons of the same kind as the parties would give to it in the same circumstances.

B.   Factors relevant to interpretation

Now that it is established that the main criterion for interpretation is the common intention of the parties and how a reasonable party would interpret the used words, the next question is how a court applies these criteria.

There is no problem in cases where both parties are mistaken about what a term means. To give an old example that is now highly politically incorrect: if both seller and buyer use the word *Haakjöringsköd* because they both believe this means whale meat, while it is actually Norwegian for shark meat, it is whale meat that needs to be delivered because this is what both parties had in mind when concluding the contract. The buyer can claim damages if he only received shark meat, as the German highest court decided in 1920. This is simply a matter of having the common intention of the parties (one could say: their shared subjective understanding) prevail over the objective meaning of the contract. Lawyers qualify this type of case as *falsa demonstratio non nocet* ('a wrong description does no harm'); it would fall under section 1 of the just quoted Art. 5:101 PECL.

Falsa demonstratio

Equally simple is the case in which parties are not mistaken about the meaning of a term (as above), but in which their common understanding of a word differs from its usual meaning. If a motorcycle fan has always referred to her Harley Davidson motorbike as her 'little trike', and then sells 'my trike' for €3,000 to her uncle who knows of this odd habit, the uncle can protest if he is delivered a child's tricycle. Article 5:101 s. 2 PECL reflects this.

Common understanding

Things become more difficult if parties use truly ambiguous clauses. Civil law jurisdictions allow the court to look at a range of different circumstances in interpreting such clauses. This is well reflected in Art. 5:102 PECL, which states:

Ambiguous clauses

> In interpreting the contract, regard shall be had, in particular, to:
> a. the circumstances in which it was concluded, including the preliminary negotiations;
> b. the conduct of the parties, even subsequent to the conclusion of the contract;
> c. the nature and purpose of the contract;
> d. the interpretation which has already been given to similar clauses by the parties and the practices they have established between themselves;
> e. the meaning commonly given to terms and expressions in the branch of activity concerned and the interpretation similar clauses may already have received;
> f. usages; and
> g. good faith and fair dealing.

How to apply these factors can be exemplified by reference to a German case about a so-called 'first demand guarantee' (*Bürgschaft auf erstes Anfordern*, 1992). Such a – very perilous – guarantee allows the creditor to obtain immediately from the surety the promised sum; any defences that the debtor is not obliged to pay are postponed to a later stage and could at best lead to a claim for restitution if the surety paid without a valid ground. In the case decided by the *Bundesgerichtshof* the surety was the wife of a man whose business partner had borrowed money from the plaintiff. Her husband had talked her into giving the guarantee. She was a layperson who believed that she had given only a 'normal' guarantee. When the plaintiff brought a claim for payment she pleaded that she did not mean to be bound to a demand guarantee, prompting the court to interpret the declaration she had made. The court found decisive how the creditor had to understand this declaration according to good faith and commercial practice. It then continued in the following way:

> Even if the plaintiff, when it formulated its terms, deliberately chose wording that banks regularly use for first demand guarantees, it could not assume, on that ground alone, that the defendant intended to be bound to such a guarantee. From the point of view of the creditor, who initiated and formulated the guarantee, the intention of the guarantor can only have been in accordance with what she understood the wording submitted to her to mean. This is why the plaintiff must accept the declaration of guarantee as having the meaning which she can objectively derive from it in the circumstances of the case.
>
> However, the wording of the agreement in question ('The guaranteed sum shall become immediately payable upon demand or upon this deed being first produced …') corresponds to the standard formulation as it has come to be used in banking transactions for demand guarantees. Such circumstances lying outside of the declaration itself can be taken into account in the interpretation, in so far as they allow the recipient of the declaration to draw a conclusion as to its meaning. (…) That is not the case here, as the plaintiff could not assume that the defendant knew or should have known the meaning of the wording of the agreement in banking operations. (…) A demand guarantee is a typical banking transaction. It is little known outside of banking circles. The plaintiff has not argued that the defendant had experience with respect to credit securities in general or about demand guarantees in particular; nor did the plaintiff argue that the defendant was informed of the specificities of a demand guarantee.

The proper interpretation of the guarantee was therefore that it was only a 'simple' guarantee and not a demand guarantee. This meant that the surety could validly invoke the reasons why she did not want to pay the creditor. It is not difficult to see various elements of Art. 5:102 sub a PECL coming back in the decision:

a: 'the circumstances in which the contract was concluded': the defendant was talked into the guarantee by her husband;

b: 'the conduct of the parties': the creditor did not inform the defendant about the risks of the guarantee and used only a standard formulation in the contract;

c: 'the nature and purpose of the contract': a demand guarantee is a dangerous transaction that can be very burdensome for the debtor;

e: 'the meaning commonly given to terms and expressions': there is a specific meaning given to a demand guarantee, but only in banking circles. The specific meaning of the term was not known to the defendant.

Expertise

A relevant factor not mentioned in Art. 5:102 PECL, but highly relevant in most jurisdictions, is the position of the parties and what knowledge and experience can be expected of them. This element was mentioned in the Dutch *Haviltex* case (see above) and is also relevant for the German court: the defendant was an inexperienced layperson who did not have to know about the true meaning of the guarantee and who did not have an expert present when the contract was made.

Parol evidence

Although the English approach to interpreting ambiguous clauses is not fundamentally different, courts are bound by the so-called *parol evidence rule*. This rule of evidence entails that in a written contract evidence extrinsic to the express terms of the contract cannot be taken into account. Draft contracts, letters, statements by witnesses or documentation from the pre-contractual negotiations between the parties cannot play a role in ascertaining what the contract terms 'actually' say. If Abimbola rents office space from Cherida and the contract contains an ambiguous clause about the time of payment of the rent, Abimbola cannot point at a prior oral agreement that he was allowed to pay only at the end of each three-month period instead of at the beginning. This means that English lawyers would have difficulty in accepting points a. and b. of Art. 5:102 PECL as relevant factors for interpretation (and for reasons set out later in this chapter the same is true for point g. on good faith and fair dealing).

C. Maxims of interpretation; *contra proferentem* rule

Civil codes in the French legal tradition typically provide rules of thumb to help interpret contracts. In the French Civil Code these *maxims of interpretation* are for example laid down in the Arts. 1189–1192, but they can also be found in the Italian, Spanish and Belgian Codes. Although two hundred years of experience show that these rules are not of too much practical use, the drafters of some new codifications still chose to adopt them (notable examples are the Arts. 1425–1432 of the new Civil Code of Quebec of 1994

BOX 7.1

UNAMBIGUOUS CLAUSES: *CLAUSES CLAIRES ET PRÉCISES*

Interpretation is a highly factual exercise. This explains why the highest courts in Europe have difficulty in providing lower courts with guidance on how to interpret – other than that interpretation needs to be objective. This is also true for the French *Cour de Cassation*, that refuses to review the interpretation of contracts in decisions of lower courts. But there is one interesting exception to this. Constantly, since 1872, in case law the French court has held that if a clause in a written contract is unambiguous (a *clause claire et précise*), the court is not allowed to interpret it. If the lower court give it a meaning other than the 'clear' objective one, the *Cour de Cassation* can quash the decision for distorting the intention of the parties. For much the same reason – fear that the court would get too much discretionary power in striking down the parties' agreement – the old Dutch Civil Code of 1838 contained the provision (Art. 1378) that: 'If words of a contract are clear, one can not deviate from these through interpretation.' This is of course a highly questionable approach: a clause is never clear as such and always need to be interpreted before one can say that it is 'clear'. But through this technique the *Cour de Cassation* (and

the same is true for the Italian *Corte di Cassazione*) is able to exercise some control over interpretation. A recent example is the case *Emil Cioran* (2012). A few years before his death in 1995 the French-Romanian writer Emil Cioran had written a holographic testament leaving his property to his partner. The testament read: 'I, the undersigned Emil Cioran, holding residence in (…), name as my heir for all my goods Ms. (…), holding residence in (…). In case Ms. (…) dies earlier, I name as my heir for all my goods Mr. (…), my brother, holding residence in (…).' After not only Cioran himself, but also his partner had died, a *brocanteuse* was hired by the partner's brother to empty the house. She found a great many unpublished manuscripts in the cellar. Cioran's partner had donated all manuscripts to the University of Paris who therefore claimed to be their owner. Although this was not a contract but a testament, the *Cour de Cassation* applied the doctrine of *clauses claires et précises* and held that interpretation of the testament was not allowed as it was clear in itself. Despite its questionable meaning, the French lawmaker decided in 2016 to codify the doctrine in Art. 1192 CC.

and Art. 1268 of the new Romanian Civil Code of 2011). Thus, the interpretation is preferred that gives an ambiguous clause some effect rather than none at all (Art. 1191 CC). Clauses must also be interpreted in the light of the entire contract (Art. 1189). Some of these rules can also be found in the PECL, that adds the provision that individually negotiated terms take preference over those which are not (Art. 5:104) and that in case of a discrepancy between two language versions of one contract the interpretation that accords to the original version of the contract prevails (Art. 5:107).

The best-known rule of interpretation, and one that is important in practice, is the so-called *contra proferentem rule*. This rule entails that an ambiguity in a written contract must be interpreted against the person who drafted it. This gives a clear incentive to the drafter to put the contract in clear terms, providing deterrence against sloppy drafting. The rule cannot only be found in some national codes (e.g. Arts. 1190 and 1602 *Code Civil*), but is also laid down in European Directive 93/13 on Unfair Terms in Consumer Contracts. Article 5 (2) states:

> In the case of contracts where all or certain terms offered to the consumer are in writing, these terms must always be drafted in plain, intelligible language. Where there is doubt about the meaning of a term, the interpretation most favourable to the consumer shall prevail.

As a result, all European Member States have adopted the *contra proferentem* rule in any event for general conditions in consumer contracts (see for example § 305c (2) BGB, Art. L 211-1 French Consumer Code, s. 69 Consumer Rights Act 2015 and Art. 6:238 (2) BW). Some of these jurisdictions also apply the rule to commercial contracts (as is also possible under Art. 5:103 PECL).

Ad hoc gap filling

Once it is established what is the proper meaning of the words explicitly used by the parties, the contract can still be incomplete. This is because a contract can never provide for all eventualities. The court then has to supplement the interpreted party agreement through gap filling. As was seen in the introduction to this chapter, this can take place on an ad hoc basis and by use of default rules. The first method – ad hoc gap filling – means that a lacuna in a specific contract of the two specific parties is filled with terms that are necessary for the working of the contract and that the parties would have agreed upon if they had thought about it. The presumed intention of the parties (their 'hypothetical will') serves as the basis for this – admittedly speculative – exercise. Art. II-9:101 DCFR puts it like this (Arts. 6:102 PECL and 4.8 PICC provide similar provisions):

> (1) The terms of a contract may be derived from the express or tacit agreement of the parties, from rules of law or from practices established between the parties or usages.
> (2) Where it is necessary to provide for a matter which the parties have not foreseen or provided for, a court may imply an additional term, having regard in particular to:

(a) the nature and purpose of the contract;

(b) the circumstances in which the contract was concluded; and

(c) the requirements of good faith and fair dealing.

(3) Any term implied under paragraph (2) should, where possible, be such as to give effect to what the parties, had they provided for the matter, would probably have agreed.(…)

Germany

All jurisdictions accept this ad hoc gap filling to give meaning to the contract, albeit under different names. It is applied in much less obvious cases than the car keys example mentioned before. In German law this is *ergänzende Vertragsauslegung* (supplementing interpretation of the contract, based on the general provision on interpretation of § 157 BGB). It entails that in case the parties have omitted to say something, the court must – in the wording of the *Bundesgerichtshof* – 'discover and take into account what, in the light of the whole purpose of the contract, they would have said if they had dealt with the point in question, acting pursuant to the requirements of good faith and sound business practice' (*Swapping doctors*, 1954). In that case, a doctor who had swapped practices with a colleague was barred from opening a new practice in the vicinity of his old one for a reasonable period of two to three years.

France

The French speak of *interprétation créatrice* (constructive interpretation), which they base on Art. 1194 *Code Civil*. This provision states: 'Contracts are binding not only as to what is therein expressed, but also as to all the consequences which equity, usage or statute give to the contract.' There is a huge amount of case law based on this article that obliges parties to comply with all kinds of pre-contractual duties to inform, advise and warn their counterpart (see Chapter 8). But the article is also applied in other cases. In one decision, a radio station had commissioned an author to write a radio play, had accepted the play without objections and had paid for it, but subsequently refused to broadcast the play on the radio. The court held that broadcasting was part of the agreement even though parties had not explicitly discussed this at the time of contracting (*Radio play*, 1974).

In civil law jurisdictions there is a close relationship between interpretation, ad hoc gap filling and the so-called *principle of good faith (reasonableness and fairness)*. This principle will be discussed in more detail in Chapter 8, but what interests us here is that the principle obliges parties to a contract to take into account each other's interests. In civil law the duty to interpret the contract in a reasonable way and to fill lacunae are seen as following from this principle. This is even explicitly laid down in Art. 6:248 (1) of the Dutch Civil Code, which states: 'A contract not only has the effects agreed upon by the parties, but also those which, according to the nature of the contract, result from statute, usage or the requirements of good faith (reasonableness and fairness).'

English law does not regard ad hoc gap filling as a means of interpretation. Instead it speaks of *terms implied in fact*. Again, these are terms that are not explicitly laid down in the contract, but of which it is assumed that parties would have included them if they had directed their minds to it. English courts have developed two tests to find this unexpressed intention. The first one is often called the 'officious bystander' test and was formulated by MacKinnon LJ in *Shirlaw v Southern Foundries* (1939):

> *Prima facie* that which in any contract is left to be implied and need not be expressed is something so obvious that it goes without saying; so that, if while the parties were making their bargain, an officious bystander were to suggest some express provision for it in the agreement, they would testily suppress him with a common, "Oh, of course!"

The second test is called the 'business efficacy' test. The leading case is *The Moorcock* (1889). Parties had entered into a contract that allowed the plaintiff to unload his boat *The Moorcock* at the wharf of the defendant. The boat was damaged when the unloading took place at low tide and hit the hard ground of the riverbed. It was not explicitly stated in the contract that the boat had to be moored safely, but the Court of Appeal implied such a term arguing that this 'must be necessary to give the transaction such business efficacy as the parties must have intended'. In other words: the defendant should have warned the plaintiff of the unevenness of the riverbed. Any other view would have meant that the plaintiff had only bought 'an opportunity of danger'. Consequently the boat owner could claim damages for breach of contract.

Both tests largely overlap. They concur in only allowing the court to imply a term if the contract is ineffective without it, and if the term is so obvious that it goes without saying that it must be part of the contract. These are strict criteria that only lead to inclusion of terms in fact if really necessary. Not just any 'reasonable' term can be implied with the argument that it is a term that a reasonable person would have agreed to; instead it is about the hypothetical intention of *these* parties.

Gap filling through default rules

While ad hoc gap filling provides solutions that are tailor-made for the specific contract of the parties, the second method of gap filling provides standard solutions for problems typical to a certain type of contract. These *default rules* exist for all contracts regulated in civil codes, such as contracts of sale, employment and lease. In the common law comparable standards exist under the heading of *terms implied in law*. These sometimes flow from statutes (in particular the Sale of Goods Act 1979), but are more often developed by the courts. The different terminology used in English law reveals a deeper truth: while civil law jurisdictions are happy to say that these rules are simply imposed by the legislator, English law finds this public interference with the contract more problematic and prefers to say that they are implied with the contract. English law thus gives pride of place to the parties.

Ratio

By providing default rules the legislator or court offers a service to the contracting parties. It saves them the expense of time and money to negotiate about terms that most probably will not have to be invoked anyway. Instead they can rely on rules that balance the parties' interests in a just way. However, if parties prefer to make their own terms the default law will yield to this contrary agreement. It is thus extremely useful for parties to be able to rely on provisions such as: sold goods must be of satisfactory quality (e.g. Sale of Goods Act 1979, s. 14 (2) and Consumer Rights Act 2015, s. 9); any sold good must be suitable for normal use (e.g. § 434 BGB); the rent is due at the beginning of the lease period (e.g. § 556b (1) BGB); the employee is entitled to a reference at the end of the employment (e.g. Art. 7:656 BW and *Spring v Guardian Assurance plc*, 1994); and the lender of a thing must tell the borrower about defects that may cause harm to the person who uses it if he knows of the defects (e.g. Art. 1891 CC). Each system of national contract law typically has hundreds of such default provisions.

Liverpool City Council v Irwin

The difference between statutory default terms typical to civil law jurisdictions and terms implied in law by the English courts can be illustrated by reference to the case of *Liverpool City Council v Irwin* (1977). Mr. and Mrs. Irwin were the tenants of a flat on the ninth floor of a 15-storey, high-rise block in Liverpool. The common parts of the building were constantly vandalised with the result that the stair lights failed, lifts did not work and the garbage chute was usually blocked. Together with other tenants Mr. and Mrs. Irwin withheld their rent. When the landlord (the city of Liverpool) brought an action to evict them, they counterclaimed that there was a duty on the part of the landlord to keep the common parts of the building in a decent state and properly lit. The City Council denied the existence of such a duty: there was no contract that listed such an obligation on the landlord. The House of Lords, however, held that the landlord had 'an obligation to take reasonable care to keep the common parts of the block in reasonable repair and usability'.

This obligation is implied in any relationship between landlord and tenant, or as Lord Wilberforce put it:

> such obligation should be read into the contract as the nature of the contract itself implicitly requires, no more, no less: a test in other words of necessity. The relationship accepted by the Corporation is that of landlord and tenant: the tenant accepts obligations accordingly, in relation *inter alia* to the stairs, the lifts and the chutes. All these are not just facilities, or conveniences provided at discretion: they are essentials of the tenancy without which life in the dwellings, as a tenant, is not possible. To leave the landlord free of contractual obligation as regards these matters, and subject only to administrative or political pressure, is, in my opinion, inconsistent totally with the nature of this relationship. The subject matter of the lease (high-rise blocks) and the relationship created by the tenancy demands, of its nature, some contractual obligation on the landlord.

This does not mean that this obliges the landlord to achieve the actual *result* that the common parts are always in a state of repair. Damage done by vandals and possibly by (the children of) the tenants themselves cannot be prevented at all times or repaired every day. It is therefore sufficient if all reasonable care is taken (in this case the court found that the City Council had indeed exercised all necessary care). French lawyers would speak of an *obligation de moyens* (in contrast to an *obligation de résultat*).

Civil law jurisdictions reach the same result by applying statutory default provisions. These are the provisions that French, German and Dutch courts would probably use to decide a similar case in their jurisdiction:

> **Art. 1719 CC:** 'A lessor is bound, by the nature of the contract, and without need of any particular stipulation:
> 1° To deliver the thing leased to the lessee and, where the main dwelling of the latter is concerned, a decent lodging. In case a residential dwelling is not fit for this use, the lessor cannot claim the nullity of the lease or its termination in order to evict the resident;
> 2° To maintain that thing in order so that it can serve the use for which it has been let;
> 3° To secure to the lessee a peaceful enjoyment for the duration of the lease;
> 4° To secure also the permanence and quality of plantings.'

> **§ 536 (1) BGB:** 'If the leased property at the time of putting it at the disposal of the lessee has a defect which removes its suitability for the contractually agreed use, or if such a defect arises during the lease period, then the lessee is exempted for the period when suitability is removed from paying the rent. (...)'

Art. 7:204 (2) Dutch Civil Code: 'A defect is a quality or characteristic of the leased property or another circumstance not attributable to the lessee, as a result of which the leased property cannot provide the lessee the enjoyment which a lessee, at the moment on which the lease agreement was concluded, can expect of a well maintained property of the kind to which the lease agreement relates.'

Art. 7:206 (1) Dutch Civil Code: 'If the lessee desires so, the lessor must cure a defect, unless this is impossible or would require expenditures which in the given circumstances cannot reasonably be expected to be made by the lessor.'

 TOPICS FOR REVIEW

Contents of the contract
Incomplete contracts
Interpretation
Subjective interpretation
Objective interpretation
Factors relevant to interpretation of a contract
Parol evidence rule
Doctrine of unambiguous clauses
Maxims of interpretation
Contra proferentem rule
Ad hoc gap filling
Hypothetical will of parties
Terms implied in fact
Default rules
Terms implied in law
Landlord's duty to keep a building in a reasonable state of repair

 FURTHER READING

- Hugh Beale et al, *Cases, Materials and Text on Contract Law, Ius Commune Casebooks for the Common Law of Europe*, 2nd ed., Oxford (Hart Publishing) 2010, Chapter 13–15.
- Claus-Wilhelm Canaris and Hans Christoph Grigoleit, 'Interpretation of Contracts, in: Arthur Hartkamp et al (eds.), *Towards a European Civil Code*, 4th ed. Nijmegen (Ars Aequi) 2011, Chapter 26.
- Jacques Herbots, 'Interpretation of Contracts,' in: Jan M. Smits (ed.), *Elgar Encyclopedia of Comparative Law*, 2nd ed., Cheltenham, UK; Northampton, MA, USA (Edward Elgar) 2012, Chapter 35.
- Nicole Kornet, *Contract Interpretation and Gap-filling: Comparative and Theoretical Perspectives*, Antwerp (Intersentia) 2006.
- Hein Kötz, *European Contract Law Vol. 1* (translated by Tony Weir), Oxford (Oxford University Press) 1997, Chapter 7.
- Francois Terré, Philippe Simler and Yves Lequette, *Droit civil: les obligations*, 11th ed., Paris (Dalloz) 2013, Book 1, Title 1.

8

The principle of good faith and policing unfair contract terms

 CHAPTER OVERVIEW

This chapter discusses two main topics:

- the central role of the **principle of good faith** (reasonableness and fairness) in civil law jurisdictions and its absence in English law;
- the legal techniques to restrict the use of **unfair contract terms**, in particular with a view to policing exemption clauses and unfair terms in general conditions in consumer contracts.

The principle of good faith

It is self-evident to continental lawyers that the principle of good faith (*bonne foi, Treu und Glauben, redelijkheid en billijkheid*) has a central role to play in the law of contract. All civil codes adopt a provision on this principle. In chronology of their being enacted, the French, German and Dutch Code state the following:

> **Art. 1104 (1) CC:** 'Contracts must be negotiated, formed and performed in good faith.'

> **§ 242 BGB:** 'The debtor is obliged to perform in such a manner as good faith requires, regard being had to general practice.'

> **Art. 6:248 BW:** '1. A contract not only has the effects agreed upon by the parties, but also those which, according to the nature of the contract, result from statute, usage or the requirements of reasonableness and fairness.
> 2. A rule binding upon the parties as a result of the contract does not apply to the extent that, in the given circumstances, this would be unacceptable according to criteria of reasonableness and fairness.'

Civil law courts have given these articles a wide application, sometimes going far beyond the original intent of the legislator. Good faith plays a role in the entire life of the contract, from the very first negotiations until the very last part of the performance, and is seen by many civil lawyers as the highest norm of contract law, described by some even as the 'queen of rules'. The importance of good faith as a 'super-provision' is already more clear in the Dutch provision, but is best grasped by the PECL that declares good faith the immediate counter principle of the freedom to contract and dictates that each contracting party must mandatory respect it across the board:

> **Art. 1:102 (1) PECL:** 'Parties are free to enter into a contract and to determine its contents, subject to the requirements of good faith and fair dealing, and the mandatory rules established by these Principles.'

> **Art. 1:201 PECL:** '(1) Each party must act in accordance with good faith and fair dealing.
> (2) The parties may not exclude or limit this duty.'

Standing opposite civil law jurisdictions and the PECL is English law that does not recognise a general principle of good faith. In this chapter the role of good faith will first be examined in the civil law (A), followed by an analysis of why it is much less important in England (B).

A.   Understanding good faith in the civil law

It probably takes an outsider to best describe what good faith in civil law means. The English judge Lord Bingham describes it as follows in *Interfoto Library Ltd v Stiletto Ltd* (1988):

> In many civil law systems, and perhaps in most legal systems outside the common law world, the law of obligations recognises and enforces an overriding principle that in making and carrying out contracts parties should act in good faith. This does not simply mean that they should not deceive each other, a principle which any legal system must recognise; its effect is perhaps most aptly conveyed by such metaphorical colloquialisms as 'playing fair', 'coming clean' or 'putting one's cards face upwards on the table'. It is in essence a principle of fair and open dealing (…).

What Bingham describes here is so-called 'objective' good faith. At various places in this book we encountered a different type, namely subjective good faith which refers to a subjective state of mind of a person who does not know nor has reason to know of a certain fact, and therefore acts 'in good faith' (or 'not in bad faith'), as in the case where he relies on the apparent intention of the other party to be legally bound. Objective good faith is something else, which is exactly the reason why the German Code refers to it with the different term '*Treu und Glauben*' and the Dutch Code with the term 'reasonableness and fairness'. Unlike subjective good faith, reasonableness and fairness is

Norm a *norm* for the contracting parties: it sets a standard of conduct that requires each party to take the interests of the other party into account. This sounds rather vague and thus immediately reveals an important characteristic of

Open-ended good faith: the norm is *open-ended*. This means that it depends on the circumstances of the case how the norm is applied, giving much discretionary power to the courts. Civil law courts have often used the good faith provision to 'break open' contracts the enforcement of which they deemed grossly unfair. They have even used the provision as a vehicle to develop whole new fields of law, such as pre-contractual duties to inform the other party in French law, rules on hardship ('unforeseen circumstances') in German law, and control of general conditions in both French and German law and various other jurisdictions. The legislator is never able to foresee all situations that end up in the courts – and when it is able to, it is seldom on time or even willing to enact a new statute. Courts can then use the good faith provision to keep the law in sync with societal developments.

Danger The freedom that the courts allow themselves can of course be seen as being at odds with the constitutional separation of powers, and therefore as a threat to legal certainty and predictability (for which there is no better word than the German term *Einzelfallgerechigkeit*, justice in each individual case). In 1933, for example, the German jurist Justus Wilhelm Hedemann launched an attack on the German § 242 BGB in a famous booklet called *Die Flucht in die Generalklauseln: eine Gefahr für Recht und Staat* ('The escape into general clauses: a danger for law and state'). This did not prevent the German courts from using the good faith provision whenever they felt the need for it. At the risk of generalising too much, courts in Central and Eastern Europe are more reluctant to lead the way in developing private law through open-ended norms, perhaps caused by the socialist heritage of a strong administration and legislator.

Three functions Until now nothing has been said about the actual application of good faith. The best way to describe the substantive law is by identifying the three *functions* that good faith has in civil law jurisdictions: the supplementing function, the interpretative function and the restrictive function.

Supplementation The supplementing function (*fonction complétive, Ergänzungsfunktion, aanvullende werking*) allows a court to fill gaps in the party agreement. We encountered this function already in Chapter 7 under the heading of ad hoc gap filling. It was seen that good faith can give rise to a great variety of supplementary duties that arise under the contract: duties of information, co-operation, protection, loyalty, disclosure, etc. These obligations may already exist in the pre-contractual stage and often extend until after the contract was performed. Sometimes there is a more specific statutory provision on which these duties can be based (such as § 157 BGB in Germany), but even if such a provision is missing civil law jurisdictions are still willing to accept this function. The underlying rationale is that parties are in the same boat when they conclude a contract, calling for reasonable behaviour from them both. In 1931 the French author René Demogue put it like this: 'The contracting parties form some kind of microcosm; it is a small society in which each of them must work towards a common goal that is the sum of the individual goals pursued by each.' Art. 1:202 PECL provides a good example of what such a microcosm entails. It states: 'Each party owes to the other a duty to co-operate in order to give full effect to the contract.' This duty to co-operate naturally exists in long-term contracts, but also in other cases. If contractor A is to build an office building for B and A is unable to proceed with the works because B refuses to apply for a building permit or does not give the information necessary to obtain this permit, B violates his duty to co-operate. In the same vein it is true that if the building is to be erected in Yemen, and B accidentally hears that a terrorist group is planning to kidnap foreigners in the place where the work is to be performed, he should immediately inform A about this.

In particular French and German courts have developed extensive systems of collateral duties on the basis of good faith that exist next to the explicit contractual obligations that follow from the party agreement. In both jurisdictions one speaks of protective duties (*obligations de sécurité, Schutzpflichte*), an obligation to protect the other party, for example against physical damage from slipping over a vegetable leaf in a supermarket (see Box 14.1), and of duties to inform (*obligations d'information, obligations de renseignement, Auskunftspflichten, Aufklärungspflichten*) that should allow the other party to carry out the contract (e.g. provide a manual for the sold machine) or to help a party make up its mind about entering into the contract at all (e.g. advise a patient that silicone implants need regular replacement). The recently introduced French Art. 1112-1 CC takes this duty to extremes by imposing a general obligation to give information. It reads:

> 'The party who has information which is of decisive importance for the consent of the other, must inform the other of it where the latter legitimately does not know the information or relies on his fellow contracting party.'

Second, parties are also bound by the principle of good faith when they interpret their contract (*fonction interprétative, Auslegung nach Treu und Glauben*). Interpretation is not something that only the courts engage in: it is primarily a duty of the parties to give a meaning to the contractual terms that fit their common goal. The rule that interpretation must be line with how reasonable parties would construe the contract, as was discussed in Chapter 7, also follows from the standard of good faith that parties are obliged to apply towards each other. If an insurance contract covers theft in case of 'illegitimate entry' into the house of the insured, and a thief enters the house by claiming that he is a telephone repairman, the insurer cannot claim that the thief was let into the house by the insured and therefore does not have to pay.

The third function of good faith is to restrict the exercise of contractual rights. This restrictive or limiting function (*fonction limitative, unzulässige Rechtsausübung, beperkende werking*) is the most spectacular application because it allows a party to escape from a binding contract. But to sacrifice the binding force of contracts for the sake of doing justice in the circumstances of the case is not something that a court would do light heartedly. The Dutch Art. 6:248 (2) BW therefore rightly states that good faith can only restrict a right if it would be 'unacceptable' for a party to invoke this right. The court will only intervene in extreme cases. The situation that one must primarily think of is that of abuse of rights: although a party has a contractual or statutory right, it is prevented from exercising this right because of its own previous behaviour. In a seminal Dutch case the bank of Mr. Saladin told him that they had a special opportunity for him. As a faithful client he could buy shares in the Waterman Pen Company. He was told by the bank that buying these shares would be without risk. When this turned out to be untrue, and the shares dropped in value, Mr. Saladin claimed the losses he had suffered to a total of fl80,000 (€36,000). The bank subsequently invoked an exemption clause in the contract, stating that 'we cannot assume any responsibility for this transaction'. The Dutch *Hoge Raad* held that whether it could be contrary to good faith for the bank to invoke the clause depended on the assessment of several factors, such as 'the gravity of the fault, the nature and other contents of the contract, the societal position of the parties and their mutual relationship, the way in which the term came into existence, and the extent to which the other party was aware of the aim of the term'. This is an outcome that most, if not all, civil jurisdictions would accept, albeit not necessarily on the basis of the good faith provision. Thus, French law no doubt accepts that good faith can also restrict a contractual right, but it finds the basis for this in the liability for tort of Arts 1240–1241 *Code Civil*, under which the rules on abuse of right (*abus de droit*) were developed.

Hardship

The restrictive function of good faith can also come into play in cases other than abuse of rights. The best-known example concerns the doctrine of *unforeseen circumstances* or *hardship* (*imprévision, Wegfall der Geschäftsgrundlage, onvoorziene omstandigheden*), discussed in more detail in Chapter 11. Each contract is based on the assumption of the contracting parties that the circumstances under which the contract is concluded will not change too much. If I buy a quantity of crude oil, I assume that the price at which I can resell it remains within certain margins. I also expect that transport of the oil will remain possible and will not be hindered by an unexpected outbreak of war in the Middle East. However, even if these expectations are not met, it follows from the principle of binding force of contract that I am still bound to the contract. Only in highly exceptional circumstances do some jurisdictions allow a party to escape from the contract in cases where its performance would be excessively onerous because of an unforeseen and unforeseeable change of circumstances. Although these legal systems now have a statutory basis for this (see e.g. Art. 1195 CC, § 313 BGB and Art. 6:258 BW), the underlying motivation is again the good faith principle: in case of a truly fundamental change of circumstances, a reasonable party cannot hold the other to the concluded contract.

The most famous applications of the doctrine of unforeseen circumstances can be found in Germany in the 1920s, when inflation was proverbially high (at one point in time it took 4 billion German Mark to buy one American dollar). The highest German court of that time (the *Reichsgericht*) had to decide on various occasions whether a debtor should be allowed to pay only the nominal value of a debt that had originated before the First World War – which would have meant that he would have received the counter performance practically for free. The court refused to allow this principle of 'Mark equals Mark' and even fixed new exchange rates, basing these revolutionary decisions on § 242 BGB. In the case *Luderitzbucht Mortgage* (1923), for example, the owner of a mortgaged property was obliged by the court to pay the mortgagee an additional sum above the nominal value of the mortgage, reasoning that:

> The legal possibility of a revalorisation of debts out of mortgage is to be recognised according to present German law, especially according to § 242 BGB. In particular in the case of mortgage debts it must be taken into account that normally the debtor has received a corresponding compensation having regard to the much increased value of the land (...).

Despite the fact that the doctrine of unforeseen circumstances is not accepted as such in English contract law (see further Chapter 11), Art. 6:111 PECL adopts it as a 'European' principle. This lengthy provision well reflects that the doctrine can only be applied in exceptional cases and that the result is not that the contract is invalid, but that it must be adapted to meet the changed circumstances. This adaptation is primarily left to the parties themselves; the court is only allowed to step in if they do not reach agreement about new conditions:

(1) A party is bound to fulfill its obligations even if performance has become more onerous, whether because the cost of performance has increased or because the value of the performance it receives has diminished.

(2) If, however, performance of the contract becomes excessively onerous because of a change of circumstances, the parties are bound to enter into negotiations with a view to adapting the contract or terminating it, provided that:

(a) the change of circumstances occurred after the time of conclusion of the contract,

(b) the possibility of a change of circumstances was not one which could reasonably have been taken into account at the time of conclusion of the contract, and

(c) the risk of the change of circumstances is not one which, according to the contract, the party affected should be required to bear.

(3) If the parties fail to reach agreement within a reasonable period, the court may:

(a) end the contract at a date and on terms to be determined by the court; or

(b) adapt the contract in order to distribute between the parties in a just and equitable manner the losses and gains resulting from the change of circumstances.

In either case, the court may award damages for the loss suffered through a party refusing to negotiate or breaking off negotiations contrary to good faith and fair dealing.

B.   English law: no general principle of good faith

English law does not accept a general principle of good faith. Unlike most other common law jurisdictions and unlike Scots law, English law regards the need to take into account the interests of the other party in any type of contract as contrary to the very nature of contracting. The most famous formulation of this position can be found in the decision of the House of Lords in *Walford v Miles* (1992). Although the following quote from Lord Ackner in that case is restricted to pre-contractual negotiations, it can be seen as evidence of the reluctance of English law to accept a general principle of good faith:

the concept of a duty to carry on negotiations in good faith is inherently repugnant to the adversarial position of the parties when involved in negotiations. Each party to the negotiations is entitled to pursue his (or her) own interest, so long as he avoids making misrepresentations. A duty to negotiate in good faith is as unworkable in practice as it is inherently inconsistent with the position of the negotiating parties. (...)

Policy reasons

Contracting parties, in particular if they are involved in commercial transactions, are generally considered to contract 'at arm's length'. It is therefore not surprising that English law also lacks a theory of abuse of rights: if a party has a right, it must be able to exercise it at all times. As Pearson LJ put it in the case *Chapman v Honig* (1963), ' a person who has a right under a contract or other instrument is entitled to exercise it and can effectively exercise it for a good reason or a bad reason or no reason at all'. It may not be honourable if the landlord gives notice to his tenant only because the tenant has given evidence against him in a dispute with another tenant, but this is not a matter that should influence the landlord's exercise of rights.

So why does English law not recognise a general principle of good faith? The usual explanation given is that English law is more morally insensitive than civil law jurisdictions. English law is designed in the interests of economic efficiency, while the civil law ranks solidarity higher. This purportedly makes English law a better law for commercial parties. The comparative lawyer Kahn-Freund famously said: 'It certainly seems that the English law of contract was designed for a nation of shopkeepers. If that be so, the common lawyer might retort, then the French system was made for a race of peasants.' This is reiterated in the following quote of the English commercial lawyer Roy Goode:

> The predictability of the legal outcome of a case is more important than absolute justice. It is necessary in a commercial setting that businessmen at least should know where they stand. (...) The last thing that we want to do is to drive business away by vague concepts of fairness which make judicial decisions unpredictable, and if that means that the outcome of disputes is sometimes hard on a party we regard that as an acceptable price to pay in the interest of the great majority of business litigants.

The English author Roger Brownsword sums up the various arguments against a general principle of good faith that have been brought forward over the years, including the ones just mentioned. First, good faith requires the parties to take into account the legitimate interests of one another, which would go against the individualistic and liberal ethic of English contract law that is based on adversarial self-interested dealing. Second, good faith would be too vague: it is not clear how far the restrictions on the pursuit of this self-interest should go. This threatens legal certainty. Third, even objective good faith sometimes still requires an inquiry into the state of mind of the

BOX 8.1

AN ALTERNATIVE EXPLANATION FOR THE ABSENCE OF A GENERAL PRINCIPLE OF GOOD FAITH IN ENGLISH LAW

The Australian professor Fred Ellinghaus (1989) gives an alternative explanation for the absence of a general principle of good faith in English law. He does not seek the explanation in deep-rooted values about a country's society and economy, but claims that the outlook of a country's contract law depends to a large extent on the types of cases decided by the highest courts. In comparing Australian and English contract law, Ellinghaus argues that a:

> law of contract devised by a court most often confronted with one type of contract will differ from that devised by a court most often confronted with another type of contract. A court of ultimate appeal which draws on its own precedents in the development of a particular body of doctrine will naturally be influenced by the data most often placed before it.

Most cases litigated before the UK Supreme Court (and previously the House of Lords) are about carriage of goods, contracts of insurance and charter parties. The then judge in the House of Lords Lord Goff once said:

> One feature of our legal system which I find many of our continental friends are unable to

understand or unwilling to accept is the worldwide importance of the English commercial court, of English commercial arbitration and of English commercial law. Yet this is a fact of life. (…) I here refer not so much to London as a financial centre, but to London as the centre of the world's shipping, the centre of nearly all the world's commodity trades, and the centre of the world's insurance. One result of this is that more commercial arbitrations are held each year in London than in the rest of Europe put together (. . .). Yet another is, of course, the English Commercial Court itself (. . .) which must, I imagine, be by far the most important court in the world for the resolution of international commercial disputes. Certainly there is nothing like it anywhere else in Europe. You can judge its international character by the fact that, in one year during which I had the honour to preside over the court, in every single case tried in the court either one or both parties came from overseas.

It is not difficult to contrast this with the cases that come before the highest courts in France and Germany that are much more often purely domestic and typically involve consumers.

parties because it is dependent on the reasons why a party acted in a certain way. Fourth, good faith impinges on the autonomy of the contracting parties. If it regulates the behaviour of the parties, it restricts their autonomy and this is inconsistent with the fundamental philosophy of freedom of contract. Finally, English law has little sympathy for good faith because it fails to recognise that contracting contexts are not all alike. Contract law must be sensitive to context, and therefore also to different types of contracts: a commercial contract on commodity sales is different from a consumer contract.

Much can be said against these arguments. It is, for example, not clear at all that a liberal ethic is best for a well-functioning economy: trust and co-operation may be of equal importance. The legal certainty argument can also be turned upside down: the good faith principle can also provide security against opportunism and unfair dealing, making a party more willing to enter into a contract with someone it does not know. Finally, it is not true that good faith must be applied regardless of context, but rather it equips courts with an instrument to respond to the different circumstances of the case.

The absence of a general principle of good faith does not mean that good faith plays no role at all in English law. There are three different ways through which good faith enters English contract law.

Functional equivalents

First, English law adopts several doctrines that may not be called 'good faith', but that comparative lawyers are eager to recognise as fulfilling a similar function as in the civil law. The interpretation of a contract in line with how reasonable parties would understand it is one example. Another example is gap filling through terms implied in fact (see Chapter 7).

Contracts uberrimae fidei

Second, good faith is explicitly recognised as an important norm in some special contracts and relationships. Certain contracts are considered to be *contracts 'uberrimae fidei'* (Latin for 'of the utmost good faith'). This is for example the case for contracts of insurance, suretyship, partnership and employment. The main consequence of this is that parties must disclose information to their counterpart. Thus, in an insurance contract a person taking out insurance must inform the insurance company of any fact it considers relevant for the insurer's decision to accept her. This is a matter of trust among the parties. In the case of *International Management Group UK Ltd v Simmonds* (2003), IMG acquired the television rights for the matches of the Sahara Cup (a cricket tournament between India and Pakistan). It insured against the risk of the matches being cancelled without telling the insurer that it was aware of rumours that the Indian Government would not allow the Indian team to participate. When India indeed banned the tournament, IMG could not claim payment on the insurance policy as it had breached its duty to inform the insurer in a contract that required the utmost good faith. The importance of trust becomes even more evident if one realises that an insurance company also need not pay out anything if the non-disclosed fact is unrelated to the claim. If someone with a life insurance policy does not tell the insurance company about a heart condition, the insurer can invalidate the contract even if the insured dies in a plane crash.

Fiduciary relationships

Next to these contracts of the utmost good faith, there are also certain relationships that are considered as being governed by good faith. These so-called

BOX 8.2

A NEW ERA FOR GOOD FAITH IN ENGLISH LAW?

The present English approach is one in which good faith is only accepted in some piecemeal contracts and relationships. This does not mean that no pleas have been made in favour of a more principled approach that recognises good faith as an overriding principle for any contract. In the recent case of *Yam Seng Pte Ltd v International Trade Corp Ltd* (2013) the High Court (in a decision taken by Leggatt J) ruled that any hostility of the English courts to a general duty of good faith in contracts is misplaced. The court found that a general duty of good faith must be implied into a long-term distribution agreement. In this case, the parties entered into an agreement giving the claimant the exclusive rights to distribute eau de toilette, deodorant and shower gel bearing the name 'Manchester United' in the Middle East, Asia, Africa and Australasia. After a year the claimant informed the defendant that it had terminated the contract because of breach: the defendant shipped products too late and refused to supply all the ordered products. To substantiate his claim, the claimant asserted that there was an implied term in the agreement that the parties would deal with each other in good faith. The court followed this analysis, concluding that the agreement contained an enforceable implied obligation on the parties to act in good faith, and that the defendant breached this obligation by knowingly concealing from the claimant the true situation concerning the defendant's pricing arrangements in a crucial distribution channel in Singapore. This breach justified the claimant's termination of the distributorship, and its subsequent damages claim.

It is interesting to note that the court found the basis for this duty of good faith in commercial dealings in the contract itself: the duty of good faith was implied in fact (see Chapter 7). This would in particular be the case in long-term relational contracts requiring extensive co-operation, such as joint ventures and franchise and distribution agreements. This gives the English duty of good faith a less fundamental character than its civil law counterpart. Leggatt J even stated that parties would be able to exclude such a duty – something that would not be possible in a civil law jurisdiction where good faith provides a mandatory rule that the parties cannot deviate from. It remains to be seen to what extent the decision of Leggatt J is only an isolated case of a lower court or the beginning of a new era for good faith in English contract law.

fiduciary relationships exist between solicitor and client, doctor and patient and principal and agent (as for example in case of financial intermediaries). In each of these cases the fiduciary owes a duty to disclose important information to the other party.

Third, as a result of the European Directive on Unfair Terms in Consumer Contracts (on which more below), the UK has adopted the notion of good

Unfair terms

faith in consumer contracts. The Consumer Rights Act 2015 (which contains the UK implementation of the directive) closely follows the directive by prescribing that contractual terms, which 'contrary to the requirement of good faith' cause a significant imbalance in the contract to the detriment of the consumer, are not binding on the consumer, regardless of whether they were individually negotiated or not. It is understandable that the English courts have had difficulties in applying this provision which, in the words of the House of Lords in *Director General of Fair Trading v. First National Bank* (2001), imports the 'notion of fair and open dealing' into English law. This explains why the UK Competition and Markets Authority published a 140-page document containing guidance on how to apply the unfair terms provisions of the CRA 2015.

BOX 8.3

THE DOCTRINE OF *IUSTUM PRETIUM*

It has not always been the case that the substantive fairness of the contract was irrelevant. Both in the Canon law of the Middle Ages and later in Natural law, it was well accepted that there must be some equivalence between the mutual performances of the parties. It was seen as immoral not to pay a just price (usually referred to with the Latin term *iustum pretium*). The consequence of this was that a contract could be avoided for *laesio enormis* (literally 'substantial impairment', a gross disproportion between the mutual performances). The difficulty, however, was to establish what exactly a 'just' price or a 'gross' disproportion were: it seems difficult to decide upon this in the absence of an objective criterion. However, some of the early Civil Codes did codify the doctrine. Thus, § 934 of the Austrian ABGB (1812) allows a party to invalidate the contract if the value of its performance is more than half of the other party's performance (*Verkürzung über die Hälfte*). This seemingly extreme rule is mitigated by several exceptions, such as the contract cannot be invalidated by a commercial party, if a party knew of the value of the good, or if it is impossible to establish its 'real' value. This still leaves some space for the application of the rule. In a recent case decided by the Austrian court someone had bought a second-hand car through eBay for €4,000 but the buyer found out later that the car had so many defects that its actual value was between €500 and €1,600. The buyer was therefore allowed to invalidate the purchase. As § 934 ABGB prescribes an objective equivalence between performance and counter performance, it does not matter whether the buyer had seen the car before concluding the contract (*Bastlerfahrzeug*, 2007). Article 1674 of the French *Code Civil* also allows the seller to avoid the contract, but only in case of an immovable where the seller suffers a loss greater than seven-twelfths of the price, and the immovable is not meant to be a gift. This provision does not play a prominent role in practice.

Policing unfair contract terms

No legal system regards a contract as invalid simply because there is an imbalance between performance and counter performance. A contract is never unfair only because one party agrees to pay 'too much'. To hold otherwise would be paternalistic and a negation of the premise that people who are sound of mind can very well look after themselves. It was seen in Chapter 1 that this is sometimes referred to as the irrelevance of so-called 'substantive fairness'. In order to invalidate a seemingly unfair contract, one always needs something extra. This could be a party who is not competent to make up its own mind (legal incapacity: Chapter 5) or a so-called 'defect of consent'. This means that a party was not able to form its intention in a sufficiently free manner because it was deceived by its counterpart (see for this and other defects of consent Chapter 9).

This explains why a party only very rarely argues that the entire contract is unfair. It is much more frequent that someone seeks to invalidate a specific clause in the contract that is disadvantageous to him. If products are delivered too late or not at all, the buyer may counter that his contract contains a clause that limits or excludes the possibility to claim performance or damages. These so-called *limitation* or *exemption clauses* are typically found in general conditions that the buyer probably did not read before entering into the contract – and if he had, he would not have been able to change their contents anyway. This buyer has no interest in the invalidation of the contract as a whole because this would mean that he would have to return the goods he was interested in. He only wants to be able to set aside the specific clause, and subsequently enforce its rights under the contract. The question is to what extent such a clause can indeed be invalidated. This section therefore examines what techniques courts and legislators use to police unfair contract terms. A distinction is made between the general doctrines of private law that courts have available (A) and the specific controls that legislators have put in place in the last few decades to police unfair contract terms (B).

Exemption clauses

A. General controls

General conditions are used in almost any consumer contract and are also very common in commercial transactions. It is not difficult to see why this standard form contracting is so popular. It saves parties from having to negotiate and draft contract conditions for every new contract. This lowers the transaction costs, which is not only in the interest of the party using the general conditions (the 'user'), but also of the other party, who is subsequently able to (for example) buy the product or service at a lower price.

Three problems

However, the use of general conditions is not without problems. There are three problems in particular. First, it is not self-evident how a set of rules drafted by one party can become part of an individual contract with somebody else who was not involved in the drafting (the incorporation problem). Second, interpretation of standard terms in line with the parties' intentions is difficult if one of the parties was not involved in the drafting of the terms. This raises the question of how to interpret general conditions (the interpretation problem). Third, the conditions may be unbalanced and unfairly favour the party who drafted them (the fairness problem). The latter problem is particularly cumbersome in B2C-transactions as the standard contracts in those cases are typically not negotiable and tend to be a take-it-or-leave-it type of affair: the only alternative to accepting the contract, with all the conditions attached to it, is to reject it. To speak of a *contract of adhesion* well reflects this phenomenon.

Incorporation

A court can tackle the incorporation problem by holding that the general conditions did not become part of the contract, and that the ensuing gap simply has to be filled with the statutory and judicial default rules. This technique offers a solution in cases where the other party is simply not aware of the fact that general conditions are used. This is easy to establish if the user did not say anything about this at the time of contracting. If Anna gets lost on her way from Bucharest to Brasov, checks into a hotel, and finds a notice in the room that the hotel accepts no liability for lost property, this is not a clause on which the hotel can rely. If Anna finds out the next morning that her Furla bag has disappeared, the court can easily establish that the exemption clause did not become part of the contract, which was made at the reception desk and not at any later stage. But also in less obvious cases courts have often been willing to help a weaker party by holding that the general conditions did not become part of the contract in cases where the reference to the general conditions is obscure, e.g. is hidden on the back of a form, or is only in small print.

Interpretation

General contract law can also assist in addressing the interpretation and fairness problems. As it is typical for general conditions to be unilaterally drafted by one party, the court can choose to interpret the conditions to the detriment of the drafter (*contra proferentem*, now laid down in Art. 5 (2) of the Directive on Unfair Contract Terms, as seen in Chapter 7). If a car (that normally has space for five persons) carries six people and is involved in an accident, the insurance company cannot rely on the clause that it need not pay out in case the car carries an 'excessive load'. An English court interpreted the term 'load' narrowly, only covering goods and not people (*Houghton v Trafalgar Insurance Co*, 1954). And if an exemption clause unfairly benefits

Fairness
the user, it could – under the restrictive function of good faith – be contrary

to reasonableness and fairness to invoke the clause. Art. 8:109 PECL reflects this: 'Remedies for non-performance may be excluded or restricted unless it would be contrary to good faith and fair dealing to invoke the exclusion or restriction.'

B.   Specific controls

In the 1970s – when the use of general conditions in B2C transactions boomed as a result of increasing consumption – it became clear that the above-mentioned general controls were not sufficient to protect consumers. This led in many jurisdictions to the introduction of specific legislation to address the three identified problems of general conditions. Thus, Germany introduced its Act on General Conditions (AGBG) in 1976 (its provisions became part of the BGB in 2002), the UK its Unfair Contract Terms Act (UCTA) in 1977 and Consumer Rights Act in 2015, and France its Act on the Protection and Information of the Consumer of Products and Services ('*Loi Scrivener*') in 1978 (now part of the Consumer Code). The exact scope of these statutes differs from one country to another: while the UCTA – the title which is a bit of a misnomer – only applies to exemption clauses (in B2B and C2C contracts and also if individually negotiated) and the CRA to consumer contracts, the French statute covers any contractual clause, but is also limited to consumer contracts. The German statute has the widest scope of application as it deals with any possibly unfair term in both B2B- and B2C-contracts.

Incorporation

The incorporation problem is addressed in German law by the rule that a clause in general conditions which is 'so unusual that the other party to the contract need not expect to encounter it' is not part of the contract (§ 305c (1) BGB). Particularly for consumer contracts this is further specified in section 2 of § 305 BGB:

> Standard business terms only become a part of a contract if the user, when entering into the contract,
> 1. refers the other party to the contract to them explicitly or, where explicit reference, due to the way in which the contract is entered into, is possible only with disproportionate difficulty, by posting a clearly visible notice at the place where the contract is entered into, and
> 2. gives the other party to the contract, in an acceptable manner, which also takes into reasonable account any physical handicap of the other party to the contract that is discernible to the user, the opportunity to take notice of their contents, and if the other party to the contract agrees to their applying.

This fits in with the English judicial approach of 'reasonable notice'. English courts require the user of general conditions to take reasonable steps to bring them to the notice of the recipient. What is reasonable depends on the contents of the terms: the more onerous or unusual they are, the greater the degree of notice that is required. Lord Denning's 'red hand rule', which he defined in *Spurling Ltd v Bradshaw* (1956), states:

Red hand rule

> the more unreasonable a clause is, the greater the notice which must be given of it. Some clauses which I have seen would need to be printed in red ink on the face of the document with a red hand pointing to it before the notice could be held to be sufficient.

A famous application of this rule is *Interfoto Picture Library v Stiletto Ltd* (1988). Advertising agency Stiletto had borrowed photos from picture library Interfoto with a view to establishing if they were fit to be used in an advertising campaign. A fee would have to be paid if any of the pictures were in fact used. When Stiletto received the 47 photos, a delivery note included the condition that if the pictures were kept for more than 14 days, a holding fee of £5 per photo per day had to be paid. Stiletto had not read the conditions and only returned the photos after a month. It subsequently received an invoice to pay almost £4,000. The Court of Appeal found that Stiletto was not liable: the term was very onerous and therefore Interfoto should have drawn Stiletto's attention to it in an explicit way. Just assuming that the other party reads the delivery note is not enough in a case like this, in which the holding fee is very high.

Fairness

When it comes to the fairness problem, an important policy question is *who* should address it. It may be that the fight against powerful parties imposing onerous general conditions on their counterparts should not be left to individual consumers: individual parties may simply not be willing to go through the costs and efforts to address a court when being confronted with an onerous clause. This may call for government intervention and this is exactly the reason why the French statute of 1978 did not give a general mandate to the court to strike down unreasonable terms, but introduced an administrative control instead. The *Loi Scrivener* created a government committee (*Commission des clauses abusives*) that is empowered to prohibit certain unfair terms in B2C-contracts by decree (see now Art. L 212-1 Consumer Code). Unfortunately, however, the only decree issued was in 1978 when the committee prohibited both clauses in sales contracts which restrict the buyer's right to claim damages in case of breach by the seller, and clauses in any type of contract which allow a professional party to unilaterally modify the characteristics of the product or service. The subsequent inactivity of the government committee led the French *Cour de Cassation* in its famous *Minit France* decision of 1991 to change the nature of the protection: in a rare case of French judicial activism, the highest court allowed the lower courts to declare unfair terms inapplicable out of their own motion. This is now also codified in Art. 1171 CC.

In Germany the possibility of the court striking down an unfair term was already accepted in the 1976 Act. § 307 (1) BGB states:

> Provisions in general conditions are ineffective if, contrary to the requirement of good faith, they unduly disadvantage the other party to the contract with the user. An undue disadvantage may also arise from the provision not being clear and comprehensible.

Grey and black list

It is not clear from this provision when exactly there is an 'undue' disadvantage. This is why §§ 308 and 309 BGB provide two lists of unfair terms that can be relied upon by consumers. § 308 – the so-called 'grey list' – lists terms that are not binding if they contain disproportionate elements. Whether this is the case or not still has to be decided upon by the court in an evaluation ('Wertung') of the circumstances of the case. § 309 – the 'black list' – lists terms that are considered not binding under any circumstances. For example, a contract clause is not binding if it excludes or limits the liability for damage from injury to life, body or health due to negligent breach by the user, or liability for other damage arising from a grossly negligent breach by the user' (§ 309, no. 7 BGB). This technique of using grey and black lists was taken over by both the French (Arts. R 212-1 and R 212-2 Consumer Code) and the Dutch legislator (Arts. 6:236 and 6:237 BW).

Unfair Contract Terms Act

The UK Unfair Contract Terms Act 1977 gives courts wide powers to control clauses that exclude or limit liability. Its exact scope of application is complicated, but the statute essentially distinguishes between exemption clauses that are ineffective as such, and clauses that are ineffective if they do not meet the requirement of reasonableness in much the same way as black and grey lists do. Ineffective as such are for example clauses that limit the liability of a business for death or personal injury caused by negligence (s. 2 (1)). Subject to the test of reasonableness are, for example, clauses that exclude or limit liability for non-performance or for performance which is substantially different from what was agreed upon, unless it is reasonable to do so (s. 3). Since the entry into force of the Consumer Rights Act 2015, the UCTA no longer applies to consumer contracts. S. 61-76 CRA 2015 now provide the relevant rules for unfair terms used in these contracts.

EU law

In 1993 the European legislator decided to put a European layer on top of these national measures. Directive 93/13 on Unfair Terms in Consumer Contracts prohibits terms in general conditions that are unreasonably onerous for the consumer. Its most important provisions are the following:

> **Art. 3:** 1. 'A contractual term which has not been individually negotiated shall be regarded as unfair if, contrary to the requirement of good faith, it causes a significant imbalance in the parties' rights and obligations arising under the contract, to the detriment of the consumer.' (…)
> 3. 'The Annex shall contain an indicative and non-exhaustive list of the terms which may be regarded as unfair.'

> **Art. 4:** '1. (…) the unfairness of a contractual term shall be assessed, taking into account the nature of the goods or services for which the contract was concluded and by referring, at the time of conclusion of the contract, to all the circumstances attending the conclusion of the contract and to all the other terms of the contract or of another contract on which it is dependent.
> 2. Assessment of the unfair nature of the terms shall relate neither to the definition of the main subject matter of the contract nor to the adequacy of the price and remuneration, on the one hand, as against the services or goods supplies in exchange, on the other, in so far as these terms are in plain intelligible language.'

> **Art. 6 (1):** 'Member States shall lay down that unfair terms used in a contract concluded with a consumer by a seller or supplier shall, as provided for under their national law, not be binding on the consumer and that the contract shall continue to bind the parties upon those terms if it is capable of continuing in existence without the unfair terms.'

Inspired by the German example, the Annex to the directive contains a 'grey' list of 17 clauses 'which may be regarded as unfair' (see Art. 3 (3) of the directive). It must be noted that the directive only offers minimum harmonisation: Member States are allowed to grant consumers a higher level of protection if they deem this fit. This explains why the national implementations of the directive widely differ. Some Member States (such as Germany, the Netherlands and the Nordic countries) did not have to change much in their pre-existing national law, while France was among the countries that had to adopt a grey list of unfair terms. The UK implemented the directive in the Consumer Rights Act 2015.

It has already been mentioned that judicial review may not be the most effective means of policing unfair terms. Consumers often lack the time, money and energy to go to court over the relatively small amount of money involved in the average consumer transaction. The same is true for a smaller company that is confronted with a counterpart with more bargaining power. The adverse effect of this is that companies may be inclined to continue to use their onerous clauses, capitalising on the incapacity or unwillingness of the weaker party to go to court. This explains why Art. 7 of Directive 93/13 obliges Member States to ensure the existence of 'adequate and effective means' to prevent the continued use of unfair terms. As a result, Member States have introduced various 'public reviews' that make the control of unfair terms not dependent on an individual party taking action. Such public reviews are for example exercised by the Commission on abusive clauses in France (see above), the Competition and Markets Authority in the UK, the *Autoriteit Consument en Markt (ACM)* in the Netherlands and by a Consumer Ombudsman in Nordic countries. Such public bodies are usually allowed to obtain the assurance of a company that it will no longer make use of unfair terms, and impose fines or even initiate criminal proceedings if they continue their unfair trade practices.

Collective
action

Next to action by public bodies, many jurisdictions also allow (private) consumer associations to pursue a so-called 'collective action' (*action collective, Verbandsklage, collectieve actie*). In a collective action the consumer association asks on behalf of the consumers it unites for an injunction to prohibit the continued use of an abusive clause. This often-effective possibility can for example be found in the German *Unterlassungsklagengesetz* (Act on Actions for Injunctions), the French Consumer Code (Art. 621-7), the UK Competition Act 1998 and in Art. 6:240 BW.

⊶ TOPICS FOR REVIEW

Objective and subjective good faith
Good faith as an open-ended norm
Functions of good faith
Unforeseen circumstances
The role of good faith in English law
Arguments in favour and against a general principle of good faith
Contracts of the utmost good faith
Fiduciary relationships
Unfair contract terms
Iustum pretium
Laesio enormis
Usefulness of general conditions
Three problems of general conditions
Exemption clauses
General and specific controls
Relevant factors for the scope of application of specific controls (consumer and non-consumer; general conditions and negotiated terms; exemption clauses and other terms; B2B and B2C)

Reasonable notice
'Red hand' rule
Black and grey lists
EU directive on unfair contract terms
Public review
Collective action

 FURTHER READING

– Hugh Beale et al, *Cases, Materials and Text on Contract Law, Ius Commune Casebooks for the Common Law of Europe*, 2nd ed., Oxford (Hart Publishing) 2010, Chapter 16.
– Roger Brownsword, *Contract Law: Themes for the Twenty First Century*, 2000, Chapter 5.
– M.P. Ellinghaus, 'An Australian Contract Law?', *Journal of Contract Law* 1 (1989), 13 ff.
– Roy Goode, 'The Concept of Good Faith in English Law,' in: *Saggi, Conferenze e Seminari*, 1992.
– Martijn W. Hesselink, *Towards a European Civil Code*, 4th ed. Nijmegen (Ars Aequi) 2011, Chapter 27.
– Otto Kahn-Freund, Claude Lévy and Bernard Rudden, *A Source-book on French Law*, 1979.
– Hein Kötz, 'Towards a European Civil Code: The Duty of Good Faith', in: Peter Cane and Jane Stapleton (eds.), *The Law of Obligations: Essays in Celebration of John Fleming*, Oxford 1998, 243 ff.
– Hans-W. Micklitz, Jules Stuyck and Evelyne Terryn (eds.), *Cases, Materials and Text on Consumer Law, Ius Commune Casebooks for the Common Law of Europe*, Oxford (Hart Publishing) 2010.
– UK Competition & Markets Authority, *Unfair Contract Terms Guidance*, 31 July 2015, CMA 37.
– Thomas Wilhelmsson, *Towards a European Civil Code*, 4th ed. Nijmegen (Ars Aequi) 2011, Chapter 25.
– Reinhard Zimmermann and Simon Whittaker (eds.), *Good Faith in European Contract Law*, Cambridge (Cambridge University Press) 2000.

Part Four

Vitiating factors

Once it has been established that the contract is formed through offer and acceptance, the parties agree on their obligations and it is clear what the contents of the contract are, the contract may still not be binding. The law recognises two factors that vitiate (invalidate) the consent of the parties. These **vitiating factors** are:

1. Factors that made a party form its intention in the wrong way. If someone is threatened to conclude a contract or mistakenly believes that it buys a valuable painting while it does not, this could be a reason for invalidation of the contract. These **defects of consent** are examined in Chapter 9, together with the English doctrine of **misrepresentation**;
2. Factors that make a contract prohibited because their formation or performance is against the law or constitutes a violation of public policy or good morals. These **prohibited contracts** are discussed in Chapter 10.

A vitiating factor makes a contract void or avoidable, depending on the vitiating factor in question and the jurisdiction involved. If it is **void**, no contract has in retrospect come into being: if a party still needed to perform, it no longer has to do so. In cases where performance has already taken place, it will have to be reversed: the price and the delivered goods or services need to be given back in so far as this is still possible. If the contract is **avoidable**, the party not in breach can decide if it wants to end the contract or not. If it decides to do so, the results are the same as in case of a void contract.

9

Defects of consent and misrepresentation

CHAPTER OVERVIEW

A contract is always concluded on the basis of certain assumptions (for example, the purchased painting is by Rembrandt, the hired musician is able to play Mozart). If these assumptions prove wrong (the painting is made in China, the musician only knows how to play the Birdie Song), this usually comes at the risk of the disappointed party. But sometimes the law gives relief, in particular if the misapprehension is induced by false statements or unpermitted silence of the other party. This chapter examines the grounds for avoidance of a contract in case of:

- a **defect of consent (mistake, fraud, threat** or **undue influence);**
- **misrepresentation** (in English law).

Disappointment

Anyone concluding a contract does so on the basis of certain assumptions, motives and expectations. I can book a cruise to the North Pole, expecting not only to see polar bears and killer whales, but also assuming I will be able to party with like-minded people of my own age. And if I sell a painting for only €100, it must be because I believe it is made by an unknown painter and not by Van Gogh. These assumptions and expectations are in principle of no relevance to the law: as long as they are not explicitly mentioned to the other party as being vital for someone's consent (through which they, if the other party agrees, become part of the party agreement), they remain in the realm of a party's personal reasons to contract. However, sometimes the law must intervene. In the example above it is possible that I made it clear to the travel agency why I booked the trip: can I then avoid the contract when I accidentally hear, just before the date of embarkation, that all my fellow travellers are retired Russians who go to bed after dinner? And what if the buyer of the painting is an expert in nineteenth century art who was aware of its true value but understandably did not tell me? Should I then be able to claim back the painting or should I have better investigated what its true provenance was? These are questions that the law discusses under the headings of defects of consent and (in English law) misrepresentation.

Civil law

The civil law usually approaches these questions from the perspective of the party in error. If the intention to be bound is the most essential element in the formation of a contract, then his intention must be properly formed. In cases where there is a 'defect' in the intention – because it is based on a wrong assumption – this must affect the validity of the contract. A party must therefore be able to invalidate the contract in cases where the defect is serious enough. Civil law countries traditionally accept three *defects of consent* (*vices du consentement, Willensmängel, wilsgebreken*): mistake, fraud and threat. Civil codes usually group these three grounds for avoidance together in one section (see for example Arts. 1130 ff. *Code Civil* and §§ 119 ff. BGB; see however Arts. 3:44 and 6:228 Dutch BW). In addition to these three grounds, several jurisdictions also allow avoidance of the contract for *undue influence*.

English law

The starting point of English law is different. It does not begin with the (defective) intention of the party in error, but from the party who *caused* the error. This party may have made false statements or – exceptionally – remained silent while it ought to have spoken. English law therefore requires a so-called *misrepresentation* in order for the contract to be avoided by the innocent party. It was only in the nineteenth century that, under continental influence, English law also carved out a place for avoidance on the basis of mistake not caused by a misrepresentation (a so-called self-induced misapprehension), but the scope of this possibility has remained very limited. As the English lawyer John Cartwright puts it: 'English law rarely allows a remedy for mistake' (practically speaking only the 'common mistake', explained below, is accepted). The underlying policy reason behind this different approach is – as we saw before – that English law puts great emphasis on protecting the reasonable reliance of the other party who believes an agreement did come into being. Avoidance for mistake would frustrate this reliance.

We will now look at these grounds for avoidance in more detail. This chapter first examines mistake (A), fraud (B), threat (C) and undue influence (D), and then continues to study misrepresentation under English law (E).

A.   Mistake

Rules on the avoidance of a contract for mistake (*erreur, Irrtum, dwaling*) can be found in any civil code and soft law instrument on contract law. Some of these provisions are reproduced below.

Art. 1130 (1) CC: 'Mistake, fraud and duress vitiate the consent where they are of such a nature that, without them, one of the parties would not have contracted or would have contracted on substantially different terms.

Art. 1132 CC: 'Mistake of law or of fact, as long as it is not inexcusable, is a ground for avoidance of the contract where it bears on the essential qualities of the performance owed or of the other contracting party.'

§ 119 BGB: '(1) A person who, when making a declaration of intent, was mistaken about its contents or had no intention whatsoever of making a declaration with this content, may avoid the declaration if it is to be assumed that he would not have made the declaration with knowledge of the factual position and with a sensible understanding of the case.
(2) A mistake about such characteristics of a person or a thing as are customarily regarded as essential is also regarded as a mistake about the content of the declaration.'

§ 122 BGB: '(1) If a declaration of intent is (…) avoided under §§ 119 and 120, the person declaring must, if the declaration was to be made to another person, pay damages to this person, or failing this to any third party, for the damage that the other or the third party suffers as a result of his relying on the validity of the declaration; but not in excess of the total amount of the interest which the other or the third party has in the validity of the declaration.
(2) A duty to pay damages does not arise if the injured person knew the reason for the voidness or the voidability or did not know it as a result of his negligence (ought to have known it).'

Art. 6:228 BW: '1. A contract which has been entered into under the influence of a mistake and which would not have been concluded had there been a correct assessment of the facts, is avoidable:
   a. if the mistake is caused by information given by the other party, unless this party could assume that the contract would have been concluded even without this information;
   b. if the other party, in view of what it knew or ought to have known about the mistake, should have informed the mistaken party;
   c. if the other party, at the moment of concluding the contract, has based itself on the same incorrect assumption as the mistaken party, unless the other party, even if there had been a correct assessment of the facts, would not have had reason to understand that the mistaken party would therefore be prevented from entering into the contract.
2. The avoidance cannot be based on a mistake as to an exclusively future fact, or on a mistake for which, given the nature of the contract, common

opinion or the circumstances of the case, the mistaken party should remain accountable.'

Art. 4:103 PECL: '(1) A party may avoid a contract for mistake of fact or law existing when the contract was concluded if:
  (a) (i) the mistake was caused by information given by the other party; or
      (ii) the other party knew or ought to have known of the mistake and it was contrary to good faith and fair dealing to leave the mistaken party in error; or
      (iii) the other party made the same mistake,
  and
  (b) the other party knew or ought to have known that the mistaken party, had it known the truth, would not have entered the contract or would have done so only on fundamentally different terms.
(2) However a party may not avoid the contract if:
  (a) in the circumstances its mistake was inexcusable, or
  (b) the risk of the mistake was assumed, or in the circumstances should be borne, by it.'

Although these provisions show differences in the details, it is possible to derive from them some common requirements that any legally relevant mistake must meet.

Contract

The first requirement is that there must be a contract that can be avoided. This is not as self-evident as it seems. It transpired in Chapter 4 that a mistake sometimes prevents a meeting of the minds, namely if parties are the victim of a misunderstanding as to what the terms of the contract actually mean. There is, for example, a lack of consent (*dissensus*, sometimes also referred to as a *mutual mistake*) if parties made a contract, but it is unclear who is the buyer and who is the seller. Another example is if parties agree that goods will be shipped on the vessel called *Peerless*, but each party refers to a different ship both named *Peerless*. Such a misunderstanding can prevent the contract from coming into being at all, unlike the type of cases discussed here in which a contract does exist, but can be invalidated by the party in error.

Misapprehension

Second, there must be a misapprehension of the correct situation by one party or by both parties (the actual 'mistake'). What matters in any jurisdiction is that a party is mistaken about a *fundamental* (some jurisdictions would call it an essential or material, but in any event a not trivial) characteristic of the good (the purchased diamonds turn out to be 'blood diamonds'; the used car is a lemon) or about an essential quality of a person (a party mistakenly believes its future employee will get a work permit; the recently contracted professional cyclist turns out to have used EPO). A trivial mistake would for example be to err about the fact that the bought painting used to hang in the artist's bedroom, a circumstance that is not likely to be of any relevance.

Third, the contract would not have been concluded under the same conditions on a correct assessment of the facts. In other words: there must be a causal link between the mistake and the conclusion of the contract. So a party paying €70,000 for a copy of Grotius' *On the Law of War and Peace* published in 1625 would surely not have paid this price if it had known that it was not a first edition, but only a reprint from the nineteenth century.

Causal link

Fourth, it must be clear to the other party that the mistaken party, had it known the truth, would not have entered into the contract (or at least not on the same terms). The other party need not know about the mistake itself, but it must know, or ought to have known, that the mistaken party regarded a certain quality as vital. If I buy a used car and the seller tells me that the vehicle is still in good shape, I cannot avoid the contract on the basis of a mistake if I bought the car with the intended purpose of street racing and in the process of Tokyo-drifting the engine blows up. I should have told the seller that I wanted to use the car for this purpose, in which case he may have told me that the car was not fit for such extreme use. And if I do not tell my landlord that I wish to use the leased premises to start a restaurant, I cannot complain that she did not tell me that the property can only be used for residential purposes. This is simply a matter of protecting reasonable reliance: if the other party is unaware of my wishes, it should not be confronted with a claim for avoidance for mistake.

Apparent importance

Fifth, the mistake must fall under one of three categories. These are explicitly summed up in Art. 6:228 Dutch BW and Art. 4:103 PECL, but also aptly reflect the law of other civil law jurisdictions.

Situation

a.   The mistake is caused by incorrect information given by the other party

This is probably the most important reason why a legally relevant mistake occurs in a civil law jurisdiction. If Sylvia tells an antiques dealer that she is interested in tableware made in Maastricht between 1860 and 1950 and she subsequently buys a teapot depicting the *Aw Brök* because the dealer tells her it was made by local ceramics manufacturer Sphinx, she can avoid the contract for mistake if it turns out that the pot is a recent copy from China. It does not matter that the dealer believed that the information he provided was incorrect (but if he knew, this qualifies as fraud). Similarly, if Adela rents her holiday home to Jiangqiu, telling him that it is at a very quiet spot, Jiangqiu can avoid the contract for mistake if – unknown to both of them – it turns out that the house is under the flight path of the recently opened landing strip of the nearby airport.

A party cannot rely on just any information. A seller may recommend her products as 'unique', 'the best' and 'the cheapest', but such sales talk does not usually contain statements from which rights will arise. However, more concrete statements made by the other party can become part of the contract itself: if a seller says that the product is fit for a certain use ('the crane is allowed to drive on public roads') or has a certain quality (a 'gold' ring), there is no reason to bring in the rules on mistake (and some jurisdictions even prohibit this): the buyer can simply bring a contractual remedy, such as a claim for performance, damages or termination (see on these remedies Part 5).

In English law a false statement as discussed here does not qualify as mistake, but may constitute a case of misrepresentation (see below, sub-section E).

b.   The mistake is caused by non-disclosure by the other party

In civil law countries a legally relevant mistake can also be caused by the silence of the other party. This would not be the case if everyone were allowed to contract at arm's length and did not need to disclose any information. However, as was seen in Chapter 8, the principle of good faith necessitates that a party sometimes has to meet a pre-contractual duty of disclosure (*obligation de renseignement, Aufklärungspflicht, mededelingsplicht*). It is decisive as to whether a party can reasonably expect to be informed about certain matters before entering into the contract, as is well captured by Art. II-3:101 (1) DCFR:

> Before the conclusion of a contract for the supply of goods, other assets or services by a business to another person, the business has a duty to disclose to the other person such information concerning the goods, other assets or services to be supplied as the other person can reasonably expect, taking into account the standards of quality and performance which would be normal under the circumstances.

Although it differs from one jurisdiction to another when exactly this criterion is met, it is possible to list the factors that play a role here. Art. 4:107 (3) PECL provides an illustrative list:

> In determining whether good faith and fair dealing required that a party disclose particular information, regard should be had to all the circumstances, including:

(a) whether the party had special expertise;
(b) the cost to it of acquiring the relevant information;
(c) whether the other party could reasonably acquire the information for itself; and
(d) the apparent importance of the information to the other party.

The starting point in any jurisdiction must be that people do not have to share the information that they have on the qualities or saleability of a good or service. Often this information is acquired through one's own efforts, by costly research, by training or by experience and the duty to give it away would gravely weaken the incentive of people to inform themselves before entering into a contract. A society that values initiative and education cannot be of a different view. This explains why a buyer in principle need not tell the seller about a likely surge in the market for a certain product, and why an art collector can usually remain silent if he discovers a valuable painting at a flea market. But things may be different if the knowledge of a party is the result of chance, in particular if it would be expensive for the other party to obtain the same information. A car dealer is supposed to give information about the state of the cars it is selling because it would be much more costly for the non-professional buyer to inform himself. This is true in particular if the information relates to the safety of the car. It can be expected from a professional seller that he investigates the safety of the car (do the brakes still work?) before he sells it to an average consumer. A layperson selling a car will have to give such information if she knows about it, as she should also spontaneously disclose that the house she is selling suffers from damp – unless this is easy to discover by the buyer himself. So if construction works are going on next to the house at the time of concluding the contract, the buyer cannot avoid the contract for mistake because the seller did not disclose that a new motorway was being built. In the same vein, German and French case law firmly hold that the seller of a house must tell the prospective buyer that there is woodworm affecting the floors unless this is clearly visible to the buyer.

When to disclose

What to disclose

Although English law does not allow a claim for mistake for non-disclosure, it is exceptionally possible that non-disclosure qualifies as misrepresentation (see below, subsection E).

c.   Common mistake

In case of a common (or 'shared') mistake, both parties have the same misapprehension of reality. It may be that seller and buyer mistakenly believe the painting to be by Mondrian, or that landlord and tenant are wrong in thinking that the apartment is not subject to rent control. The law also allows the parties to avoid such a contract for mistake. This is explicitly laid down in Art. 6:228 (1) sub c Dutch BW, but it is also true in other jurisdictions. Practically speaking, common mistake is also the only type of mistake that is recognised in English law.

The interesting thing about common mistake is that both parties are allowed to avoid the contract. This calls for an assessment of who should bear the risk of the wrong assumption. In the German *Matchfixing* case (1975) a football club in the *Bundesliga* had transferred a player to a club in the lower *Regionalliga*. Both parties were unaware of the fact that the player had accepted a bribe when he played a match for the selling club against Arminia Bielefeld. When the player confessed and was banned by the national German Football Association, the buying club avoided the transfer agreement and claimed back the transfer money. The court reasoned entirely on the basis of who should bear the risk of the player no longer being allowed to participate in the German competition. The court held that this risk fell on the selling club as this was where the player worked at the time of the bribe. The buyer could therefore invalidate the transfer and claim back the transfer fee.

Risk

The sixth, and the final common requirement to establish mistake, is that the mistake must not come at the risk of the mistaken party. A seller may have explicitly stipulated that he is not liable for defects in the goods: this will prevent the mistaken buyer from avoiding the contract (at least in so far as the exemption clause is upheld by the court). But the mistake can also come at a party's risk because it is inexcusable. If it is the mistaken party's own fault that its expectations were not met, it has no relief. Whether or not this is the case, again depends greatly on what can be expected from a party. Should the seller of a painting first have investigated himself what its true provenance was before selling it far below the market value? And should a buyer of a

Duty to investigate

house bring in an expert to discover any hidden defects such as a rotten floor? It is clear that the answer to these questions also depends on whether the other party has a duty to disclose. If the seller must disclose information about the characteristics of the good, this effectively means that the buyer need not investigate. Whether a duty to investigate exists depends on the relative expertise and experience of the parties, as well as on the costs of the investigation.

The end result of this extensive survey of the requirements for a legally relevant mistake must be that, although mistake has a prominent place in the civil codes, its practical significance is fairly limited. Not only will a statement about the quality of a good or a person often give rise to a claim for non-performance – which is much easier to prove than mistake –, but the mistake itself will have to meet strict requirements in order for the avoidance of the contract to be successful.

B.   Fraud

Mistake offers relief to a party who is under a misapprehension that is self-induced or caused by the other party's statement or silence. It does not matter whether the other party knew it was not telling the truth. But sometimes the other party deliberately deceives its counterpart. A can sell a car to B after having turned back the mileage on the car's odometer from 200,000 km to 20,000 km. And C can sell a house to D after having repainted the walls to conceal a rotten area. The law qualifies such wilful deception, regardless of whether it comes in the form of an explicit lie or unpermitted silence, as *fraud* (sometimes also called *deceit*). It regards such trickery as so much against what is required from a contracting party that it adopts special rules on this defect of consent. All civil codes and international instruments therefore make clear that fraud (*dol, arglistige Täuschung, bedrog*) is a ground for avoidance of the contract or other juridical act:

> **Art. 1137 CC**: 'Fraud is an act of a party in obtaining the consent of the other by scheming or lies.
> The intentional concealment by one party of information, where he knows its decisive character for the other party, is also fraud.'

> **§ 123 (1) BGB**: 'Whoever has been induced to make a declaration of will by fraud or unlawfully by threats may rescind the declaration.'

> **Art. 3:44 BW**: '1. A juridical act may be annulled when it has been entered into as a result of threat, fraud or abuse of circumstances.
> (...)
> 3. Fraud occurs when someone induces another person to execute a certain juridical act by deliberately making an incorrect statement, by deliberately concealing a fact that had to be disclosed, or by another artifice. Endorsements in general terms, even if they are untrue, do not as such constitute fraud.'

> **Art. 4:107 PECL**: '(1) A party may avoid a contract when it has been led to conclude it by the other party's fraudulent representation, whether by words or conduct, or fraudulent non-disclosure of any information which in accordance with good faith and fair dealing it should have disclosed.
> (2) A party's representation or non-disclosure is fraudulent if it was intended to deceive.'

In practice a party who believes itself to be the victim of fraud will base its claim on both mistake and fraud. If the victim can indeed prove that the other party had the intention to deceive, this allows not only the avoidance of the contract, but also a claim for damages (in tort, or based on some special provision such as Art. 4:117 PECL). This is particularly useful if the deceived party has incurred costs in reliance on the validity of the contract. If the seller clocked the odometer to deceive the buyer about the age of the car and the car breaks down shortly after delivery, the buyer can not only avoid the contract (and therefore claim back the contract price), but also sue the seller for the reasonable costs of a rental car. The situations that qualify as fraud in civil law systems are likely to fall under fraudulent misrepresentation in English law, but only if based on a party's statement: keeping silent usually will not qualify as misrepresentation (see below, subsection E).

Damages

C. Threat

A third reason for avoidance of a contract is threat. If Bonnie puts a gun to Clyde's head while telling him to sign a document, every jurisdiction would allow Clyde to invalidate the contract at a later stage. The threat need not be physical: if my boss increases my salary after I tell her that I might tell her husband about her affair with the janitor, she can avoid my new employment contract. Here the law intervenes to ensure that only truly, freely exercised autonomy is a source of binding obligations. Threat (*violence, widerrechtliche Drohung, bedreiging*) is not only recognised as a ground for avoidance of a contract in English law (where it is often called *duress*), but is also accepted as a defect of consent in civil codes and international instruments. The defect lies not so much in a misapprehension of the correct situation, but in the fact that a party concludes a contract out of fear of harm to itself, its property, its honour, or its family members.

> **Art. 1140 CC**: 'There is duress if one party contracts under the influence of a constraint which makes him fear that his person or his wealth, or those of his near relatives, might be exposed to considerable harm.'

> **Art. 3:44 (2) BW**: 'Threat occurs when someone induces another person to execute a certain juridical act by unlawfully threatening him or a third party with harm to his person or property. The threat must be of such a nature that a reasonable person would be influenced by it.'

> **Art. 4:108 PECL**: 'A party may avoid a contract when it has been led to conclude it by the other party's imminent and serious threat of an act:
>   (a) which is wrongful in itself, or

(b) which it is wrongful to use as a means to obtain the conclusion of the contract, unless in the circumstances the first party had a reasonable alternative.'

There is a thin line between the illegitimate threat that allows a party to avoid the contract and claim damages on the one hand, and legally accepted pressure or acting in line with social and economic circumstances on the other. In times of food shortage a seller is undoubtedly allowed to ask a higher price than is normal. It is also perfectly legitimate if I threaten my car dealer that I will go to his competitor if he does not lower the price of the car I am interested in buying. Conversely, it is always unlawful to threaten to do something that is against the law, such as to threaten with physical violence or theft. But things can be more difficult. Is it unlawful harassment if I tell my debtor, long overdue with her payment, that if she does not accept a low price on a new contract, I will file for her bankruptcy? And what if I happen to know about her criminal past or that of her wife: can I threaten to report this to the police in order to get a more favourable deal? Although the acts I threaten with are not unlawful in themselves, the law does usually allow avoidance of the contract in such cases. The reason for this is that the threat is unrelated to the obligation of the other party. One is allowed to file for someone's bankruptcy or to report a crime to the police, but only to ensure a fair insolvency or criminal prosecution, not to achieve a low price on a contract.

D. Undue influence

Next to the three traditional defects of consent mistake, fraud and threat, some jurisdictions have in the course of the last century supplemented the judge's toolbox with a fourth ground for avoidance of the contract. This was motivated by the wish to give relief to a vulnerable party that, to its great economic disadvantage, is exploited by somebody else. It was seen in Chapter 8 that a disparity in the value of the mutual performances is in itself never a reason for invalidity of the contract, but this fourth ground for avoidance allows a party to escape the contract if an excessive disparity is caused by *undue influence*. The exact requirements and names differ from one jurisdiction to another. While French law classifies exploitation of a party's weakness as a special case of threat (Art. 1143 CC), German law introduced a separate provision on usury (*Wucher*) in § 138 (2) BGB. This provision comes close to the European model provided by the PECL:

> **§ 138 BGB**: '(1) A juridical act which violates good morals is void.
> (2) In particular, a juridical act is void by which a person, by exploiting the predicament, inexperience, lack of sound judgement or considerable weakness of will of another, causes himself or a third party, in exchange for an act of

performance, to be promised or granted pecuniary advantages which are strikingly disproportionate to the performance.'

Art. 4:109 PECL: '(1) A party may avoid a contract if, at the time of the conclusion of the contract:
>   (a) it was dependent on or had a relationship of trust with the other party, was in economic distress or had urgent needs, was improvident, ignorant, inexperienced or lacking in bargaining skill, and
>   (b) the other party knew or ought to have known of this and, given the circumstances and purpose of the contract, took advantage of the first party's situation in a way which was grossly unfair or took an excessive benefit.
> (2) Upon the request of the party entitled to avoidance, a court may if it is appropriate adapt the contract in order to bring it into accordance with what might have been agreed had the requirements of good faith and fair dealing been followed.
> (3) A court may similarly adapt the contract upon the request of a party receiving notice of avoidance for excessive benefit or unfair advantage, provided that this party informs the party who gave the notice promptly after receiving it and before that party has acted in reliance on it.'

Double test

Both provisions require not only the deliberate exploitation of the vulnerable position of one party, but also an excessive advantage resulting from this for the other. The tests for procedural and substantive fairness (see Chapter 1) are thus combined. If I fancy the house next to mine and do the weekly shopping for the aged and physically disabled couple living in it because they have no one else to turn to, this is no doubt noble behaviour on my part. However, if my neighbour's husband dies after a marriage of 60 years and I tell his grieving and lonely widow that I am only willing to continue the shopping if she moves to a nearby flat and sells her house to me far below the market value, she can avoid the contract (or claim its adaptation under Art. 4:109 (3) PECL). My conduct would not qualify as mistake, fraud or threat, but surely it is wrongful exploitation. The same is true if you are involved in a car accident while in Sardinia and your friend is seriously injured. If, in the absence of any other means of transport, the only way to get to a good hospital is with the local taxi, but the driver charges you ten times as much as the normal amount, your vulnerable position allows the taxi driver to obtain an excessive benefit. You will almost certainly accept the price, but are allowed to invalidate the contract in a later stage.

Undue influence

English law lacks a general doctrine of wrongful exploitation. Such a case may qualify as duress, but it is more likely that the court will avoid the contract by applying the equitable doctrine of *undue influence*. This requires not only a manifest disadvantage, but also that the parties have been in a special relationship of trust (the same type of fiduciary relationship we encountered before in Chapter 8). This should have allowed them to rely on the other party's expertise and advice. Examples are the relationships between child and parent, patient and doctor, client and lawyer and husband and wife, but a relationship of trust can also simply follow from the facts of the case. If such trust is abused, it is open to the court to avoid the contract. An illustrative case is *Lloyd's Bank Ltd v Bundy* (1975). Bundy and his son were both clients of Lloyd's Bank. When the son ran into financial difficulties, he asked the bank for a loan. The bank agreed to this on the condition that the father, who was a small farmer, would put up his farm for security. The bank employee did not say anything to the father about the financial problems of the son and did not give him the opportunity to ask for independent advice. The court found not only a manifestly disadvantageous transaction for the father, but also a relationship of trust (on the facts of the case): the father had been a client of the bank for a long time and could have expected to have been duly informed. Lord Denning went even further and proposed to introduce a general principle of English law of inequality of bargaining power. The courts did not accept this proposal, but in his formulation we can clearly see the same elements coming back as were encountered in the civil law approach:

> The English law gives relief to one who, without independent advice, enters into a contract on terms which are very unfair or transfers property for a consideration which is grossly inadequate, when his bargaining power is grievously impaired by reason of his own needs or desires, or by his own ignorance or infirmity, coupled with undue influences or pressures brought to bear on him by or for the benefit of the other.

PICC

Dutch law and the UNIDROIT Principles of International Commercial Contracts proffer interesting variations on the common theme in two different directions. While the Dutch Art. 3:44 (4) BW on abuse of circumstances (*misbruik van omstandigheden*) does not require a disparity between the mutual performances and is satisfied with mere abuse, the PICC, in contrast, only requires an excessive disadvantage in its provision on *gross disparity*. The way in which this disadvantage comes about is only one of the relevant factors in deciding whether relief must be offered. With this, the PICC arguably go furthest in accepting substantive unfairness as a ground for avoidance of the contract – which may be surprising in view of their scope of application (international commercial contracts).

> **Art. 3:44 (4) BW**: 'Abuse of circumstances occurs when someone knows or should understand that another person is induced to execute a juridical act

as a result of special circumstances, such as a state of necessity, dependency, wantonness, abnormal mental condition or inexperience, and promotes the realisation of that juridical act, although what he knows or should understand should lead him to refrain from doing so.'

Art. 3.2.7 PICC: '(1) A party may avoid the contract or an individual term of it if, at the time of the conclusion of the contract, the contract or term unjustifiably gave the other party an excessive advantage. Regard is to be had, among other factors, to
   (a) the fact that the other party has taken unfair advantage of the first party's dependence, economic distress or urgent needs, or of its improvidence, ignorance, inexperience or lack of bargaining skill, and
   (b) the nature and purpose of the contract.
(2) Upon the request of the party entitled to avoidance, a court may adapt the contract or term in order to make it accord with reasonable commercial standards of fair dealing.
(3) A court may also adapt the contract or term upon the request of the party receiving notice of avoidance, provided that that party informs the other party of its request promptly after receiving such notice and before the other party has reasonably acted in reliance on it. Article 3.2.10 (2) applies accordingly.'

E.   Misrepresentation

a.   No general duty to disclose information

As noted above, civil law jurisdictions are willing to accept a general duty to disclose information to the other party. In cases where this leads a party to conclude a contract under a misapprehension, that party can avoid the contract for mistake. English law is different. Consistent case law since the nineteenth century holds that there is no general duty to disclose facts known to one party but not to the other, at least not in commercial transactions. The leading case is *Smith v Hughes* (1871) in which the seller knew that the buyer (a racehorse trainer) wanted to buy a quantity of old oats, but still sold him new ones (green oats that horses do not eat). The buyer was bound to the contract. The court reasoned in the best English tradition of separating morals from law. Blackburn, J held:

> The buyer persuaded himself they were old oats, when they were not so; but the seller neither said nor did anything to contribute to his deception. He has himself to blame. The question is not what a man of scrupulous morality or nice honour would do under such circumstances. (...) Whatever may be the case in a court of morals, there is no legal obligation on the vendor to inform the purchaser that he is under a mistake, not induced by the act of the vendor.

Caveat emptor

This view is traditionally recapped in the maxim *caveat emptor* (Latin for 'let the buyer beware'): a purchaser must ask questions, or investigate himself, in the absence of a duty of the seller to volunteer information. The ratio for this position is again related to the assumption in English law that it is a good thing if commercial parties deal at arms' length – next to the already mentioned argument that it would be a disincentive to the acquisition of information if it is to be shared with one's counterpart.

The absence of a general duty to give information does not mean that English law does not accept the need to inform the other party in some well-defined situations. It was seen in Chapter 8 that in contracts of the utmost good faith and in fiduciary relationships, a sometimes far-reaching duty to disclose could arise. This duty can also follow from statute or from a European rule (as was seen in Chapter 6). Even more important than this is the effect the law gives to not informing the other party about any matter that makes the quality of the goods unsatisfactory. According to s. 14 of the Sale of Goods Act 1979 (in B2B contracts) and s. 9 (1) Consumer Rights Act 2015 (in B2C contracts), the uninformed buyer can assume that the supplied goods are of satisfactory quality and can bring contractual remedies if they are not.

b. Misrepresentation

While mere silence is in principle no ground for avoidance of the contract under English law, this is different in case of an untrue statement. The phrase 'silence is golden' seems to have been invented for English law: a party can remain silent, but if it does speak it must make sure that it is telling the truth. If it provides incorrect information, the other party may be able to avoid the contract (*rescission*) or claim damages on the basis of *misrepresentation*.

Types of misrepresentation

Misrepresentation can be defined as a spoken or written untrue statement of fact which induces a party to conclude a contract. Silence can only constitute misrepresentation in the rare cases in which there is a duty to speak (see above). English law distinguishes between three types of misrepresentation, dependent on the mind of the party making it:

- *Fraudulent* misrepresentation exists if a party *knows* it is making a false statement, of which we saw examples in subsection B above. In this case a party has the deliberate intention to deceive, allowing the other party to avoid the contract and claim damages on basis of the tort of deceit.
- *Negligent* misrepresentation exists if a party carelessly makes a representation while having no reasonable basis to believe it to be true. This party does not lie, but is careless in saying what it says. If a real estate agent

BOX 9.1

TERMS, REPRESENTATIONS AND MISREPRESENTATIONS

The conclusion of most contracts is preceded by negotiations or at least by statements of both parties. If Fatima wants to have a garage built, the contractor may say things about the price, the time it will take, who will do the work, what exactly is included in the contract price, how the electricity is supplied, and which colour the stones will be. Unlike civil law systems, English law classifies such statements as either representations or terms. A *term* is a promise that becomes part of the contract, meaning that it allows an action for breach of contract in case the promisor does not perform. A *representation* is a statement which asserts the truth of a given state of facts. It may encourage a party to make the contract but is not part of the contract itself. In case the representation is false (it states facts that are untrue), it can give rise to an action for *misrepresentation*. Misrepresentation is therefore an untrue statement of fact (not a mere opinion) which induces a party to conclude a contract. It is dependent on the parties' intentions whether a statement is a term or a (mis) representation. One practical rule is that if a contract is put into writing, the written contract is usually regarded as containing terms while any previously made oral statements are representations. Another rule of thumb is that a party with special knowledge or expertise is more likely to state terms. In *Dick Bentley Productions Ltd v Harold Smith (Motors) Ltd* (1965), for example, Bentley bought a car from car dealer Smith, relying on Smith's statement that the car had travelled 20,000 miles after a new engine and gearbox had been put in. Soon after the purchase it became clear that the car had done much more and was in need of new repairs. The court found that the professional dealer's statements were terms, allowing Bentley to claim damages.

states that the house it is trying to sell is very quiet, it is making a negligent misrepresentation if the house next door is in fact undergoing a lengthy and noisy renovation. The agent did not know about this (otherwise this would be a case of fraudulent misrepresentation), but the statement is made in a careless way because he assumed something that he should have investigated before saying anything. Negligent misrepresentation allows the other party to avoid the contract and claim damages under S. 2 (1) of the Misrepresentation Act 1967.

The question when exactly a statement is made in a negligent way can be difficult to answer, but section 2 (1) of the Misrepresentation Act can be of great help to the disadvantaged party. The provision reverses the burden of proof by stating that if a party is induced to conclude a contract by another party's misrepresentation, it can claim damages unless the other party can prove that at the time of concluding the contract it believed its statement to be true and had reasonable grounds to believe this. This provision proved helpful in the illustrative case of *Spice Girls Ltd v Aprilia World Service BV* (2002). On 6 May 1998 the Spice Girls entered into a contract with the Italian manufacturer of scooters Aprilia. Aprilia would sponsor the tour of the Spice Girls (according to the contract consisting of five members) in return for the right to use Spice Girls' images and their participation in the filming of an Aprilia TV commercial. On 29 May, shortly after the conclusion of the contract and the shooting of the commercial, Gerri Halliwell ('Ginger Spice') left the group. As a result, Aprilia refused to pay under the sponsorship contract and claimed back the costs of making the commercial and plans to launch a 'Spice Sonic' scooter, arguing that the group already knew about Halliwell leaving before the conclusion of the contract and should have disclosed this to Aprilia. The court agreed and held the Spice Girls liable for negligent misrepresentation. The representation consisted of allowing Halliwell to participate in the commercial, with which the group represented that she would stay on as a member for the period the commercial would be used. It would have been difficult for Aprilia to prove that the Spice Girls actually knew of Halliwell leaving the group, but as a result of section 2 (1) of the Misrepresentation Act it did not have to prove this – the Spice Girls could not prove they did *not* know about Halliwell leaving and were therefore liable.

- *Innocent* misrepresentation exists if an incorrect statement is made without fault, meaning that a party believed its statement to be true and could also reasonably believe this to be the case. If you sell your stereo to somebody else, telling the buyer that 'it functions well' (which you believe to be true because you have not used the stereo in the last few years), this is an innocent misrepresentation. It allows a party to avoid the contract, unless the court regards this to be a too severe sanction and wants to award damages instead (Misrepresentation Act, s. 2 (2)).

 TOPICS FOR REVIEW

Defects of consent
Fundamental mistake
Types of mistake
Mistake in English law
Duty of disclosure
Duty to investigate
Fraud
Threat
Undue influence
Abuse of circumstances
Gross disparity
Terms and representations

Caveat emptor
Misrepresentation
Types of misrepresentation
Remedies for misrepresentation

 FURTHER READING

– Hugh Beale et al, *Cases, Materials and Text on Contract Law, Ius Commune Casebooks for the Common Law of Europe*, 2nd ed., Oxford (Hart Publishing) 2010, Chapters 10 and 11.
– John Cartwright, *Towards a European Civil Code*, 4th ed. Nijmegen (Ars Aequi) 2011, Chapter 23.
– Catherine Elliott and Frances Quinn, *Contract Law*, 10th ed., Harlow (Pearson) 2015, Chapters 9 and 10.
– Hein Kötz, *European Contract Law Vol. 1* (translated by Tony Weir), Oxford (Oxford University Press) 1997, Chapters 10 and 11.
– Anthony Kronman, 'Mistake, Disclosure, Information and the Law of Contracts', *Journal of Legal Studies* 7 (1978), 1 ff.
– Ewan McKendrick, *Contract Law*, 11th ed., Basingstoke (Palgrave Macmillan) 2015, Chapters 12 and 13.
– Ruth Sefton-Green (ed.), *Mistake, Fraud and Duties to Inform in European Contract Law*, Cambridge (Cambridge University Press) 2005.

10

Prohibited contracts

CHAPTER OVERVIEW

Freedom of contract finds its limits in mandatory law, public policy and good morals. Even if contracting parties intend to be bound, and their consent is not affected by mistake, fraud, threat, duress or misrepresentation, their contract can still be void or unenforceable if its conclusion or performance violates a statute or fundamental principles of society. This chapter examines these **prohibited contracts**.

Despite the great importance the law attaches to the principle of freedom of contract, parties are not free to enter into any contract whatever its contents. Every legal system puts limits on the freedom of contracting parties by declaring contracts void or unenforceable if they are contrary to mandatory law, public policy or good morals (*bonos mores*). If Marjolein agrees to sell nuclear arms to a terrorist group, or if Jens agrees to kill someone in return for a sum of money wired to his Swiss bank account, not many people would doubt that these contracts interfere with the public interest and should therefore not be enforceable. Even if it is unlikely that Marjolein and Jens, or their counterparts, would sue each other in court, the law cannot do without rules on prohibited contracts. If a court happens to come across one, it is to declare the contract invalid out of its own motion.

All jurisdictions concur in declaring a contract unenforceable if it infringes a statute or public policy or good morals – although the exact formulation naturally differs somewhat from one country to another. The relevant provisions of the French, German and Dutch codes are the following (English law could also very well live with what these provisions express):

> **Art. 6 CC**: 'Statutes relating to public policy and morals may not be derogated from by private agreements.'

> **Art. 1162 CC**: 'A contract cannot derogate from public policy either by its stipulations or by its purpose, regardless of whether the latter was known to all the parties or not.'

§ **134 BGB**: 'A juridical act which violates a statutory prohibition is void, unless the statute leads to a different conclusion.'

§ **138 (1) BGB**: 'A juridical act which violates good morals is void.'

Art. 3:40 BW: '1. A juridical act that by its contents or implications violates good morals or public policy, is null and void.
2. A juridical act that violates a statutory provision of mandatory law is null and void; if, however, this statutory provision is only intended to protect one of the parties to a multilateral juridical act, the juridical act is only avoidable; in both cases this applies in so far as the provision does not imply otherwise.
3. Section 2 does not apply to statutory provisions which do not purport to invalidate juridical acts contrary to them.'

These dry provisions raise two main questions. The first question (A) is when exactly a contract goes against a statutory prohibition, public policy (*ordre public, openbare orde*) or good morals (*gute Sitten, goede zeden*). Public policy or good morals (taken together in the remainder of this chapter) are open-ended clauses that leave much discretion to the court. This is on the one hand a good thing because it allows the courts to deal with changing conceptions of what should be prohibited. What was seen as immoral in the 1950s (e.g. to let a house for use as a brothel) may today be accepted, and what was a hundred years ago perfectly permissible (e.g. to agree to organise a goose-pulling competition) is seen today as unacceptable (in this example because it entails intolerable cruelty against animals). On the other hand, it can be difficult for a court to decide what public policy or good morals requires. Judges are not allowed to impose their own standards, but rather must feel out what society as a whole believes to be morally unjustifiable. And while this may still be possible within one national society, it is highly improbable that there is one, uniform, global, or even European, conception of what parties can freely agree upon. This explains why the PECL only contain a very shallow provision on prohibited contracts (Art. 15:101), which merely states that a contract is of no effect to the extent that it is 'contrary to principles recognized as fundamental in the laws of the member states of the European Union'.

The second question (B) is what must be the effect of a prohibited contract if it has already been performed. It seems self-evident that a prohibited contract cannot be enforced and does not allow a claim for damages in case of non-performance. This is because State courts must refuse to assist in upholding prohibited contracts. But what if one party, or both parties, have

Two questions

already performed under the contract (arms dealer Marjolein and hitman Jens received their money)? Are their partners in crime then allowed to claim back the payment, or would this mean that the court unjustifiably lends its services to parties to a prohibited transaction?

A. When is a contract prohibited?

a. Statutory illegality

All jurisdictions contain statutory provisions that prohibit the conclusion of certain types of contracts. For example, encouraging someone to commit a crime by paying this person money (as in the case of the hitman) is a criminal offence (namely *incitement*). The same is true for knowingly buying stolen property (*fencing*). Both crimes are prohibited by statute. Such statutory illegality can often also be categorised as being against public policy or good morals (the hitman's contract does not only violate a provision of criminal law, but is naturally also against public policy or good morals), but the important advantage of being able to refer to a statutory provision is that the court no longer needs to ask itself what public policy or good morals exactly require. In the unlikely event that the incited party or fencer claims payment before the court, the court will declare the contract void and reject the claim. Another example concerns trade in human organs: many countries have adopted a statute that prohibits the selling of body parts. Violation of such a statute will also make the contract void.

Sanction It was seen in Chapter 6 that not all contracts violating a statutory rule will be declared void. Sometimes a provision only aims to protect one party to the contract, as in the case where consumer suretyship is not made on a written form, which only makes the contract avoidable by the guarantor. This is explicitly laid down in Art. 3:40 (2) BW, but it is also accepted in the case law of other jurisdictions. It could even be that a statutory provision prohibits a contract, but does not purport to invalidate it in any way (as Art. 3:40 (3) BW states). An example of this is the rule that prohibits shops selling products after hours, such as the UK Sunday Trading Act 1994 and the Berlin *Ladenöffnungsgesetz*. Such statutes do not mean to invalidate the contract with a customer who happened to be in need of a product at an unusual hour, but only provide administrative sanctions for the retailer (for example that she must pay a fine to the authorities).

Art 101 TFEU An important example of statutory illegality following from European law can be found in Art. 101 TFEU. This provision prohibits agreements between competitors that restrict competition on the European internal market, such as cartels and price-fixing agreements. The provision reads as follows:

> 1. The following shall be prohibited as incompatible with the internal market: all agreements between undertakings, decisions by associations of undertakings and concerted practices which may affect trade between Member States and which have as their object or effect the prevention, restriction or distortion of competition within the internal market (…)
> 2. Any agreements or decisions prohibited pursuant to this Article shall be automatically void.

If the agreement has an appreciable effect on competition (which is usually the case if a share of at least 5 per cent of the market is affected by the illegal deal), it is not only void but the European Commission is also allowed to impose fines on the companies involved. These fines usually attract a lot of publicity. The highest cartel fine imposed so far was in 2008 when a cartel of four car class producers, who together controlled 90 per cent of the European market, were fined €1.3 billion.

Performance illegal

In the above examples, the *formation* of the agreement itself is prohibited. But it can also be that a contract is legally concluded, with illegality only arising at the time of *performance*. If A agrees with B to transport goods from Latakia to Rotterdam, this is a perfectly valid contract. Nowhere in a statute is it written that a transport contract is illegal. But if shortly before the transport is to take place the Dutch Government prohibits the import of any products from Syria, transporting the goods becomes an illegal act.

Motive unknown

There is one category of illegal agreements that merits special attention. It is not always apparent to the other party that the contract is concluded to engage in an illegal activity. If I were to buy a knife in a nearby supermarket with the aim of killing my neighbour, it is not likely that I will tell the seller about this motive. But if the other party should reasonably know about my intentions, this contract is arguably void as well. This is why most jurisdictions hold that if both parties are aware of the illegality (either in formation or performance of the contract), neither party can enforce it. But if the other party did not know about the illegal performance, the innocent party can still enforce the contract. If a taxi driver agrees to drive my guests from Maastricht to Brussels in a taxi that does not have a licence to operate on Belgian soil, the actual performance of the contract is against the law. But as long as I do not know of this, I can normally sue the driver in case of non-performance (for example, because she is too late or causes an accident in which my guests are hurt).

b.   Contracts against public policy or good morals

While it is relatively easy to determine that a contract violates a statutory rule, it is often more difficult to establish that the agreement of the parties goes against public policy or good morals. The code provisions mentioned above do not give much guidance. The term 'good morals' is supposed to refer to the common decency of reasonable persons, while 'public policy' refers to fundamental principles of society. But these descriptions do not help much in understanding what the statutory texts mean. The new French Art. 1162 CC no longer even mentions good morals at all and regards these as part of the overall concept of public policy. The best way to grasp the gist of these provisions is by looking at some categories of cases.

1.   *Contracts unduly restricting personal, artistic or economic freedom*

Personal freedom

Contracts that unduly restrict a party's personal, artistic or economic freedom are contrary to public policy or good morals. If you agree to be my house sitter while I am away on holiday, I will not be able to enforce the clause in our contract that you must stay inside the house for the four weeks that I am away. Slavery is too strong a word for this, but our agreement is no doubt seen by society as an unpermitted burden on your personal freedom. And if a writer or a musician promises a publisher or a record company to offer all his future works to the latter, this is also seen as a too severe restriction of the artist's freedom. In this type of case the German Supreme Court once held that allowing such an agreement to be binding on the artist would lead to a 'one-sided burden, which constrained his economic and personal freedom to an unacceptable extent' (*Vorrechtsvertrag Verfasser*, 1956). This would have been different if the contract had contained a time limit of, for example, five years. Yet another example from German law was seen in the previous chapter: if a party's vulnerable position is exploited by somebody else, this could constitute such a violation of someone's freedom that the contract is void for undue influence (§ 138 (2) BGB).

Artistic freedom

Waiver

A party could also be tempted to *waive one of its fundamental rights*. Although fundamental rights traditionally only work in the 'vertical' relationship between the State and the citizen, they often reflect common societal standards that also have value in the 'horizontal' relationship between citizens. It would therefore be contrary to public policy or good morals to make the purchaser of a house agree to no longer exercise his religion in return for a lower price on the contract. Similarly, Evy will not be able to enforce Ben's promise that he will never marry anyone else but her (which would be a clear violation of Ben's right to family life). Also contrary to public policy is a clause (for example in general conditions) that excludes a party from access to court in case of a dispute, which is seen as a violation of the right to a fair trial as protected by Art. 6 of the ECHR. Also other agreements that go against freedom of religion, freedom of speech or other fundamental rights are usually unenforceable.

Economic freedom

Another important category of possibly unduly restrictive agreements is that of *contracts in restraint of trade.* These are contracts in which a party agrees to restrict his economic freedom, particularly his freedom to trade or to conduct his profession or business. An employment contract can contain the clause that an employee, after her employment has ended, is not allowed to start her own business or work for a competitor. It is even very common that the seller of a business agrees not to set up a similar business in order to avoid customers following the seller. The law looks with suspicion upon such agreements. On the one hand, it is clear that the employer and purchaser of the business have an interest in restricting the activities of their former employee and competitor, but on the other hand enforcement of such clauses could deprive them of the possibility of making a living for themselves (and would also infringe upon the public interest of free competition). In particular people such as lawyers, accountants, doctors and hairdressers could be hit hard by such a non-competition clause. This explains why contracts in restraint of trade and non-competition clauses are only considered valid if they are restricted in scope (the exact type of activity or clients must be defined, e.g. only clients advised in the year prior to departure cannot be approached), time and place (e.g. only a prohibition to compete within 20 kilometers from the original workplace and only for a period of two years).

Restraint of trade

2. *Contracts against moral views believed to be held in society*

The category of cases discussed above (*subsection 1*) typically involves agreements that are one-sided in the sense that one party clearly benefits from the contract. In each of these cases, one could also ask whether the other party would really have accepted the conditions of the contract if it had been completely free to design it in accordance with its own desires. But there are also contracts that are deemed to violate the interests of the community at large. In this category, there is no question that both parties wanted to enter into the contract, but the contract is believed to be against the moral views that society holds dear. An obvious example is to have somebody else write your bachelor thesis (or any other academic paper): both you and your ghostwriter profit from this, but society finds it unacceptable. The cases that have come before the courts in the last hundred years offer a nice perspective on changing views of morality.

In any event until the Summer of Love – and probably for some time afterwards – agreements promoting 'sexual immorality' were, together with gambling contracts, a main category of contracts held void for violating good morals. It was considered immoral to let a house be used as a brothel, or for cohabitants (if married to somebody else) to agree on their mutual financial obligations in the common household (or, in the language of times foregone 'to pay a mistress'). Just at the end of the Victorian era, the English court still held void a contract under which a person was paid a fee by a lonely single to find her a marriage partner (*Hermann v Charlesworth*, 1905).

All these examples have become redundant. The frontiers of today's sexual morality lie somewhere else. Not many European jurisdictions would still disallow a claim of a prostitute or a call girl for the agreed price. The English Court of Appeal also held a contract to advertise for telephone sex lines in magazines perfectly valid, arguing that, although 'distasteful', sex lines were generally accepted by society (*Armhouse Lee Ltd v Chappell*, 1996). In the same vein, not many people have sleepless nights – at least not because of the infringement of standards of morality – if they are confronted with so-called 'casual dating' sites that actively promote adultery under the slogan 'Life is short, have a second love.'

Surrogate
motherhood

The more important cases today are concerned with topics such as surrogate motherhood and trading in body parts and human blood. In the last 30 years cases of surrogate motherhood have come before the courts in a wide variety of countries. This is the result of better techniques of artificial insemination, but the phenomenon itself is as old as the Old Testament. In Genesis 16 the following story is told:

> Now Sarah, Abraham's wife, had borne him no children. But she had an Egyptian slave named Hagar; so she said to Abraham, "The Lord has kept me from having children. Go, sleep with my slave; perhaps I can build a family through her." Abraham agreed to what Sarah said. So after Abraham had been living in Canaan ten years, Sarah his wife took her Egyptian slave Hagar and gave her to her husband to be his wife. He slept with Hagar, and she conceived.

While Hagar was the child's genetic mother, surrogate motherhood (a woman agreeing to bear and give birth to a child for a person or a couple with a view to that person or couple adopting or taking legal custody of the child) today often consists of carrying a child that is genetically unrelated to the woman who delivers it. Jurisdictions around the world differ widely in their approach to holding such surrogacy agreements enforceable or not. The French Civil Code, in a chapter on 'respect of the human body' introduced by the French legislator in 1994, explicitly declares void 'all agreements relating to procreation or gestation for the sake of somebody else' (Art. 16-7 CC). If a surrogacy agreement (*maternité pour autrui*) was made and the surrogate mother does not want to keep the child, the intended parents are even excluded from the possibility to adopt it. German law is equally strict and introduced in 1998 a new § 1591 BGB, which concisely states: 'The mother of a child is the woman who gave birth to it.' The other extreme is India, where commercial surrogacy (meaning that the surrogate mother receives a fee for her services) is perfectly legal, making it a leading country in so-called fertility tourism. Clinics in India even offer full packages for foreigners including the hiring of Indian surrogate mothers, fertilisation and delivery of the baby for a price ranging between €15,000 and €90,000. In between these two extremes are the UK and the Netherlands that allow only altruistic surrogacy, which means that the intended parents and surrogate mother (*draagmoeder*) can validly agree on reimbursement of the latter's medical and other expenses, but not on an enforceable obligation of the surrogate mother to give the newborn to the intended parents or to be paid a fee. While this is established case law in the Netherlands, the UK adopted legislation on this in the form of the Surrogacy Arrangements Act 1985, which states:

> S. 1A: No surrogacy arrangement is enforceable by or against any of the persons making it.'
> S. 2: No person shall on a commercial basis do any of the following acts in the United Kingdom, that is –
> > (a) initiate or take part in any negotiations with a view to the making of a surrogacy arrangement,
> > (b) offer or agree to negotiate the making of a surrogacy arrangement, or
> > (c) compile any information with a view to its use in making, or negotiating the making of, surrogacy arrangements;
> and no person shall in the United Kingdom knowingly cause another to do any of those acts on a commercial basis.

3.   *Other contracts*

The very nature of an open-ended clause such as public policy or good morals makes it impossible to list all categories of agreements that might fall under it. When US Supreme Court justice Potter Stewart asked himself how to define the open-ended term 'hardcore pornography', he replied: 'I know it when I see it.'

BOX 10.1

SHOULD A SURROGATE MOTHERHOOD CONTRACT BE ENFORCEABLE?

Views on the legitimacy of surrogate motherhood differ widely from one country to another. The general stance among EU Member States is one of disapproval: at most the agreement to reimburse medical and other expenses is seen as valid. The idea that the intended parents should be able to enforce the contract and claim 'back' the baby from the woman who gave birth is usually regarded as morally and legally wrong. But is it? The task of academic lawyers is not to take moral convictions at face value, but to find rational arguments. This necessarily involves contrarian thinking: one must argue against the majority view, regardless of how unpopular it may be. It is therefore interesting to contrast the opposition against the validity of commercial surrogacy with the views of Richard Posner. Posner, a former judge and law professor at the University of Chicago, is one of the most cited legal authors worldwide. In his pioneering textbook on *Economic Analysis of Law*, he takes issue with the famous case of *Baby M* (1988), in which the Supreme Court of New Jersey found the enforcement of a commercial surrogacy contract against public policy. In this case, William Stern and his wife entered into a surrogacy agreement with Mary Beth Whitehead, a woman they found through a newspaper advertisement. The contract held that Mary Beth would agree to be inseminated with William's sperm, deliver the baby, and then abandon her parental rights in favour of William's wife. However, Mary Beth decided to keep the baby and was subsequently sued by the Stern couple to be recognised as the

child's legal parents. The court, however, recognised Mary Beth as the legal mother because she gave birth, but William was awarded legal custody as this was regarded to be in the child's best interest. Mary Beth was allowed to visit the child.

The *Baby M* decision makes excellent reading as it lists all the main arguments against allowing enforcement of a surrogacy contract (and these arguments matter regardless of the jurisdiction in which the contract is concluded). Let us have a look at the court's arguments (according to Posner showing 'a lack of economic sophistication') and at how Posner retorts.

- *Court*: allowing the claim would mean that the child finds itself immediately after birth in a tug of war between contending mother and father. *Posner*: this tug of war is only the result of present legal uncertainty. If it is settled that a surrogate contract can be enforced, the surrogate mother will no longer challenge the contract.
- *Court*: the purpose of the surrogacy contract was to give the father the rights to the child by destroying the rights of the mother. *Posner*: the court overlooks that without a contract no child would have been born in the first place. The purpose of the contract was not to destroy the mother's right, but to encourage one woman to help another woman. A contract is in this sense immensely productive: it helps to realise something that would otherwise not have been possible.

➡

←

- *Court*: allowing surrogacy probably means that the baby will go the highest bidders, regardless of whether they are suited as parents. *Posner*: unlike paintings by Van Gogh, there is no fixed supply of babies. Supply will increase if money can be earned and the ensuing competition among surrogate mothers will force down the price. The court should therefore not be worried that adoption is only available to the wealthy (who, incidentally, are also the first to adopt in case adoption is regulated by the State).

- *Court*: the shortage of babies for adoption will lead to middlemen who get paid to increase the supply of babies [so the type of surrogacy clinics we saw that exist in India, JMS]. *Posner*: this is certainly true, but this is not an argument against but for baby brokers. There are not enough babies offered for adoption precisely *because* middlemen are not allowed to bring together demand and supply and are not allowed to be paid for this. It must be noted that, in one of the most famous law articles of the 1970s, Posner and his colleague Elisabeth Landes argued in favour of creating a market for babies. If a mother is allowed to put up her child for adoption, this would not only remedy the shortage of adoption babies, but it could also lead to fewer children being neglected by their parents, and to benefits for a mother who may not want to be burdened with the need to carry a baby for nine months. Moreover, an illegal market for babies probably already exists today and would disappear if one could validly contract about parental rights.

- *Court*: infertile couples with a low income will not find surrogate mothers. *Posner*: this argument is the 'jurisprudence of envy'. Even if it were true that poor couples cannot afford the price of a surrogate mother, they are not helped by a rule that prohibits infertile high income couples from hiring one.

- *Court*: 'There are, in short, values that society deems more important than granting to wealth whatever it can buy, be it labor, love, or life.' *Posner*: it is not clear how these values are served by refusing to allow the enforcement of a surrogacy contract.

One need not agree with all of Posner's counterarguments to see that there is (much) more to prohibiting surrogacy contracts than mere 'morality'.

B.   The effect of a prohibited contract; recovery of money or goods

It has already been pointed out that illegality does not necessarily mean that a contract is void. We saw that a statutory provision sometimes only aims to protect one party to the contract, in which case it is only avoidable by this party (e.g. when a consumer suretyship is not made in writing). We also saw that a prohibition on making a certain type of contract does not always aim to invalidate the contract itself (meaning the contract is neither void nor voidable), as in case of legislation restricting shopping hours. But *if* the contract is void or avoided for illegality, the consequence is that no party can sue for performance or for damages resulting from breach of contract. This is a logical consequence: State courts cannot be expected to assist a person who bases their claim on an illegal or immoral act.

However, a practical difficulty arises if a party (or both parties) have already performed the prohibited contract. The normal consequence of a contract being void or avoided (for example on the ground of legal incapacity or mistake) is that each of the parties can claim restitution of what it has already supplied under the contract. So in case of a sales contract the buyer can recover the money paid and the seller can claim the goods back. But this is not the self-evident outcome in case of a prohibited contract. The mafia boss who paid the hitman for his much-needed services should not be able to recover the paid sum. The Romans certainly thought so. The Digest (the most important part of the *Corpus Iuris Civilis*) devotes an entire title (Book 12, Title 5) to 'The action for recovery if the cause is immoral or unlawful.' Here we find the views of the great Roman jurists Julius Paulus and Domitius Ulpianus on the consequences of respectively bribing a judge, sexual immorality and paying hush money to an unwelcome spectator:

> 3. *Paulus* (...): Where both the giver and the recipient are guilty of immoral conduct, we hold that no action lies for recovery as, for instance, where money is paid in order to pervert a judgment.
> 4. *Ulpianus* (...): The same applies where something is given for sexual malpractice, or where someone caught in adultery buys his way out: no action for recovery will then be available (...).

In pari delicto This rule of Roman law is still known today as the *in pari delicto* rule: in cases where both parties have unclean hands because they willingly acted against a statute or against public policy or good morals, they cannot recover anything. This rule can be found in the German BGB (§ 817) and is accepted in most other jurisdictions as well. The lucky consequence of the *in pari delicto* rule is that if only one of the parties is primarily responsible for the illegality, and the other party is relatively innocent, the latter's claim for restitution is allowed. An example is provided by the limitations that many jurisdictions pose on the payment of so-called 'key money' when renting a house or a room. A tenant must naturally pay the rent, and possibly a refundable deposit not exceeding a reasonable amount (for example two or three months of rent), but the payment of a non-refundable sum to the landlord when the lease is concluded is a fatal recipe for abuse and therefore often prohibited. Even if the tenant knew that this practice is illegal when he paid the key money, he can reclaim the money. His 'fault' is only little compared to that of the landlord.

The extent to which both parties were at fault or intended to infringe upon statutory or fundamental norms is not the only factor that plays a role in deciding whether or not restitution should be granted. Another relevant factor is the purpose of the rule. One can well argue that a difference must be made between a contract that amounts to a gross infringement of fundamental values (the hitman's agreement to kill someone) and a contract that only violates an administrative provision (such as a provision on rent control or the need for a licence). This multi-factor approach, which makes it dependent on a range of factors whether a claim for recovery is possible, is gradually becoming the accepted view in the whole of Europe. Art. 15:104 PECL reflects the progressive solution that we need in this complicated matter.

> (1) When a contract is rendered ineffective under Articles 15:101 or 15:102, either party may claim restitution of whatever that party has supplied under the contract, provided that, where appropriate, concurrent restitution is made of whatever has been received.
> (2) When considering whether to grant restitution under paragraph (1), and what concurrent restitution, if any, would be appropriate, regard must be had to the factors referred to in Article 15:102 (3).
> (3) An award of restitution may be refused to a party who knew or ought to have known of the reason for the ineffectiveness.
> (4) If restitution cannot be made in kind for any reason, a reasonable sum must be paid for what has been received.

The factors referred to in Art. 15:102 (3) are the following:

> (a) the purpose of the rule which has been infringed;
> (b) the category of persons for whose protection the rule exists;
> (c) any sanction that may be imposed under the rule infringed;
> (d) the seriousness of the infringement;
> (e) whether the infringement was intentional; and
> (f) the closeness of the relationship between the infringement and the contract.

The provision no longer starts from the *in pari delicto* rule, but states instead that a claim for restitution must be available if this is appropriate, which is made dependent on six factors to be weighed in the circumstances of the case.

 TOPICS FOR REVIEW

Prohibited contracts
Statutory illegality
Contracts against public policy or good morals

Prohibited formation and prohibited performance
Illegal motive unknown to the other party
Agreements prohibited under Art. 101 TFEU
Public policy or good morals as an open-ended concept
Agreements violating a person's personal, artistic or economic freedom
Waiver of fundamental rights
Contracts in restraint of trade and non-competition clauses
Surrogate motherhood contracts
Arguments pro and contra the enforceability of surrogate motherhood contracts
Effects of prohibited contracts
Recovery of money or goods
In pari delicto rule

 FURTHER READING

– Hugh Beale et al, *Cases, Materials and Text on Contract Law, Ius Commune Casebooks for the Common Law of Europe*, 2nd ed., Oxford (Hart Publishing) 2010, Chapter 12.
– Catherine Elliott and Frances Quinn, *Contract Law*, 10th ed., Harlow (Pearson) 2015, Chapter 11.
– Hein Kötz, *European Contract Law Vol. 1* (translated by Tony Weir), Oxford (Oxford University Press) 1997, Chapter 9.
– Ewan McKendrick, *Contract Law*, 11th ed., Basingstoke (Palgrave Macmillan) 2015, Chapter 15.
– Hector L. MacQueen, *Towards a European Civil Code*, 4th ed. Nijmegen (Ars Aequi) 2011, Chapter 24.
– Richard A Posner and Elisabeth M. Landes, 'The Economics of the Baby Shortage', *Journal of Legal Studies* 7 (1978), 323 ff.
– Richard A. Posner, *Economic Analysis of Law*, 9th ed., New York (Wolters Kluwer) 2014, Chapter 5.

Part Five

Contractual remedies

This part examines the contractual remedies, which are available when the other party does not perform its contractual obligations. In a normal situation both parties perform in conformity with what they agreed upon, leading to **discharge** of the contract by performance. But it can also happen that a party is in breach of what was agreed upon. The tenant can refuse to leave the apartment, the hairdresser can set up shop next to his former employer, and the ordered products may not be delivered on time, or not at all. This raises the question of what the disappointed creditor can do. Depending on whether the exact requirements for each of these remedies are met, there are five possible actions:

- bring a claim for **performance** of the contract and, in case of consumer sale, bring a claim for **price reduction** (Chapter 11);
- claim **damages** for non-performance (Chapter 12);
- **terminate** the contract, possibly preceded by **withholding performance** (Chapter 13).

11

Performance

CHAPTER OVERVIEW

The question addressed in this chapter is whether a party to a contract can compel the other party to perform *in natura*. While in civil law jurisdictions there is no doubt whatsoever that performance is a right of the creditor, this is different in English law, which regards specific performance as an exceptional remedy that is only available if a claim for damages would not do adequate justice. This chapter examines:

- the availability of the action for **performance** in **civil law** and **common law**;
- how to **execute** a court order for performance;
- when the action for performance cannot be brought because of **impossibility** (frustration) or because it requires **personal services** or **constant supervision** of compliance by the court;
- when **unforeseen circumstances** can be invoked;
- **repair, replacement** and **price reduction** in consumer sales as laid down in the Consumer Sales Directive;
- the solution proposed by the **PECL**.

The principle of binding force of the contract would be futile in cases where a party could escape from being bound to its agreement. However, there are two fundamentally different ways in which one can reason about what it means to be 'bound' to a contract.

Civil law

First, one can argue that this must mean that the creditor can go to court and actually force the debtor to perform *in natura*; so he can obtain a court order that the goods must be delivered, that the former employee must refrain from competition, or that the contractor must build the house. The position of the civil law is that binding force of the contract means that in principle the creditor is allowed to claim performance in any case. Civil law jurisdictions thus tend to regard a contract as a moral device: promises must be kept.

Common law

Second, one can argue that binding force means primarily that the creditor is allowed to claim monetary compensation where the debtor does not perform. If A agrees to sell two tons of bananas or 100 barrels of oil to B, and A does not deliver, then why would B not be satisfied with obtaining damages? If A compensates B for the costs he incurred in concluding the contract as well as for the lost profits, this prevents A from having to find substitute goods to deliver to B while B obtains the money value of the contract. This is, of course, different if a party has an interest in obtaining a specific good (like a house or a rare painting), but in the case of products that are readily available on the market, this is a commercially viable solution. This is the position of English law. In his famous book *The Common Law* (published in 1881), the American jurist Oliver Wendell Holmes put it like this: 'The only universal consequence of a legally binding promise is, that the law makes the promisor pay damages if the promised event does not come to pass. In every case it leaves him free (...) to break his contract if he chooses'. This quote reveals that in the common law a contract is not primarily seen as a moral device, but as an economic one. If one assumes that a contract is concluded to make a profit, it is just as good (and perhaps even better) to get the money value as it is to obtain performance *in natura*.

This difference between the civil law and the common law approach to performance sets the agenda for this chapter. First, several civil law jurisdictions are examined (A), followed by a survey of English law (B). Separate attention is paid to the doctrine of unforeseen circumstances (C) and to the European solution in the PECL and in the European directive 1999/44 on sale of consumer goods (D).

A. Civil law: Performance as the routine remedy

1. General

In civil law jurisdictions it is self-evident that the contracting parties can claim performance (*exécution en nature, Erfüllung, nakoming*) of the contract. This is so obvious that not all civil codes have, in fact, explicitly codified the rule. In Germany it can be derived from § 241 (1) BGB, which states that the creditor is entitled 'to demand performance from the debtor' while according to Art. 1221 of the French Civil Code a party can require the other 'to perform in kind unless performance is impossible.'

It is of course dependent on the contract itself at what point such a claim for performance can be brought. If the parties have agreed that delivery is due on 1 May, it is only from this day onward that performance can be claimed. The law supplements the gap in case no time was fixed for performance. For example, § 271 (1) BGB and Art. 6:38 BW specify that performance can then be demanded 'immediately', which means that the debtor has as much time as he reasonably needs to carry out his obligations (a similar rule is provided by Art. 7:102 PECL).

Futile defect

The general availability of the claim for performance implies that it is difficult for the debtor to argue that the creditor has only little interest in performance compared to the disproportionate efforts that the debtor may have to go through. The performance must in general entirely match what the parties agreed upon. In a Dutch case in which the tiles of the façade of a newly built office building showed cosmetic defects through corrosion the court still allowed a claim for performance (meaning that the debtor had to replace the tiles), even though the costs of replacement amounted to Fl. 6 million (€2,730,000) and the defects were hardly visibly from the street (*Multi Vastgoed v Nethou*, 2001). French courts also used to allow a claim for performance in cases where the creditor seemed to suffer only little harm or inconvenience. In a case in which a swimming pool was built with three instead of four steps, the contractor could still be obliged to perform correctly (*Piscine*, 1984). In the extreme case of *Belhadj v Les Batisseurs du Grand Delta* (2005), a family house had been built that was 33 cm lower than agreed upon. This did not make it unfit for its purpose and use, but still the court allowed the claim to demolish and rebuild the house. This decision seems contrary to what reasonableness and fairness require in the contractual relationship, and it would probably be decided differently today. The new Art. 1221 CC (introduced in 2016) now requires the court to deny a claim for performance if there is a manifest disproportion between its cost to the debtor and its interest for the creditor. The German § 275 BGB also offers space for denying the claim in case of a futile defect. It states that the debtor may refuse performance 'to the extent that performance requires expense and effort which, taking into account the contents of the obligation and the requirements of good faith, is grossly disproportionate to the interest in performance of the creditor'.

2. Impossibility of performance

Even if the claim for performance is in principle always available in a civil law jurisdiction, without the need for a requirement other than that the obligation is due, this does not mean that claiming performance is always *useful*. The court will naturally deny the claim if performance is impossible. If a house burns down the day before it has to be delivered to the buyer, it would be pointless for the court to order the seller to perform. It may be possible to bring a claim for damages or termination (if the requirements for these

BOX 11.1

HOW TO ENFORCE PERFORMANCE?

The creditor who is confronted with an unwilling debtor cannot obtain the necessary performance by way of *self-help*: for obvious reasons the law does not allow creditors to confront the defaulting party to 'convince' the latter of the need to perform by simply taking the goods or throwing out the tenant. This is why the creditor first needs to obtain a court order in which the debtor is ordered to perform his obligations. The relevant rules are to be found in the law of civil procedure. Thus, § 887 (1) of the German Code of Civil Procedure (ZPO) states that if the debtor does not perform, the creditor 'is to be authorised by the court to have performance rendered at the expense of the debtor', while Art. L111-1 of the French Code on Civil Execution Procedures confirms that 'each creditor can, under the conditions laid down by law, force his defaulting debtor to perform his obligations'.

An important question is how the creditor can exactly obtain what he is entitled to if the debtor refuses to comply with the court order. Generally this is not a problem in cases where the claim is for the payment of money (such as the price for purchased goods or the interest on a loan): a bailiff (*huissier, Gerichtsvollzieher, deurwaarder*) is then able to seize and sell the property of the debtor and give the proceeds of the sale to the creditor. Matters are equally simple – at least for the law – if the debtor is a tenant and refuses to leave the house. In that case, the bailiff can oblige the debtor to leave, if need be with the help of the police. For performance other than by payment of money or eviction, two different methods exist. The first is to make the defendant perform

himself, while the second is to have a third party perform in his place.

The usual way to make an unwilling debtor perform by himself is to impose a monetary penalty for non-compliance with the court order, often to be paid by each day or week of delay. Thus, the court can order the debtor to pay € 1,000 for each day that he refuses to deliver the goods or write a reference for his employee. This *non-compliance penalty* (*astreinte, Ordnungsgeld, dwangsom*), usually very effective as a threat of punishment, is to be paid to the creditor in France and the Netherlands, but directly to the State in Germany. As a measure of last resort the German and Dutch court may even be prepared to imprison an unwilling debtor until he has performed (*Ordnungshaft, lijfsdwang*), a method that has long been abolished in France. English law regards the non-compliance with a court order as a case of contempt of court, which can be penalised with imprisonment (committal) or a fine. It is likely that one of the reasons why English law is reluctant to allow a claim for specific performance lies in the fact that these quasi-criminal procedures are simply *too* powerful: if enforcement can only take place in a such a heavy-handed way, a court is less willing to allow it.

Performance by a third party at the debtor's expense comes in useful if performance can easily be rendered by a party other than the debtor. If a contractor fails to construct a house or install a kitchen, or if an iPhone repair shop does not do the job, enforcement can be effected by having somebody else perform instead at the cost of the debtor.

claims are met), but performance is no longer possible. Lawyers distinguish between different types of impossibility.

Absolute
impossibility

First, the most obvious type of case in which performance is impossible is that of *absolute impossibility*. This means that performance is objectively ('logically') impossible. Apart from the example of the burnt-down house, one can think of a car dealer who promises to service a car that is wrecked in a crash just before the agreed day on which the maintenance would take place. Another example is when a party needs to perform the contract personally, but is unable to do so (the lead singer of the group dies of an overdose or the hired architect goes insane). A contract can also require a party to do something that was already achieved: I hire a plumber to unplug my sink, but a plunger has already done the job. A final example is when the contract fixes a time for performance and the time has elapsed. A DJ who is to perform in Amsterdam on King's Day can no longer perform if the due date has passed. The classic case is that of ordering a wedding dress. If Alfredo agrees to deliver a snow-white fairy tale bridal to Liz for her wedding with Rita on 8 August 2008, performance has become absolutely impossible after that date (at least if we assume that Liz does not want to use the dress for her second, third or fourth marriage).

Generic goods

When courts have to decide whether performance is absolutely impossible in case of sale of goods, they can rely on a useful rule of thumb that already existed in Roman times. This rule of *genus non perit* means that in cases where so-called *generic goods* are sold, there can never be a case of absolute impossibility. Generic goods are goods that are only defined on the basis of their quantity, type, quality or weight (five bottles of Tequila, a Saab 9-3 Cabrio, a golden ring, ten tons of potatoes). The seller is always expected to find similar goods, even if the specific goods she had in mind to sell no longer exist. Products such as bananas, oil, seeds, wheat and stones can be found elsewhere, while the original manufacturer of T-shirts, chairs and tiles can be traded in for somebody else – the higher costs naturally coming at the risk of the seller. The *genus non perit* rule is thus one instance of a more general principle, namely that the impossibility of performance only exists if *any type* of performance has become impossible. The agency that promised to provide 'a pianist' (of average quality) can, in case of illness, still find somebody else. And if you promise to transport goods from Barcelona to Warsaw, you are expected to find means of alternative transport in case the Catalan air traffic controllers go on strike.

Specific goods

All this is different in case of non-generic (or *specific*) goods. If I buy a work of art by Damien Hirst, hire Armin van Buuren to play at my birthday, or have

Santiago Calatrava build my new house, these are obligations that can only be performed by these specific debtors. Hence, absolute impossibility of performance will follow from the object's decay and from the DJ and architect falling ill.

Until a hundred years ago or so, only absolute impossibility was accepted by the law as a reason for not being able to claim performance. This was in line with the liberal climate of the nineteenth century, in which the bindingness of a contract was almost absolute and the interest of the creditor in performance prevailed over that of the debtor to escape if performance would be unreasonably difficult. This has changed. A second type of impossibility of performance is recognised today under the heading of *relative impossibility*. If Samantha's ring slides off of her finger while on a boat trip on the North Sea, the jeweller in Paris to whom she sold the ring cannot claim delivery. In principle it would be possible for Samantha to organise a search and rescue operation with pontoons and divers, but the time and money this would take would be so disproportionate to the value of the ring that this is not what she is reasonably expected to do. It may be that the loss of the ring was caused by her careless behaviour, but this then only allows a claim for damages and not for performance.

It is evident that the law cannot easily accept a case of relative impossibility as this would violate the binding force of contract. Legislators and courts throughout the world have tried to find a formula that expresses when performance can no longer be demanded. Article 9:102 PECL requires that performance would cause the debtor 'unreasonable effort or expense', Art. 7.2.2 PICC that performance is 'unreasonably burdensome or expensive', the American Restatement (Second) of Contracts an 'unreasonable difficulty, expense, injury or loss' and the explanatory memorandum to the Dutch Civil Code demands 'a so exceptional effort or sacrifice that performance is practically impossible'. Finally, § 275 (2) of the German BGB allows the debtor to refuse performance if this requires expense and effort of the debtor that is 'grossly disproportionate' to the interest of the creditor in performance. These are all necessarily imperfect formulations that only beget their true meaning when applied to real cases. These cases show that there is a thin line between performance that is difficult and performance that is *too* difficult.

Sometimes a debtor argues that performance of the contract would make him go bankrupt, or in any event cause great financial difficulty. This is not an argument that courts are willing to accept. A purely financial reason does not amount to impossibility. The policy reason behind this must be that there is an alternative way to deal with financial difficulties of the debtor, namely insolvency law. Rather than allow the debtor not to perform his obligations towards one specific claimant, insolvency will allow the law to consider the interests of all creditors as well as that of the debtor in a special procedure created for this.

Moral impossibility

The cases discussed until now are sometimes referred to as *practical impossibility*. They concern situations in which performance has become so onerous that it can no longer be expected from the debtor. Two other categories of relative impossibility are moral and legal impossibility. In a case of *moral impossibility* performance by the debtor is not possible without unreasonable danger to his own (or another's) life, health or freedom. The textbook example is that of an opera singer who refuses to sing at the recital because his child is seriously ill. In the same vein, an employer cannot oblige her employees to remain at work if an epidemic disease has broken out or if temperatures at the office are too high to bear. An illustrative case from English law – which, as we shall see below, also accepts impossibility as a valid excuse for non-performance – is *Liston v SS Carpathian (Owners)* (1915). Here, the claimants were sailors on a trip from England to Port Arthur. Upon arrival in the port, located in Texas, the sailors heard that the First World War had broken out and were therefore allowed to refuse to sail back to Europe. In a German case (*Wehrdienst im Ausland*, 1983) a Turk living and working in Germany was allowed to stay away from work due to moral impossibility: he had to perform his military service in Turkey and failure to do so would have meant prosecution and possibly even the death penalty.

An interesting question is whether moral objections could also be accepted as constituting a case of moral impossibility. For example, can someone refuse to pay the electricity bill if they are against nuclear energy? Or not pay the water bill because it was cleaned using chemical techniques that were tested on animals? It is clear that this question can only arise if the consumer lacks a choice as to the available suppliers. If, for example, an electricity company exists that does not make use of nuclear energy, the morally sensitive consumer is expected to choose this company. But also in case of a monopolistic supplier it is difficult to accept impossibility because it was the customer himself who deliberately chose to *conclude* the contract, thus making his moral objections necessarily self-induced.

Legal impossibility

A final category of relative impossibility concerns cases of *legal impossibility*. It was seen in Chapter 10 that performance of the contract is sometimes prohibited by statute, public policy or good morals. This does not render performance absolutely impossible, but it does make it prohibited. Also in this case performance cannot reasonably be expected from the debtor.

3. Personal services

Sometimes contracts call for services to be delivered by a party who is the only one able to provide them. A famous photographer can agree to make a series of photos of a wealthy businesswoman or a scientist can contract with a publisher to write a book on the Higgs particle. Can such contracts for personal services be enforced in the courts? All the world's legal systems answer in the negative, allowing the drafters of the DCFR to formulate a common rule in Art. III-3:302 (3): 'Specific performance cannot (…) be enforced where: (…) c. performance would be of such a personal character that it would be unreasonable to enforce it.' Three reasons can be given for this. First, to force the debtor to perform personal services or work is seen as a too-severe interference with the debtor's personal liberty. Second, when compelled to perform such services, the debtor is not likely to deliver high-quality work. And third, the court will find it difficult to determine whether the debtor performed its obligations in the proper way. This means that the likes of David Guetta and Jürgen Habermas cannot be ordered by the court to show their artistic and academic talents. If this seems harsh on the organiser of the concert or on the publisher, one must realise that it may be possible to claim damages (Chapter 12) or terminate the contract (Chapter 13). In addition, the court can help the creditor by issuing a so-called *injunction* (an order not to do a particular thing), which forbids the debtor from performing a similar obligation at the same time for somebody else. Thus, if Guetta refuses to stand by his original agreement to perform on Ibiza because he was asked to do a better-paid gig in Berlin, the court can prevent such opportunistic behaviour by prohibiting his performance. When the German singer Johanna Wagner broke her contract to perform at Her Majesty's Theatre in London's West End because Covent Garden offered her more money, Lord Chancellor St Leonards prohibited her from performing anywhere other than in Her Majesty's Theatre:

> It is true that I have not the means of compelling her to sing, but she has no cause of complaint if I compel her to abstain from the commission of an act which she has bound herself not to do, and thus possibly cause her to fulfil her engagement' (*Lumley v Wagner*, 1852).

B. English law: Specific performance as an exceptional remedy

Unique goods

It has already been pointed out that English law adopts a different position regarding the claim for performance of the contract. In English common law such a claim does not exist. In equity, however, the court has the discretionary power in exceptional cases to grant a claim for so-called *specific performance*. The criterion is whether a common law remedy (in particular the claim for damages) would not be an adequate remedy to do justice to the obligee. Thus, if the creditor can easily find other goods that replace the performance (as in the case of generic goods), no specific performance can be claimed. This is different in case of unique goods, such as a particular piece of art, a specifically designed machine, or a teddy bear with sentimental value. In practice specific performance is mainly applied in case of sale of land and buildings. The assumption here is that the interest of the creditor can then not be estimated in money terms because each immovable is seen as unique. Section 52 of the Sale of Goods Act summarises the English position: 'In any action for breach of contract to deliver specific or ascertained goods the court may, if it thinks fit, on the plaintiff's application, by its judgment or decree direct that the contract shall be performed specifically.' English law also rec-

Impossibility   ognises that no claim lies in case of personal services (such as a contract of employment) and if performance is impossible. Impossibility is a case of *frustration* and exists if, after the contract was concluded, an event occurs which makes performance of the contract impossible. The English doctrine of frustration covers not only impossibility, but also cases that would fall under unforeseen circumstances in the civil law (although it is very rare that an English court would recognise unforeseen circumstances as a ground for escaping from the contract; see below, subsection C). A paradigmatic case of impossibility is *Taylor v Caldwell* (1863), in which the parties had entered into a contract for use of the Surrey Music Hall in London for a number of concerts. Shortly before the date of the first concert the music hall was destroyed by fire, clearly leading to the impossibility to perform and hence to frustration.

Similar to the civil law, the mere fact that performance has become more onerous is not likely to amount to frustration because of practical impossibil-
Practical impossibility   ity. In the case of *Tsakiroglou Co Ltd v Noblee Thorl GmbH* (1962), a contract had been concluded for the shipping of 300 tons of Sudanese peanuts from Port Sudan to Hamburg. Both parties assumed that the ship could navigate through the Suez Canal, but the Canal was blocked as a result of the second Arab-Israeli War of 1956. The only way to deliver the peanuts within the agreed upon time was to go via the Cape of Good Hope, a distance three times as long as what was originally envisaged. The debtor argued that the contract had been frustrated and refused to deliver the goods. However, the court found that it was still possible to perform: the fact that it was more difficult and costly did not amount to frustration.

Even if a claim for damages would not do perfect justice, performance does
not require personal services and is not impossible, English law is still hesitant to grant a decree of specific performance in case the execution of the
judgment would be difficult. This is in particular the case if the contract
requires continuous duties, as in case of long-term contracts. In *Co-operative
Insurance Society Ltd v Argyll Stores (Holdings) Ltd* (1997), for example, the
court refused to compel a supermarket to carry on a tenancy. In 1979 Co-op
had let the main unit of the Hillsborough Shopping Centre in Sheffield to
Argyll for use as a Safeway supermarket for a period of 35 years. The contract
explicitly stated that Argyll was 'to keep open the demised premises for retail
trade' during this period. This provision (a 'keep-open covenant') was motivated by the wish of Co-op to have one big 'anchor' shop in the shopping
centre that could attract many customers and thus also generate business for
the smaller shops in the centre. When in 1995 Argyll decided to close the
shop because it was no longer profitable, Co-op demanded a court order for
specific performance of the keep-open agreement. Unlike the Court of
Appeal, the House of Lords did not grant the order. It found that an order for
specific performance could not be granted in order to compel someone to
carry on a business as this would require constant supervision by the court.
This would be different if the contract is for a certain result because then the
court can easily establish whether this is reached or not. One of the other
arguments used by the court was that it is not in the public interest to require
someone to carry on business at a loss if there is a plausible alternative way of
providing compensation (namely a claim in damages). If a party were ordered
to run a business, it would effectively be locked into a hostile relationship,
which is likely to lead to a flow of complaints, solicitors' letters and new court
cases. This is, however, not the only way to deal with keep-open covenants.
In Scots law, for example, such agreements can be enforced.

C.   Unforeseen circumstances

In Chapter 8 the doctrine of *unforeseen circumstances* ('hardship' or 'supervening events') was discussed as an application of the principle of good
faith. There is a thin line between these unforeseen circumstances and cases
of practical impossibility. In theory the difference is clear: while practical impossibility renders performance reasonably impossible (the golden
ring lies at the bottom of the sea), unforeseen circumstances only render
it (much) more difficult or expensive (the market for gold unexpectedly
soars). But in practice the difference is difficult to make. This explains why
English law usually lumps the two situations together under the heading of
frustration (because the purpose of the transaction is frustrated, both in case
of impossibility to perform and in case of excessive hardship). Other juris-

dictions distinguish between the two, often leading to difficult questions of demarcation.

English law does not allow the court to amend or put an end to the contract only because the contract has become more onerous as a result of supervening events. As was seen above in the case of the *Tsakiroglou*, English courts are very hesitant to invoke the doctrine of frustration in cases other than of impossibility. It is only allowed if the supervening event radically or fundamentally changes the nature of the performance, case law in which this is recognised is extremely rare, but the position can be illustrated with two well-known cases.

Frustration

The first is one of the unusual cases in which frustration was allowed because of a supervening events In *Krell v Henry* (1903) Henry had hired a room for two days to watch the procession for the coronation of King Edward VII as the successor of Queen Victoria. Shortly after his accession, Edward fell ill and the coronation was postponed. Krell claimed payment, but the court held that the purpose of the contract was frustrated because of 'the cessation or non-existence of an express condition or state of things, going to the root of the contract, and essential to its performance'. The coronation was so central to the agreement that the parties were no longer bound when it was cancelled.

The second case is *Davis Contractors Ltd v Fareham Urban District Council* (1956). Davis had agreed to build 78 houses for Fareham for £94,000. The parties thought that it would take eight months to carry out the work, but a lack of skilled labour led to a delay of 14 months and £20,000 in extra costs. Davis's argument that the contract had been frustrated was rejected. This was simply a contract that turned out to be a bad deal for Davis, but that could also have worked out the other way if he had been able to finish the contract in less than eight months. Radcliffe LJ held:

> It is not hardship or inconvenience or material loss itself which calls the principle of frustration into play. There must be as well a change in the significance of the obligation that the thing undertaken would, if performed, be a different thing from that contracted for.

Clause

The position of English law is not as harsh as it may seem. The legal rules on impossibility, unforeseen circumstances and frustration are all default rules that parties can set aside when concluding their contract. In practice parties in any commercial contract of some value, in particular if long-term, will include a clause on the impact of unexpected events. Such a *force majeure clause* could read in this way: 'A party to this contract shall not be liable in the event of non-performance of any obligation under this contract by reason of strikes, fire, disease, Act of God, and any other incident of any nature beyond the control of the relevant party.' The clause could also include an obligation to renegotiate the contract to deal with the hardship (in which case one usually speaks of a *hardship clause*). The English reluctance to allow a party to escape from an onerous contract can be explained from this: if parties can contractually provide for unforeseen circumstances, it comes at their risk if they do not.

Unlike English law, French, German and Dutch law all accept unforeseen circumstances as a ground for termination or adaptation of the contract next to the impossibility to perform. These *imprévision, Störung der Geschäftsgrundlage* (interference with the basis of the contract) and *onvoorziene omstandigheden* all have an explicit legal basis in the civil code:

> **Art. 1195 CC**: 'If a change of circumstances unforeseeable at the time of the conclusion of the contract renders performance excessively onerous for a party who had not accepted the risk of such a change, that party may ask the other contracting party to renegotiate the contract. The first party must continue to perform his obligations during renegotiation.
> In case of refusal or failure of renegotiations, the parties may agree to terminate the contract from the date and on the conditions which they determine, or by a common agreement ask the court to adapt the contract. In the absence of an agreement within a reasonable time, the court may, on the request of a party, revise the contract or put an end to it, from a date and subject to such conditions as it shall determine.'

> **§ 313 BGB**: '1. If circumstances upon which a contract was based have significantly changed since the contract was entered into and if the parties would not have entered into the contract or would have entered into it upon different terms if they had foreseen this change, adaptation of the contract may be demanded to the extent that, taking account all the circumstances of the specific case, in particular the contractual or statutory distribution of risk, one of the parties cannot reasonably be expected to continue to be bound to the contract without adaptation.
> 2. It is equivalent to a change of circumstances if material assumptions that have become the basis of the contract turn out to be incorrect.
> 3. If adaptation of the contract is not possible or cannot reasonably be imposed on one party, the disadvantaged party may terminate the contract. In the case of a contract for the performance of recurring obligations, the right to terminate with notice takes the place of the right to terminate.'

> **Art. 6:258 BW**: '1. Upon the demand of one of the parties, the court may adapt the effects of the contract or terminate the contract in whole or in part on the

basis of unforeseen circumstances which are of such a nature that the other party, according to criteria of reasonableness and fairness, may not expect that the contract be maintained in an unmodified form. The court may give retroactive effect to the adaptation or termination.

2. The adaptation or termination of the contract is not granted to the extent that the party invoking the circumstances, in view of the nature of the contract or common opinion, should come for account of the party who invokes them.

(…).

The great advantage of the civil law approach is that it allows the court not only to terminate, but also to amend the contract. Frustration in English law automatically ends the contract, no matter whether the parties want this or not. The new French Art. 1195 CC (inspired by Articles 6:111 PECL and 6.2.3 PICC) goes even further and requires that the parties first enter into negotiations about the adaptation or termination of the contract. The court is only allowed to step in if they do not reach agreement about new conditions or about how to end the contract.

D.   European principles and the Consumer Sales Directive

It seems that the civil law and common law approaches to performance of the contract differ widely. However, the rift between the two legal families may not be as great as it appears. It was seen that in the civil law, the claim for specific performance cannot be brought in cases of impossibility or personal services. And even if the possibility does exist, it is likely that a commercial party will often prefer to claim damages instead of performance because this may be a much quicker and therefore more effective remedy than forcing the debtor to execute a court order. The remaining difference between English law and the law in the rest of Europe seems to centre on one type of case: the sale of generic goods. If A sells B a number of ordinary chairs and A refuses to deliver, B cannot require performance by A under English law, while this possibility does exist in a civil law jurisdiction.

This difference necessitated a choice by the drafters of European principles. PECL   Article 9:102 PECL reads:

(1) The aggrieved party is entitled to specific performance of an obligation other than one to pay money, including the remedying of a defective performance.

(2) Specific performance cannot, however, be obtained where:

(a) performance would be unlawful or impossible; or

(b) performance would cause the obligor unreasonable effort or expense; or

(c) the performance consists in the provision of services or work of a personal character or depends upon a personal relationship, or
(d) the aggrieved party may reasonably obtain performance from another source.
(...)

Section (d) reflects the choice made and it comes close to the common law approach. If the debtor proves that the creditor can obtain performance from another source, and may therefore reasonably be expected to make a cover transaction (buy the goods elsewhere), no action for performance can be brought.

Meanwhile, the difference between civil law and common law has further diminished as a result of EU Directive 1999/44 on sale of consumer goods and associated guarantees (usually referred to as the Consumer Sales Directive). The European legislator issued this directive to enhance cross-border shopping by consumers. It creates a set of minimum rights for consumers that are applicable no matter in which Member State they purchase their goods. Member States are allowed to offer more protection – and have often done so – but the rights given by the directive are what the consumer can in any case rely upon in a B2C-sales contract.

Consumer Sales Directive

Article 2 of the directive stipulates that the seller must deliver the goods to the consumer in conformity with the contract of sale. This means that the goods must not only comply with the description by the seller and be fit for the particular purpose that the consumer made known to the seller, and that the seller accepted at the time of conclusion of the contract, but also that the goods must be of a quality which is normal and which the consumer can reasonably expect. Article 3 subsequently lists the rights of the consumer:

(1) The seller shall be liable to the consumer for any lack of conformity which exists at the time the goods were delivered.
(2) In the case of a lack of conformity, the consumer shall be entitled to have the goods brought into conformity free of charge by repair or replacement, in accordance with paragraph 3, or to have an appropriate reduction made in the price or the contract rescinded with regard to those goods, in accordance with paragraphs 5 and 6.
(3) In the first place, the consumer may require the seller to repair the goods or he may require the seller to replace them, in either case free of charge, unless this is impossible or disproportionate.
A remedy shall be deemed to be disproportionate if it imposes costs on the seller which, in comparison with the alternative remedy, are unreasonable, taking into account:

- the value the goods would have if there were no lack of conformity,
- the significance of the lack of conformity, and
- whether the alternative remedy could be completed without significant inconvenience to the consumer.

Any repair or replacement shall be completed within a reasonable time and without any significant inconvenience to the consumer, taking account of the nature of the goods and the purpose for which the consumer required the goods.

(4) The terms 'free of charge' in paragraphs 2 and 3 refer to the necessary costs incurred to bring the goods into conformity, particularly the cost of postage, labour and materials.

(5) The consumer may require an appropriate reduction of the price or have the contract rescinded:

- if the consumer is entitled to neither repair nor replacement, or
- if the seller has not completed the remedy within a reasonable time, or
- if the seller has not completed the remedy without significant inconvenience to the consumer.

(6) The consumer is not entitled to have the contract rescinded if the lack of conformity is minor.

This lengthy provision gives the consumer the right to performance by way of repair or replacement in case the original performance revealed a lack of conformity. If either repair or replacement is impossible or not effectuated within a reasonable time, the consumer can claim an appropriate reduction of the price or 'rescission' (termination) of the contract. Next to these 'European' rights, the consumer is still able to exercise all the rights enumerated under national law, in particular the right to damages for non-performance (see Chapter 12).

It is clear why the consumer's right to repair and replacement brings English law closer to the civil law. Prior to the directive, an English consumer to whom a defective good was delivered had to have it repaired at his own cost and then claim back the money from the seller by way of damages. The alternative was to terminate the contract and buy the goods elsewhere, but both remedies are not as effective as a direct claim for repair or replacement (as is now laid down in the Consumer Rights Act 2015, s. 19 (3–4) and 23).

The directive provides a highly effective protection to the consumer, also because of a reversal of the burden of proof. If a lack of conformity becomes apparent within six months of delivery of the goods, the goods are presumed not to have been in conformity at the time of delivery (Art. 5 (3) directive). It is for the seller to prove that the defect originated after delivery, which is no easy task. If a TV or mobile phone breaks down as result of abuse by the buyer, it will be difficult for the seller to prove that the defect did not exist at the time of delivery.

TOPICS FOR REVIEW

Performance in civil law and common law
Impossibility of performance
Types of impossibility
Generic goods and specific goods
Genus non perit
Personal services
Frustration
Injunction
Keep-open covenants
Unforeseen circumstances
Force majeure and hardship clauses
Consumer rights under the Consumer Sales Directive

FURTHER READING

– Hugh Beale et al, *Cases, Materials and Text on Contract Law, Ius Commune Casebooks for the Common Law of Europe*, 2nd ed., Oxford (Hart Publishing) 2010, Chapters 18 and 23–25.
– Catherine Elliott and Frances Quinn, *Contract Law*, 10th ed., Harlow (Pearson) 2015, Chapter 15.
– Oliver Wendell Holmes, *The Common Law*, 1881, ed. Mark DeWolfe Howe, Cambridge Mass. 1963.
– Ewan McKendrick, *Contract Law*, 11th ed., Basingstoke (Palgrave Macmillan) 2015, Chapters 14 and 21.
– Reinhard Zimmermann, 'Breach of Contract and Remedies under the New German Law of Obligations', *Saggi, Conferenze e Seminari 48*, Centro di studi e ricerche di diritto comparato e straniero, Rome 2002, 17–27.
– Konrad Zweigert and Hein Kötz, *An Introduction to Comparative Law* (translated by Tony Weir), 3rd ed., Oxford (Oxford University Press) 1998, Chapters 35 and 37.

12

Damages for non-performance

 CHAPTER OVERVIEW

If a party does not perform the contract in the way agreed upon, or not at all, the creditor can exercise a contractual remedy. The creditor will, if the relevant criteria are met, be able to **terminate the contract** (Chapter 13) or claim **damages for non-performance** (this chapter). Jurisdictions differ in the extent to which they require that the non-performance is not excused ('**attributable**'), a **notice** needs to be sent, or **a second chance to perform** needs to be given to the debtor. Another relevant question is **which damages** can exactly be claimed and whether parties can agree upon a **damages clause** or not.

It was seen in Chapter 11 that contracts are usually discharged through performance, either voluntarily or through a court order. But it can also happen that a party does not perform. This chapter and Chapter 13 are devoted to the rights of the creditor in such a case of non-performance (or 'breach') of the contract. This means that we enter the *pathology* of contract law: it is not normal that contracts are not (properly) performed, but if it happens the law must provide a set of default rules that balances the interests of creditor and debtor in a fair way. On the one hand, the creditor has a clear interest in obtaining damages that put him in the same position he would have been in had the contract been properly performed; on the other hand, however, it may be that the debtor could not help his non-performance, for example the seller cannot be blamed for the fact that the object was stolen before delivery, or where a singer falls ill just before the concert takes place. The law must balance these interests and different jurisdictions do so in different ways.

The action for damages for non-performance (this chapter) and the action for termination of the contract (Chapter 13) have in common that they both require non-performance: the debtor does not do what the contract requires. The law classifies non-performance in three different ways:

- on the basis of the *type* of non-performance. Following this criterion, it is possible that a party does not perform at all (the ordered chairs are not delivered), performs defectively (the wrong chairs are delivered) or performs too late (the chairs are to be handed over before 1 March, but the seller only does so on 5 March). In addition to these three types of non-performance, it is possible that the performance itself takes place in a correct way, but collateral damage is caused in the course of performing the contract (for example, the seller breaks an antique vase in the home of the buyer while delivering the chairs). It will be shown that the relevance of this distinction lies in the question of whether any additional requirements need to be established before a claim of damages can be brought. Sometimes the creditor will first have to send a notice to the debtor or allow the debtor an additional period for performance.

Types of non-performance

- on the basis of the *reason* for non-performance: why is it that the debtor does not perform? The law distinguishes between the situation in which the non-performance is the debtor's fault (or attributable to him for another reason) and the situation in which there is *force majeure*. If a debtor who is to install central heating in a house takes a four-week holiday, causing the works to be delayed, this is a clear case of fault. But it may also be that the debtor cannot be blamed for the non-performance, but must still bear the risk (the debtor's diligently selected employee turns out to have lied about his diplomas and work experience, making him unsuitable to help with the performance of the contract). We will see that the distinction between non-excused ('attributable') and excused ('non-attributable') non-performance is relevant for the possibility to claim damages.

- on the basis of the *seriousness* of the non-performance. If someone is to deliver 300 laptop computers and delivers only five, the breach is obviously more serious than in case 299 laptops are delivered. This is relevant for the availability of the claim for termination of the contract, as will be seen in Chapter 13.

While the world's legal systems all agree that non-performance is the main requirement for claiming damages, they diverge to a greater or lesser extent when it comes to the answer to four other questions:

(a) Must the non-performance be attributable to the debtor or, in other words, is the debtor freed in case of *force majeure*? If so, what are the requirements for attributability?

(b) Which types of damages can be claimed and what are the mechanics of the damages claim?

(c) Are there any limitations on the damages the creditor can claim?

(d) Can the parties validly agree upon a damages clause?

A.   Attributability of the non-performance

It is clear that a contracting party can only claim damages from a debtor who failed to do what he promised. This requirement of non-performance (or 'breach') is what any jurisdiction accepts as a prerequisite for a damages claim. But opinions differ on whether the non-performance must be *attributable* to the debtor. 'Attributability' means that the debtor is held liable for the non-performance, either because he is to blame for it or because he must bear the risk even if he was not at fault. This can also be expressed by saying that the non-performance must be *non-excused*, or that there is no *force majeure*. Civil law jurisdictions (subsection A.1 below) all pose this requirement, while English law (subsection A.2) generally finds the fact of non-performance itself quite sufficient to bring a claim for damages. This difference is clearly caused by a different balancing of the interests of creditor and debtor: while civil law emphasises that a debtor is freed from his obligations if he cannot help his failure to perform, English law highlights the interest of the creditor who counts on obtaining what was promised to him.

1.   The civil law approach

The requirement that the non-performance must be attributable to the debtor comes out clearly in the various code provisions. The relevant articles in the French, German and Dutch Civil Codes are the following:

> **Art. 1231-1 CC:** 'The debtor is condemned, where appropriate, to the payment of damages either on the ground of the non-performance or a delay in performance of an obligation, unless he justifies this on the ground that performance was prevented by force majeure.'

> **Art. 1218 CC:** 'In contractual matters, there is force majeure where an event beyond the control of the debtor, which could not reasonably have been foreseen at the time of the conclusion of the contract and whose effects could not be avoided by appropriate measures, prevents performance of his obligation by the debtor.
> If the prevention is temporary, performance of the obligation is suspended unless the delay which results justifies termination of the contract. If the prevention is permanent, the contract is terminated by operation of law and the parties are discharged from their obligations under the conditions provided by articles 1351 and 1351-1.'

> **§ 276 BGB:** '(1) The debtor is responsible for intention and negligence, if a higher or lower degree of liability is neither laid down nor to be inferred from the contents

of the obligation, including but not limited to the giving of a guarantee or the assumption of a procurement risk. (...)
(2) A person acts negligently if he fails to exercise reasonable care. (...)'

§ 280 BGB: '(1) If the debtor breaches a duty arising from the obligation, the creditor may demand damages for the damage caused thereby. This does not apply if the breach of duty (*Pflichtverletzung*) is not attributable to the debtor.
(2) Damages for delay in performance may be demanded by the creditor only subject to the additional requirement of § 286.
(3) Damages in lieu of performance may be demanded by the creditor only subject to the additional requirements of § 281, of § 282 or of § 283.'

Art. 6:74 BW: '1. Any non-performance of an obligation obliges the debtor to compensate the creditor for the damage the latter suffers as a result, unless the non-performance is not attributable to the debtor.
2. In so far as performance is not yet permanently impossible, section 1 of this Article only applies with due observance of what is regulated in subchapter 2 on default of the debtor.'

Art. 6:75 BW: 'Non-performance is not attributable to the debtor, if he is not to blame for it, nor accountable for it by virtue of statute, a juridical act or generally accepted societal norms.'

French law

These provisions allow the creditor to claim damages whenever the non-performance is attributable to the debtor (Art. 9:501 PECL speaks of non-performance that is 'not excused'). The key question is of course what counts as an excusable obstacle to performance, meaning that the debtor is freed from the obligation to pay damages. It seems rather clear that each jurisdiction draws the line somewhat differently.

Best efforts and results

Under the French Article 1218 CC, *force majeure* requires that two conditions are satisfied: the obstacle must be '*imprévisible* and *inévitable*.' This means that the event must have been *unforeseeable* at the time of concluding the contract and must pose an *irresistible* obstacle for performance. This formulation still leaves much leeway for the courts in deciding when the debtor is freed. In the case of *La Concorde v Montagnani* (1994), Mr. Montagnani had checked into the Hotel des Lices in Saint-Tropez. Shortly after he had deposited almost €17,000 in the hotel safe, the hotel was robbed by four thieves who forced the hotel staff to open the safe. Mr. Montagnani claimed damages on the basis of non-performance by the hotel. The court did not find this a case of *force majeure*. Armed robbery in a luxury hotel is not unforeseeable and, even if it was impossible for the hotel staff to resist opening the safe (thereby making performance of the contract with the client impossible), this does not mean that the hotel could not have taken better precautions to avoid the robbery. In fact, the night porter had let in one of the robbers who had claimed that he had an appointment with a hotel guest.

Meanwhile the French position is not always as harsh on the debtor as this decision suggests. In reality an important role is assigned to the distinction between the *obligation de moyens* and the *obligation de résultat*. In the case of the first type of obligation, the debtor only needs to show that he carried out all best efforts that can be expected from a reasonable party (true to its masculine roots the French Code spoke until 2014 of the *bon père de famille* – the good housefather). In case of the obligation to achieve a result, however, the debtor must ensure that he achieves what is agreed upon in the contract. This is an important distinction in practice because if the debtor needs to procure a certain result, it is easy for the creditor to prove that the contract is not properly performed. It is subsequently up to the debtor to show that *force majeure* prevented him from performing. In the case of an obligation to use best efforts, the debtor is only liable if the creditor proves that the debtor did not try as hard as can be expected from a reasonable party, which is obviously more difficult.

This makes it important to know which obligations are for a result and which are for best efforts. Although this is a matter of interpretation of individual contracts by the courts, it is consistent case law that for example the seller's obligation to deliver goods on time, of the lessor to provide the good to the lessee, and of the ski-lift operator to keep the user safe, are all obligations to achieve a result. The same is true for the doctor's duty to use proper and clean equipment, while the doctor's obligation to treat patients, and the lawyer's obligation to represent clients, are only obligations to use best efforts. This is sound reasoning: the doctor cannot be expected to cure the patient or the lawyer to win his case.

German and
Dutch law

German law also excludes liability in damages in case the non-performance (*Pflichtverletzung*) is not attributable to the debtor. §§ 276 and 280 BGB make clear that non-performance needs to be attributable to the debtor and that this is the case if the breach is intentional or negligent (meaning that the debtor did not exercise reasonable care). Dutch law (Arts 6:74 and 6:75 BW) applies the same norm in order to be able to claim damages for non-performance (*tekortkoming*).

No fault

What the German and Dutch Code say explicitly, but what the French courts also accept, is that the debtor is not only responsible in case he is at fault.

Attributability of the non-performance can also be based on other grounds. First, an important reason can be that the parties have themselves dealt with the issue in their contract by way of a guarantee (for example by adding a clause saying: 'export guaranteed', 'sold as authentic'). Second, most jurisdictions hold the debtor responsible for the persons he uses in performing the contract (such as employees and subcontractors) as well as for any instruments he makes use of. Third, the debtor is held liable for circumstances that are foreseeable or in regard to him personally. Inexperience, inability and financial difficulty (the Germans say '*Geld hat man zu haben*', money one must have) of the debtor all count as such. Importantly, the debtor is also held liable in case he has to provide generic goods: if the seller of a quantity of bananas is unable to deliver the ones he had in mind because of an unexpected strike or fire in his supplier's premises, this is not accepted as *force majeure* because the seller will still be able to obtain bananas elsewhere. *Force majeure* would only be accepted if the entire genus is destroyed (which is highly unlikely).

Art. 8:108 (1) PECL aptly summarises the civil law position:

> 'A party's non-performance is excused if it proves that it is due to an impediment beyond its control and that it could not reasonably have been expected to take the impediment into account at the time of the conclusion of the contract, or to have avoided or overcome the impediment or its consequences.'

2.   English law

English law, unlike civil law jurisdictions, regards any contract as containing a guarantee. This means that the debtor can in principle not escape liability in damages in cases where he could not help his failure to perform. The seller must simply deliver the goods and the contractor must build the house. This doctrine of strict or 'absolute' liability for breach of contract dates back to the case of *Paradine v Jane* (1647), in which the lessee was kept to his obligation to pay rent to the landowner, even though he could not access the land for three years because it had been invaded by hostile forces during the English Civil War. The inclination of English law is not to be interested in *why* a party did not perform. In the attractive language of Sellers, J in *Nicolene Ltd v Simmonds* (1953): 'It does not matter whether the failure to fulfil the contract by the seller is because he is indifferent or wilfully negligent or just unfortunate. It does not matter what the reason is. What matters is the fact of performance. Has he performed or not?'

Frustration

The only possible way of escaping liability is to invoke the doctrine of frustration. The effect of a debtor successfully invoking frustration is that the contract comes to an end by operation of the law, which also excludes a damages claim. However, as already seen in Chapter 11 where the claim for performance was discussed, the boundaries of frustration are very limited. Frustration exists in cases of impossibility of performance because of the destruction of an essential element of the contract (such as the music hall in *Taylor v Caldwell*) or because of the death of a party who needs to perform personally (such as an employee). It also exists when performance is in principle possible, but nevertheless pointless (as in *Krell v Henry*). The authoritative criterion formulated by Radcliffe LJ in *Davis Contractors Ltd v Fareham Urban District Council* (1956) is the following:

> Frustration occurs whenever the law recognises that, without default of either party, a contractual obligation has become incapable of being performed because the circumstances in which performance is called for would render it a thing radically different from that which was undertaken by the contract.

Because it is rare that a claim for frustration succeeds, parties often allocate the risk themselves by including a *force majeure* clause in their contract. But there is still another way in which the harsh position of English law is eased. Just as in French law, not all contracts require a party to achieve a certain result. English law is happy to accept that the obligations of doctors, lawyers and other advisers are only to use reasonable care and skill. Lord Denning put it like this in *Greaves & Co v Baynham Meikle & Partners* (1975):

> The surgeon does not warrant that he will cure the patient. Nor does the solicitor warrant that he will win the case. But, when a dentist agrees to make a set of false teeth for a patient, there is an implied warranty that they will fit his gums (. . .).

B. Types of damages and the mechanics of damage claims

Delay

Until now nothing has been said about the type of damages that can be claimed. Here the creditor has a fundamental choice to make. He is (assuming that performance is still possible) allowed to hold the other party to the contract (thus: claim performance) and claim damages *next to this* for the loss he suffers as a result of the delay (*dommages-intérêts moratoires, Verzögerungsschaden, vertragingsschade*). If the car I rented is not delivered to my home at the promised time, I will not only have to take a taxi to my appointment, but also may be obliged to rent a car from a different company at a higher price. Both costs are damages for delay. The basis for claiming these damages can be found in the Arts. 1217 (that conveniently lists the available remedies) and 1231-1 CC, §§ 280, 286 BGB, Art. 6:74 BW, as well as in English common law.

Damages in lieu

If the debtor does not perform because he is unable or unwilling to do so, or if the creditor is simply no longer interested in obtaining performance (and therefore decides to terminate the contract), he will seek a different type of damages. These so-called *damages in lieu of performance* (*dommages-intérêts compensatoires, Schadensersatz statt der Leistung, vervangende schadevergoeding*) replace the performance. Claiming these should put the creditor in the same position that he would have been in had the contract been properly performed (as we will see subsection C below, this is the so-called *expectation interest*). If Rose buys 20,000 *Poeticus Narcissi* flower bulbs from her regular supplier with the intention of selling the bulbs to florists around the world, she can claim the profits that she would have made on these contracts if her supplier fails to deliver the bulbs to her. And if seller of goods A is confronted with buyer B who fails to pay the price, allowing A to terminate the contract and sell the goods at a lower price to somebody else, A can claim from B the difference between the price B had agreed to pay and the price at which the goods were sold to the new buyer. The bases for claiming these damages in lieu of performance are again the Arts 1231-1 CC and Art. 6:74 BW in French and Dutch law, while German law bases these on § 280 in combination with §§ 281–283 BGB.

Collateral damage

A third type of damages concerns *collateral damage* or consequential loss (*Mangelfolgeschäden, gevolgschade*). This is damage caused in the course of performing the contract (as in case where the painter damages the interior of his customer's home, or cattle are delivered that are infected with a disease and infect all the other cattle of the buyer). The legal bases for claiming this harm caused by the defect are Art. 1231-1, § 280 BGB and Art. 6:74 BW.

The distinction between damages for delay, damages in lieu of performance and collateral damages is highly relevant to the question at which point in time a claim for damages can be brought. It is self-evident that if proper performance is no longer possible or can no longer be expected, or if the loss is already suffered (as in case of collateral damage), the creditor must be able to claim damages without any further requirement. But this may be different in cases where the creditor claims damages for delay or damages in lieu of performance. In these cases, the interest of the debtor can require that he is first warned by way of a *notice* that damages are going to be claimed if he does not perform. It may even be that the debtor must be given *a second chance to perform* if the original performance was defective. The national rules on this question are quite technical and show so many differences in detail that French, German, Dutch and English law will be discussed consecutively.

French law

In French law a claim for damages can only be brought if the debtor is in default (*en demeure*). The creditor puts the other party in default by sending a formal notice (a *sommation* by a bailiff) or a clear letter demanding that the debtor performs, but this is not necessary in cases where the contract itself already indicates a particular time for performance or states that performance must take place immediately. A notice is obviously also unnecessary if it would be futile, as in the case of the debtor already indicating that he is not going to perform or being simply unable to do so. All this follows from the Arts 1139 and 1146 *Code Civil*:

> **Art. 1231 CC**: 'Unless non-performance is permanent, damages are only due if the debtor has previously been put on notice to perform (*mise en demeure*) his obligation within a reasonable time.'

> **Art. 1344 CC**: 'A debtor is put on notice to perform (*mise en demeure*) either by formal demand (*sommation*) or an act which gives sufficient warning, or, if this is provided for by the contract, by the mere fact that the obligation is enforceable.'

German law

The German law of contractual remedies, which was fundamentally reformed in 2002, is characterised by a high level of doctrinal precision. § 280 BGB, quoted above, makes a distinction between damages for delay and damages in lieu of performance. Damages for delay are subject to the additional requirement of § 286 BGB, which states:

> (1) If the debtor, following a warning notice (*Mahnung*) from the creditor that is made after performance is due, fails to perform, he is in default (*Verzug*) as a result of the warning notice. Bringing an action for performance and serving a demand for payment in summary debt proceedings for recovery of debt have the same effect as a warning notice.
> (2) There is no need for a warning notice if
>   1. a period of time according to the calendar has been specified,
>   2. performance must be preceded by an event and a reasonable period of time for performance has been specified in such a way that it can be calculated, starting from the event, according to the calendar,
>   3. the obligor seriously and definitively refuses performance,
>   4. for special reasons, weighing the interests of both parties, the immediate commencement of default is justified.
>   (...)

This means that the debtor must be in default (*Verzug*) before damages for delay can be claimed. This default comes about by way of a notice (*Mahnung*) and a debtor who then still does not perform. This notice is simply sent to remind the debtor that he is to perform. It does not have to meet any form, although the notice will in practice always be written (by letter or e-mail). Sometimes a notice is not needed, in particular if a time for performance has been fixed according to the calendar ('Delivery before 15 November', 'Payment within two weeks after delivery'). This is in line with the French Code and with the old legal maxim of *dies interpellat pro homine* ('an agreed upon day warns instead of the creditor').

The other type of damages mentioned in § 280 BGB are damages in lieu of performance. Claiming these will lead to loss of the right to performance. Section III of this provision distinguishes between three situations that all have their own corresponding provision in the code. First, § 283 refers to the case in which performance is impossible or where the debtor simply refuses to perform. It is quite logical that no further requirement needs to be met in this case: the creditor can claim his expectation interest, unless of course the debtor proves that the non-performance was not attributable to him. § 283 BGB: 'If, under § 275 (1) to (3), the debtor is not obliged to perform, the creditor may, if the requirements of § 280 (1) are satisfied, demand damages in lieu of performance. (…)'

Second, § 281 BGB sets an additional requirement for damages in lieu of performance in case of delay or defective performance. In that case, the creditor must first have fixed, without success, a reasonable period for performance or for remedying the defective one.

> **§ 281 BGB**: (1) To the extent that the debtor does not render the due performance or does not render the performance as owed, the creditor may, subject to the requirements of § 280 (1), demand damages in lieu of performance, if he has without result set a reasonable period for the obligor for performance or cure. (…)
> (2) Setting a period for performance may be dispensed with if the debtor seriously and definitively refuses performance or if there are special circumstances which, after the interests of both parties are weighed, justify the immediate assertion of a claim for damages.
> (3) If the nature of the breach of duty is such that setting a period of time is out of the question, a warning notice (*Abmahnung*) is given instead.
> (4) The claim for performance is excluded as soon as the creditor has demanded damages in lieu of performance.

This requirement of a second chance to perform (or *Nachfrist*) is exceptional in a comparative perspective. Even though the debtor was late in performing, or performed defectively, a claim for damages in lieu of performance can in German law only be brought if the debtor was given a second chance to perform or to perform properly. This rule, that clearly provides additional latitude to the debtor by allowing him a grace period, cannot be found in any other legal system. It is true that for example the Arts 47 and 63 of the CISG (and Art. 8:106 (1) PECL) provide that buyer and seller *may* fix an additional period of time for delivery and payment, but this is only a discretionary power of the creditor: he is not obliged to allow the debtor this extra period. The reason for the German legislator to give the seller a right to a second performance was its desire to strengthen the seller's rights vis-à-vis the buyer.

Third, § 282 BGB allows the creditor to claim damages in lieu of performance if the debtor has violated a so-called ancillary duty and the creditor can no longer reasonably be expected to accept performance. § 282 BGB states to this effect: 'If the debtor breaches a duty under § 241 (2), the creditor may, if the requirements of § 280 (1) are satisfied, demand damages in lieu of performance if he can no longer reasonably be expected to accept performance by the debtor.'

What the German code means by an ancillary duty is the type of obligation that follows from the contract although the parties have not explicitly discussed it and that does not affect the performance as such. A common example is that of the painter who paints the interior of a house in an excellent way, but who damages all kinds of objects in the house in the process (a vase on day one, a door on day two and the television on day three). This is a good reason for the creditor to lose all reliance on the painter's ability to continue work without causing further damage to his property, which then allows him claim damages in lieu of performance (and terminate the contract).

Dutch law also requires that the debtor be in default before damages can be claimed. It is again logical that default is not required if performance is impossible, but if the debtor can still perform or repair his previous defective performance the creditor is in principle obliged to send a notice to the debtor giving him a reasonable period to perform. Art. 6:82 (1) BW states to this effect: 'The debtor is in default when he is held liable for his non-performance by a written notice in which he is granted a reasonable period of time during which he still may perform, and he nevertheless fails to perform within that period.' As in French and German law, a notice is not needed if a time for performance was fixed in the contract (Art. 6:83 BW).

BOX 12.1

GOING TO COURT OR NOT? RELATIONAL CONTRACTS

The mere fact that contract law provides rules that allow a party to enforce its rights does not mean that a party is also willing to do so. Empirical work on the actual use of contract law in commercial practice, pioneered by the American author Stewart Macaulay, suggests that not many commercial parties are willing to bring their counterpart to court. This is partly due to the costs involved in litigation, but also because most parties value a good relationship with their counterpart much more than being 'right' in one particular instance. Particularly in long-term relationships parties will work towards an amicable outcome and are often flexible in finding a solution. Thus, rather than resorting to the letter of the contract, the creditor is likely to voluntarily adjust the contract price or give the debtor more time for performance. Reputational sanctions are likely to play a more important role than legal sanctions: a party who does not perform will rapidly lose its attraction for other parties.

This analysis is particularly relevant in cases of so-called *relational contracts*. Legal scholar Ian Macneil juxtaposes such contracts with discrete contracts. The typical example of a discrete contract is the purchase by a consumer of fruit at the market or a newspaper at a gas station. These contracts are of short duration, with limited personal interaction, and about easily defined objects of exchange. The cooperation between the parties is minimal. Relational contacts, such as employment and franchise contracts, are at the other end of the spectrum. Here, parties strive for a long-standing relationship in which they work closely together. Only during the course of the relationship does it become clear what the parties need to do exactly. The contract is only one aspect of the complete relationship between the parties, in which mutual trust and social sanctions are much more important than compliance with the legal rules. One could say that the distinction between discrete and relational contracts mirrors the difference between a one-night-stand and a marriage.

English law
English law, finally, does not require a notice to put the debtor in default and to exercise a remedy. In line with the more strict English approach towards contractual obligations, the expiration of the time affixed for performance is reason enough to be able to claim damages. If no time is fixed for performance, performance must take place within a reasonable time. Practice, however, shows that any sensible party – in England and elsewhere – will first fix an additional period for performance before resorting to the far going step of pursuing a legal remedy (if at all: see Box 12.1).

C. Limitations of claiming damages

Once it is established that the requirements for a damages claim are met, the question must be asked whether any limitations exist to claiming damages. These limitations do indeed exist. They relate to (1) the type of interest that is protected, (2) causation, and (3) non-pecuniary loss.

1. Expectation and reliance interest

The first way in which the law limits the recoverable damages is by allowing the creditor only to claim compensation for the real loss and deprived profits he suffers ('no damages without loss'). This means that the claimant can never claim more damages than what he loses on the contract. Article 1231-2 CC, §§ 249 ff BGB, Arts 6:95 ff. BW and Art. 9:502 PECL all provide rules to this effect. A different view would put the creditor in a better position than he was without the contract or the breach and this would of course be unacceptable. Put differently: damages in contract law are always *compensatory* and never punitive. This is in sharp contrast to the law of torts, where some jurisdictions allow a claim for punitive damages in case of intentional or grossly negligent wrongdoing.

The question that the law must answer is how the creditor is best compensated for his loss. If the suffered loss is caused by delayed or defective performance or consists of collateral damage, as illustrated by the examples above, this is usually not too difficult to establish. These damages are usually claimed next to the normal performance. But what if the creditor is no longer interested in performance and decides to terminate the contract? For this type of situation lawyers often distinguish between two types of 'interest' of the creditor: the expectation interest and the reliance interest.

As noted earlier a claim for damages in lieu of performance should put the creditor as closely as possible to the position in which it would have been if the contract had been duly performed (cf. Art. 9:502 PECL). This expectation interest (or 'positive' or 'performance interest') protects the expectations the creditor had when he entered into the contract, in particular the expectation to make a profit with the contract. But the creditor could also be interested in claiming his so-called 'reliance interest' ('negative' interest). In that case the creditor's interest is to be put into the position he was in before the contract was made. The creditor may have changed his position in reliance on the other party's promise, for example by incurring costs to conclude the contract, or by already starting the performance (hiring an employee, buying materials to construct a house, etc.). While the expectation interest

Expectation interest

Reliance interest

thus puts the creditor in the position as if the contract is duly performed, the reliance interest places him into the position as if the contract was never concluded at all. A contracting party usually has the choice between claiming either of these two interests.

Example

A concrete example can illustrate the difference between the expectation and the reliance interest. Suppose that Rose has sold a large quantity of flower bulbs to the Russian buyer Boris for €20 per bag. Boris pays upon delivery in Kaliningrad, but shortly thereafter the flower bulbs turn out to be infected with mildew. Boris now has a choice. If he chooses to claim his expectation interest, he must be put into the position he would have been in had the contract been duly performed. If we assume that the market value of the flower bulbs is identical to the price (€20), Boris' expectation was to obtain flower bulbs with a value of €20, but due to the disease they are only worth €10. Deducting the received value (€10) from the expected value (€20) means that Boris can claim damages amounting to €10 per bag. If, however, Boris claims his reliance interest, he must be put in as good a position as he was in before the contract was made. In this case, Boris's reliance interest is therefore also €10 per bag. If he had not concluded the contract, Boris would not have paid €20 and would not have received defective flower bulbs only worth €10. The reliance interest is thus calculated by deducting the received value (€10) from the paid price (€20), so in this case €10.

In this example the expectation and reliance interest are the same because the paid price is identical to the market value. But this need not be the case. If Rose has made a good bargain and the flower bulbs only had a value of €17 euro, Boris's expectation interest would be €17 and he would only be able to claim €7 per bag (the expected value of €17 minus the real value of €10). In this case, Boris could better claim his reliance interest, which naturally remained the same: the paid price (€20) minus the received value (€10), which equals €10. If, on the other hand, the contract was to Boris's advantage because the real value of the flower bulbs was higher than the contract price (say €23 per bag), Boris would certainly claim the expectation interest of €13 per bag (the value of €23 minus the paid price of €10). It thus depends on how advantageous the contract to each of the parties is whether one is better off claiming expectation or reliance damages.

2.   Causation

A second limitation to a damages claim lies in the requirement that the damage must have been caused by the non-performance. It is obvious why the law would require such causation: the debtor cannot be held responsible for losses that he did not cause. However, the question whether there is a legally relevant causal lien between breach and damage is not always easy to answer. If my taxi to Amsterdam airport is late and I consequently miss my flight to Rome, a whole range of events can follow from this. Not only will I have to take the next flight at an extra cost to be paid to the airline, I also have to buy myself drinks and dinner while waiting. I may get robbed at the airport. I could also miss an important appointment in Rome at which I expected to conclude a contract that would have made me €100,000 in profits. I go bankrupt as a result of missing this deal, which leads to my wife leaving me. The subsequent divorce makes me so depressed that I end up in a hospital and lose my job. Now, all these events are 'caused' by the non-performance of the taxi company: had the taxi been on time, all this would (most probably) not have happened. But the law certainly does not allow me to claim compensation for all these events. This is because the legal concept of causation is different from the one used in physics or normal life. German lawyers speak about 'adequate' causation, Dutch lawyers about 'reasonable' causation, French lawyers limit compensation to the 'immediate and direct' consequences of the breach, and English law asks whether the damage is not too 'remote.' All these expressions aim to denote a similar thing: it must be reasonable to hold the debtor liable for the damage.

Foreseeability

An important factor in any jurisdiction when assessing causation is whether the loss was foreseeable by the debtor at the time of contracting. In the English case of *Hadley v Baxendale* (1854) it was formulated in this way; that the debtor is liable for loss which arises in 'the usual course of things' or that 'may reasonably be supposed to have been in the contemplation of the parties at the time when they made the contract, as the probable result of the breach of it'. Article 9:503 PECL does not aim to say anything else: 'The non-performing party is liable only for loss which it foresaw or could reasonably have foreseen at the time of conclusion of the contract as a likely result of its non-performance, unless the non-performance was intentional or grossly negligent.'

In the above example I will be able to claim the costs of rescheduling to a later flight and possibly the reasonable costs of a dinner as the loss that the taxi company could reasonably foresee, but not any of the more remote losses.

Factors

Factors other than foreseeability are also likely to play a role when establishing a causal link between the non-performance and the damage. Article 9:503 PECL explicitly mentions the factor that the breach is intentional or grossly negligent. If A, as the organiser of a major art fair, hires B to erect stands and a week before the opening of the event B demands an increase of the contract price, which A refuses, this may lead to extended liability of A towards the various art dealers aiming to exhibit at the fair. Some art dealers may hold A liable for lost opportunities to sell. Even though this type of damage was not foreseeable for B, he may still be liable for these damages because of the fact that the breach was intentional. This would have been different if the reason for not erecting the stands was because of a lack of skilled employees. A must still bear the risk for this, leading to attributable non-performance, but he is then no longer liable for any unforeseeable losses.

3.   Non-pecuniary loss

A third point of interest is whether only financial loss (such as economic loss and medical costs in case of physical harm) can be compensated in case of non-performance, or also so-called *non-pecuniary loss*. Non-pecuniary loss (or immaterial damage) cannot be undone with money and is therefore difficult to quantify. The photo shop that I asked to digitise my wedding photos accidentally puts them in the shredder, or the veterinarian I asked to vaccinate my six-year old dog for rabies kills it when the assistant hands her a needle with way too much of the vaccine. In both cases my material damages are low (no one would have wanted to buy my photos and my dog was a mongrel with low-market value), but I am obviously angry, devastated and hurt. Should I therefore be able to claim non-pecuniary damages (*préjudice moral, Schmerzensgeld, smartengeld*) for mental distress? Unlike their colleagues in the United States, European courts (and legislators) are reluctant to allow this: no matter how much distress the breach of contract is causing, money is not going to make this good. In addition, there is the fear of a litigation culture: if any form of inconvenience or disappointment would be a reason for a damages claim, the courts would be flooded with claimants. This explains why non-pecuniary damages are only allowed in a limited number of cases and why the awards are usually not very high.

Pleasure contracts

The type of contracts for which courts are often willing to recognise that non-pecuniary damages must be paid in case of non-performance are contracts of which the main purpose is pleasure, relaxation and peace of mind. The distress of having lost one's wedding photographs surely falls into this category: the whole aim of having a photographer take pictures, or to have them digitised, is the pleasure of looking at the photographs in the hopefully many years that the marriage will last. If the taxi does not show up to get the passenger to a concert of the Rolling Stones, the passenger cannot only claim the money he spent on the ticket, but also a fair sum of damages to compensate him for his disappointment of not attending the performance. In the

English case of *Farley v Skinner* (2001), Mr. Farley had bought a house in the countryside after retirement. The house was 20 km from Gatwick airport, but a surveyor had advised him that the house was unlikely to be affected by any noise. After moving in, Mr. Farley discovered that reality was very different: airplanes tended to circle above the house in case of congestion. He was awarded £10,000 for the distress and inconvenience of the noise. The court acknowledged that this was not a contract whose only object was pleasure, relaxation and peace of mind (Mr. Farley also simply needed a place to live), but the peace and quiet of the countryside was surely an important reason for him to buy the house.

It is no surprise that many court cases on non-pecuniary loss deal with spoilt holidays. What if one books a first-class seat on the train from Brussels to Saint-Raphael on the warmest day of the year, but the air-conditioning and water supply on the train fail and the staff tell the passengers that the train will not go any further than Metz and that they should find their own way to the Cote d'Azur? Courts would not find it difficult to allow non-pecuniary damages. The best-known holiday case is *Simone Leitner v Tui Deutschland* CJEU (2002), decided by the Court of Justice of the European Union (CJEU). The Austrian family Leitner had booked a two-week, all-inclusive holiday to a Turkish holiday resort. After one week of unspoilt holiday pleasure, 10-year-old Simone Leitner (together with many other hotel guests) started to show symptoms of Salmonella poisoning due to the food offered in the resort. Her parents had to look after her for the rest of the holiday. The parents brought a claim against TUI for loss of holiday pleasure. Austrian law had until then not recognised a claim for non-pecuniary loss for breach of contract. But it had, as every other European Member State, implemented the EU Directive on package travel (now Directive 2015/2302). This directive states that the retailer of a package travel is liable in damages to the consumer for the proper performance of the contract. This raised the question whether such 'damages' could also include a claim for lost holiday pleasure. The CJEU held that it did, meaning that immaterial damages for breach of a package travel contract must now in principle be allowed in any EU Member State. Article 9:501 (2) PECL goes much further than this and firmly states for breach of any type of contract: '(2) The loss for which damages are recoverable includes: (a) non-pecuniary loss (…)'

D.   Damages clauses

It has been seen many times before in this book that contract law often only provides default rules. Within the limits set by mandatory law parties can make their own clauses if they believe this better suits their interests. The same is true in the field of damages. Parties can in principle agree on an amount of damages to be paid in case of non-performance. For example, when booking a flight the contract is likely to contain a clause that if the consumer cancels the trip the travel company is allowed to keep a percentage of the contract price. Building contracts typically contain the clause that if the work is not finished on time, the builder is to pay a specified sum to the aggrieved party.

Two types of such damages clauses can be distinguished. First, the sum speci-

Liquidated damages fied in the contract can be based on a real assessment of what the likely damage will be in case of non-performance. The big advantage of such a *liquidated damages clause* (or *agreed damages clause*) is not only that the creditor no longer needs to prove what its actual damage is, but also that parties know in advance for which amount they are liable in case of breach. It does not matter that the real loss turns out to be higher or lower. If A agrees to build a house for B and to finish the work before 1 June, the contract can provide that A has to pay €500 for each week of delay. Consequently, if A completes the house on 29 June B can claim €2,000 as agreed damages (even if B's actual loss is greater or smaller). The law accepts these clauses as valid. Second, parties can agree on a specified sum to be paid in case of non-performance as an inducement to a party not to breach the contract. In such a *penalty clause*

Penalty clause the sum is not a reasonable pre-estimate of the likely damages, but a much higher amount. A penalty clause thus does two things: not only does it allow the parties to avoid the difficult calculation of the real damages (as in liquidated damages clauses), but it also serves as a way to pressure the debtor to perform.

It is clear that a penalty clause can lead to excessive liability and must therefore be looked at with some suspicion. For example, if a contract for the supply of an academic gown (price: €1,000) stipulates that €20,000 must be paid in case the customer refuses to pay the price and take delivery of the gown, this is a highly disproportionate sanction. It is likely that a much lower penalty would be sufficient to coerce the buyer to perform. This is why the law is reluctant to accept just any penalty clause as valid. Under English law, for example, only liquidated damage clauses are valid. Penalty clauses will not be enforced because the courts do not see punishment of a party in breach as a purpose of contract law. However, this does not mean that a damages clause cannot validly aim to deter the debtor from breaching the contract. In the case of *ParkingEye v Beavis* (2015), a car park had charged Mr. Beavis £85 for overstaying, by almost an hour, his two hours of free parking. Even though this was not a reasonable pre-estimate of the likely damages, the Supreme Court still found this clause valid. It considered that a stipulated sum is not a penalty if it protects a legitimate interest of the creditor in the performance of the contract (here funding the car park and ensuring free parking space for everyone) and the agreed sum is not out of all proportion to that interest (which was held not to be the case here). French, German and Dutch law do regard damages clauses valid (both for liquidated damages and as a penalty), but provide that these clauses can be moderated if necessary, which is highly convenient for sloppy parties who put the penalty at an unacceptably high level. Thus, § 343 BGB allows the court, at the request of the debtor, to reduce a disproportionately high penalty to a reasonable amount unless the debtor is a commercial party (§ 348 HGB). A commercial debtor may still be able to invoke the general § 242 BGB to escape the clause. Article 1231-5 CC provides that the court can even out of its own motion moderate or increase the agreed penalty if it is obviously excessive or ridiculously low. Article 6:94 BW allows this if 'fairness manifestly requires this'. In line with French, German and Dutch law, Art. 9:509 PECL also does not distinguish between penalty clauses and liquidated damages clauses, but allows the court to reduce or increase a grossly excessive agreed upon sum:

> (1) Where the contract provides that a party who fails to perform is to pay a specified sum to the aggrieved party for such non-performance, the aggrieved party shall be awarded that sum irrespective of its actual loss.
>
> (2) However, despite any agreement to the contrary the specified sum may be reduced to a reasonable amount where it is grossly excessive in relation to the loss resulting from the non-performance and the other circumstances.

TOPICS FOR REVIEW

Relational contracts
Non-performance
Attributability of non-performance
Force majeure
Obligation to achieve a result and obligation to use best efforts
Absolute contracts
Frustration
Force majeure clause
Notice
Second chance to perform
Default of debtor
Types of damages
Expectation and reliance interest
Causation
Non-pecuniary loss
Liquidated damages clause
Penalty clause

FURTHER READING

- Hugh Beale et al, *Cases, Materials and Text on Contract Law, Ius Commune Casebooks for the Common Law of Europe*, 2nd ed., Oxford (Hart Publishing) 2010, Chapter 21.
- Dagmar Coester-Waltjen, 'The New Approach to Breach of Contract in German Law', in: N. Cohen and E. McKendrick, *Comparative Remedies for Breach of Contract*, Oxford (Hart) 2005, 135–56.
- Catherine Elliott and Frances Quinn, *Contract Law*, 10th ed., Harlow (Pearson) 2015, Chapters 14 and 15.
- Lon L. Fuller and William R. Perdue, 'The Reliance Interest in Contract Damages', *Yale LJ* 46 (1936), 52 ff.
- Charles J. Goetz and Robert E. Scott, 'Liquidated Damages, Penalties, and the Just Compensation Principle: Some Notes on an Enforcement Model and a Theory of Efficient Breach', *Columbia Law Review* 77 (1977), 554 ff.
- Ole Lando and Hugh Beale (eds.), *Principles of European Contract Law Parts I and II*, The Hague (Kluwer) 2000, Chapter 9.
- Stewart Macaulay, 'An Empirical View of Contract', *Wisconsin Law Review* (1985), 465 ff.
- Ian R. Macneil, 'Relational Contract: What We Do and Do Not Know', *Wisconsin Law Review* (1985), 483 ff.
- Ewan McKendrick, *Contract Law*, 11th ed., Basingstoke (Palgrave Macmillan) 2015, Chapters 19 and 20.
- G.H. Treitel, *Remedies for Breach of Contract*, Oxford (Oxford University Press) 1988.
- Reinhard Zimmermann, 'Breach of Contract and Remedies under the New German Law of Obligations', *Saggi, Conferenze e Seminari 48*, Centro di studi e ricerche di diritto comparato e straniero, Rome 2002, 17–27.
- Konrad Zweigert and Hein Kötz, *An Introduction to Comparative Law* (translated by Tony Weir), 3rd ed., Oxford (Oxford University Press) 1998, Chapter 36.

13

Termination of the contract

 CHAPTER OVERVIEW

Contracting parties not only have the right to claim damages for non-performance of the contract. If the relevant criteria are met, the creditor may also **terminate** a bilateral contract. This chapter lays out the requirements that have to be met before a claim for termination can be brought. It will be seen that the law is reluctant to accept a claim for termination in other cases than serious non-performance. This is because it is often in the interest of the mal-performing debtor that the contract is upheld. This chapter also pays attention to the defence of **withholding performance**, which often precedes a claim for termination.

In a bilateral contract such as sale of goods, provision of services, lease or credit, each party only wants to perform because the other party is also to perform. This means that if the other party is not willing or unable to perform the contract, the very reason for being bound falls away. The contractual remedy of termination is based upon this ratio: if the other party does not perform, this allows the creditor to bring the contract to an end. The effect of termination is that each of the parties is no longer bound to perform and is usually able to claim back what has already been rendered. The ratio of termination – the equilibrium between the mutual performances would be destroyed if the creditor were not able to escape from the contract in the event that the debtor mal-performs – entails that there is no need for attributability of the non-performance to the debtor or loss to the creditor in order to bring a claim. Even if the debtor cannot help its non-performance, an action for termination can be brought.

Whether termination or not should be allowed requires the balancing of the interests of creditor and debtor. It is evident that it is a legitimate interest of the creditor to be able to terminate the contract as soon as possible if the debtor is unable or unwilling to perform or has gone bankrupt. In this case, the creditor should be allowed to free himself and find somebody else to contract with. However, it is the rightful interest of the defaulting debtor that not every minor non-compliance with the terms of the contract justifies

Interest

termination. If shop A orders 100 handmade bags from manufacturer B, and B delivers 98 bags on time but announces that the remaining two are likely to come next week, this would surely form a legitimate reason for A to claim damages for delay (in case he suffers any), but it would normally not allow him to terminate the entire contract. If it did, B would suffer a great detriment by losing all incurred expenses, as he is not able to sell the bespoke bags to somebody else. This requires a criterion to decide under which circumstances the non-performance is allowed.

The following questions must be asked:

(a) How to decide whether the non-performance allows termination?
(b) What are the mechanics of the claim for termination?
(c) Is it possible to terminate the contract before performance is due ('anticipatory breach')?
(d) What is the effect of termination?
(e) Can the creditor withhold performance?

A. When is termination allowed?

It was seen above that not every breach of contract allows the creditor to terminate the contract. Different jurisdictions adopt different approaches to limit a claim for termination. While the CISG, PECL and English law adopt a clear substantive criterion and only allow termination in case of a breach that is serious enough, French law traditionally gives the court a central role in assessing whether termination is justified. German law limits termination by requiring that the non-performance is serious enough or that the debtor was granted a second chance to perform, which he let pass. Dutch law is the odd one out by not limiting the termination action in a significant way. We will have a closer look at each of these approaches in this section.

Fundamental non-performance

It makes sense to start with the system of the PECL, which poses a clear limit on termination by requiring that the non-performance must be 'fundamental.' The relevant provisions are the following:

> **Art. 8:103**: 'A non-performance of an obligation is fundamental to the contract if:
> (a) strict compliance with the obligation is of the essence of the contract; or
> (b) the non-performance substantially deprives the aggrieved party of what it was entitled to expect under the contract, unless the other party did not foresee and could not reasonably have foreseen that result; or
> (c) the non-performance is intentional and gives the aggrieved party reason to believe that it cannot rely on the other party's future performance.'

Art. 9:301: '(1) A party may terminate the contract if the other party's non-performance is fundamental.

(2) In the case of delay the aggrieved party may also terminate the contract under Article 8:106 (3).'

The notion of fundamental non-performance (which is inspired by the CISG) makes termination only possible in case of a serious breach. One can easily relate to the three situations mentioned in Art. 8:103 PECL. In a commercial sale the time of delivery of goods is presumed to be of the essence (subpara. a). If a contractor is to build and pave a road to a new building before 1 May and on that date the road is not yet paved, making it unsuitable to drive upon, the breach deprives the creditor of what it was entitled to expect (subpara. b). If a freelancer hands in invoices for expenses he did not incur, this allows his client to terminate the freelance agreement: this is an intentional breach and the client can no longer be reasonably expected to rely on the freelancer's proper future performance.

English law allows termination (in England also referred to as *rescission for breach* or *repudiatory breach*) only in case of breach of a 'condition'. The term 'condition' has different meanings in the law. What is meant by it here is that not all contractual terms are of equal importance. If you rent a house for the holiday, the contractual term that you are allowed to make use of it during three weeks in July is more important than the term that use of the house includes free access to the local health club. English law makes the explicit distinction between terms that are 'essential' and that, in case of breach, allow termination (*conditions*) and terms that only allow a claim for damages (*warranties*). For example, the Sale of Goods Act 1979 specifies that the implied terms that the sold goods must be of satisfactory quality, fit for purpose and comply with the given description are conditions (ss 12–15). These are all terms that go 'to the root of the contract'. Parties can of course also explicitly agree that certain terms are of the essence, turning them into conditions that allow termination in case of breach. Or, as was held in *Hong Kong Fir Shipping Co. v Kawasaki Kisen Kaisha* (1962):

English law

> it is open to the parties to a contract to make it clear either expressly or by necessary implication that a particular stipulation is to be regarded as a condition which goes to the root of the contract, so that it is clear that the parties contemplate that any breach of it entitles the other party at once to treat the contract as at an end.

Articles 1224–1230 *Code Civil* form the basis for termination (*résolution*) in French law. The most relevant provisions, all introduced with the grand reform of French contract law in 2016, are the following:

French law

> **Art. 1224:** Termination results either from the application of a termination clause, or, where the non-performance is sufficiently serious, from notice by the creditor to the debtor or from a judicial decision.

> **Art. 1225 (1):** The termination clause must specify the undertakings whose non-performance will lead to the termination of the contract.

> **Art. 1226:** The creditor may, at his own risk, terminate the contract by notice. Unless there is urgency, he must previously have put the debtor in default to perform his undertaking within a reasonable time. (. . .)
> The debtor may at any time bring proceedings to challenge such a termination. The creditor must then prove the seriousness of the non-performance.

> **Art. 1227:** Termination may in any event be claimed in court proceedings.

> **Art. 1228:** The court may, according to the circumstances, recognise or declare the termination of the contract or order its performance, with the possibility of allowing the debtor further time to do so, or award only damages.

Art. 1224 CC provides the disappointed creditor with three options to part with the other contracting party. First, the parties can agree on a termination clause (the *clause résolutoire* of Art. 1225 CC) indicating the conditions that allow a party to terminate the contract (for example: 'any breach') and preferably how to realise this ('by letter'). It has become common practice in commercial contracts to include such a clause, especially because the old (pre-2016) French law made it cumbersome to terminate a contract in any other way. Second, a party can turn to the court (Art. 1227 CC) which will then assess whether the non-performance is serious enough to justify termination. The court will look at the circumstances, such as the extent to which the debtor is to blame and the loss to the creditor, and may decide to order a less intrusive remedy than termination if it deems fit (Art. 1228 CC).

As for the third option, French law recognises that it would be highly impractical if, in cases where the contract does not contain a termination clause, only a court order were able to put an end to the contract. It would mean that the creditor would have to wait endlessly before it could get rid of the defaulting debtor and conclude a cover transaction with somebody else. Art. 1226 CC therefore also allows the creditor to terminate the contract by way of notice. The protection of the non-performing party lies in the requirement that the breach must be sufficiently serious: if not, the debtor can successfully challenge the termination in court. This serves as

Unilateral termination

an effective hurdle for 'termination happy' creditors, but in obvious cases of non-performance, a creditor will eagerly accept the (low) risk that a court will subsequently leave the contract in place and make him pay damages. In the case *Abonnement téléphonique/Pigranel* (1987), the alarm system installed by the claimant had continued to go off at the wrong moment ever since it was installed. The buyer was allowed to terminate the contract in view of the seller's carelessness in installing and maintaining the alarm and the high costs of the installation and maintenance incurred by the buyer.

The core provisions on termination for non-performance (*Rücktritt*) in
German law
German law can be found in §§ 323–324 BGB:

> **§ 323**: '(1) If, in the case of a bilateral contract, the debtor fails to perform or does not perform in accordance with the contract, then the creditor may terminate the contract if he has fixed, to no avail, an additional period for performance or cure (*Frist zur Leistung*).
> (2) The additional period need not be fixed if
> 1. the debtor seriously and definitively refuses performance,
> 2. the debtor fails to perform by a date or within a period specified in the contract and, in the contract, the creditor has made the continuation of his interest in performance subject to the punctuality of that performance, or
> 3. there are special circumstances which, when weighing the interests of both parties, justify immediate termination.
> (3) If the nature of the breach of duty is such that it is not feasible to fix a period for performance, a warning notice (*Abmahnung*) is given instead.
> (...)
> (5) If the debtor has performed in part, the creditor may terminate the entire contract only if he has no interest in partial performance. If the debtor has not performed in conformity with the contract, the creditor may not terminate the contract if the breach of duty is trivial.
> (...)'

> **§ 324**: 'If the debtor, in the case of a bilateral contract, breaches a duty under § 241 (2), the creditor may terminate the contract if he can no longer reasonably be expected to uphold the contract.'

The most interesting aspect of these provisions lies in what they do *not* say: a fundamental non-performance (as in the PECL) or breach of a condition (as in English law) is not required. Nor does § 323 BGB require intervention by the court: the creditor can terminate the contract himself. And yet, also German law is eager to avoid termination for minor violations of the contract.

A minimum threshold (much lower than the one provided by the PECL, English and French law) can be found in the second sentence of paragraph (5): the breach may not be 'trivial.' But the real way in which the BGB limits termination is by summing up the types of situations in which a good ground for termination exists. Apart from the case mentioned in § 324 (that mirrors the damages claim of § 282 BGB in case of an ancillary duty, discussed in Chapter 12 subsection B) and the case in which performance is impossible (which under German law leads to automatic release from the contract: §§ 326 and 275 BGB; Art. 9:303 (4) PECL provides for the same), the three situations mentioned in § 323 (2) BGB are familiar. The PECL, English and French law would probably also qualify these cases as fundamental non-performance, breach of a condition or a non-performance that is serious enough in the eyes of the court.

Nachfrist

The real innovation that § 323 BGB brings, lies in the rule that termination is allowed in case of *any* non-performance, provided that the debtor is given a second chance to perform (para. (1)). We encountered this *Nachfrist* before in Chapter 12 subsection B, when the claim for damages based on § 281 BGB was discussed. § 323 mirrors § 281, albeit that in case a time was specified for performance (a so-called *Fixgeschäft*) the creditor is allowed to terminate the contract on the basis of § 323 (2) 2, while a claim for damages then still requires a *Nachfrist*. The main point is that German law thus makes it possible for the creditor to terminate the contract for any less than trivial breach by giving the debtor a second chance to perform. This is particularly useful in case of delay or defective performance. If A is to deliver 50 mobile phones for use by B's employees and it is unclear at which exact date delivery is due (in which case § 323 (2) 2 BGB would apply), or the delivered goods are defective, all that B needs to do is set a reasonable time for A to perform and see what happens.

Dutch law

Dutch law, finally, makes it the easiest on the creditor. Art. 6:265 BW states:

> 1. Every non-performance of a party of one of its obligations gives the other party the right to terminate the contract in full or in part, unless the non-performance, given its specific nature or trivial importance, does not justify this termination and its consequences.
> 2. In so far as performance is not permanently or temporarily impossible, the right to terminate the contract only arises when the debtor is in default.

This provision sets the threshold for termination comparatively low. Termination (*ontbinding*) is a right of the creditor and it is for the debtor to show that the non-performance does not justify the termination. Dutch

BOX 13.1

EFFICIENT BREACH

A thriving field of legal scholarship asks which rules are the most economically efficient. Pioneered by Nobel Prize winner Ronald Coase (1910–2013) and Guido Calabresi, Law and Economics applies micro-economic analysis to the law. One of the best-known theories in this field is that of *efficient breach*. This theory holds that a party should be allowed to breach ('terminate') a contract and pay damages if doing so would be economically more efficient than performing the obligations under the contract. This is a far cry from the view that a contract has binding force because morality requires it to be so. It is also inconsistent with the existing law on when a contract can be terminated. Richard Posner's *Economic Analysis of Law* gives the following well-known example of efficient breach:

> 'Suppose I sign a contract to deliver 100,000 custom-ground widgets at $10 a piece to A, for use in his boiler factory. After I have delivered 10,000, B comes to me, explains that he desperately needs 25,000 custom-ground widgets at once since otherwise he will be forced to close his pianola factory at great cost, and offers me $15 a piece for 25,000

widgets. I sell him the widgets and as a result do not complete timely delivery to A, who sustains $1,000 in damages from my breach. Having obtained an additional profit of $1,250 on the sale to B, I am better off even after reimbursing A for his loss. Society is also better off. Since B was willing to pay me $15 per widget, it must mean that each widget was worth at least $15 to him. But it was worth only $14 to A – $10, what he paid, plus $04 ($1,000 divided by 25,000), his expected profit. Thus the breach resulted in a transfer of the 25,000 widgets from a lower valued to a higher valued use.'

It is difficult to deny the logic of this reasoning. The non-performance towards A is efficient because everyone is better off: the promisor profits from his default and the promisee is in as good a position as he would have been in had the performance been rendered. The common law is sympathetic to the idea of efficient breach. The rule that the creditor is in principle only entitled to damages (and not to performance) is an incentive to breach the contract if this is efficient (for example, as in the above case, because the seller receives a better offer).

law assumes that a seller who receives €19,997 instead of the agreed upon €20,000 cannot terminate, but this is an essentially different approach to asking whether the non-performance was fundamental or serious enough.

B.   The mechanics of termination

Declaration

In any jurisdiction termination of the contract can be claimed before the court, but as noted before, this is often very impractical. This is exactly the reason why the law also allows unilateral termination by a party. But which requirements must the termination meet? Articles 1226 CC and 6:267 BW state that the terminating party must send a written declaration, while the PECL and German law provide that termination can be made by a declaration in any form (Art. 9:303 (1) PECL, § 349 BGB). An English creditor who decides to terminate (in the terminology of English law, the creditor's *acceptance of the repudiation* by the debtor) must naturally also communicate this to the defaulting debtor. Again, no form is needed, provided that the communication clearly and unequivocally indicates that the creditor wants to put an end to the contract.

Notice

It was seen in Chapter 12 that in French and German law (and the same is true for Dutch law), a damages claim can usually only be brought if the debtor is put in default by a warning notice (*mise en demeure, Mahnung*) unless this would be futile. Is such a notice also needed in case of termination? One could reason that if the breach is already serious enough to justify termination, a formal warning to the debtor that he should perform usually no longer makes much sense. However, this is not the existing law. French Arts. 1225 (2) and 1226 (1) CC require in principle that the debtor is put in default by way of notice. In German law the *Nachfrist* will usually replace the notice (see, however, § 323 (3) BGB). The Dutch Art. 6:265 (2) BW requires default (consisting of a notice unless a time was fixed for performance) in case performance is not already impossible. This is quite understandable: Dutch law is lenient on the creditor and allows termination also in case of a less serious breach.

C. Anticipatory breach

It seems obvious that a contractual remedy can only be brought in cases where the other party fails to perform. A strict application of this rule would imply that no termination (or damages) can be claimed before there is actual non-performance. But what if it is clear that the debtor will not perform or is unable to do so? It would be peculiar if the creditor must then wait until the date that performance is due. Is the creditor then allowed to treat the declaration or behaviour of the debtor to this effect as a breach of contract? Although it seems strange to hold a party in breach before performance is due, most jurisdictions make this possible by allowing a so-called *anticipatory breach*. The following provisions are evidence for this.

> **§ 323 (4) BGB**: 'The creditor may already terminate the contract before performance is due, if it is obvious that the requirements for termination will be met.'

Art. 6:80 (1) BW: 'The effects of a non-performance set in even before the claim of the creditor is due:
a. if it is certain that performance will be impossible without breach;
b. if the creditor must conclude from a statement of the debtor that he will not perform in conformity with his obligation; or
c. if the creditor has good reasons to fear that the debtor will not perform in conformity with his obligation and the debtor does not comply with a written notice of the creditor in which the debtor is asked to confirm, within a reasonable time, that he is willing to perform in conformity with his obligation. The grounds that gave the creditor good reasons to fear a non-performance of the debtor must be mentioned in this notification.'

Art. 9:304 PECL: 'Where prior to the time for performance by a party it is clear that there will be a fundamental non-performance by it the other party may terminate the contract.'

It follows from these provisions that if, for example, Mary hires Yves to renovate her flat, and two months before the work is to start Yves tells Mary that due to a busy schedule he will not be able to do the work, Mary can immediately terminate the contract. English law adopts the same position. French law, however, does not allow anticipatory breach. It is noted that jurisdictions that allow anticipatory breach will not only permit a premature claim for termination but also for damages.

D. The effect of termination

In a typical case of non-performance the creditor will combine several remedies. It is obvious that a party cannot bring a claim for performance and termination at the same time, but a claim for termination will usually be combined with one for damages for non-performance. This is self-evident: the mere termination will not make good the damage that the innocent party suffers as a result of the breach. The new Art. 1217 (2) of the French Code states what any jurisdiction accepts:

'Remedies which are not incompatible may be combined; damages may always be added to any of the others.'

The obvious aim that a creditor has with termination is to be freed from the contract. It is therefore no real question what the effect of termination is for the future: it releases both parties from their obligations to effect and to
Future receive future performance (see e.g. Art. 9:305 PECL, which speaks for all other jurisdictions).

The more difficult question is what is the effect if one or both parties have already performed part of the contract before termination. A party who already paid the price is naturally allowed to recover the money (see e.g. Art. 9:307 PECL). But what if goods were delivered? Is the seller allowed to claim these back and, if so, on what basis?

The rift in Europe is between jurisdictions that award the termination with retroactive effect and those that do not. If termination has retroactive effect (as in Italy, Spain, Bulgaria and Belgium), this means that it is as if the contract has never been concluded. The property in the goods that a party received automatically returns to the seller (assuming that the seller was the owner before delivery). This is highly practical in cases where the debtor becomes insolvent: if the seller is 'still' the owner, he can collect the goods from the debtor's home and is not bothered by claims that any other creditors may have.

If termination has no retroactive effect (as in France, Germany, England, the Netherlands and under the PECL), the property in the delivered goods remains with the party to whom the goods were transferred. In practice, however, commercial parties will agree upon a *retention of title clause*. Such a clause states that the property in the goods remains with the seller as long as the buyer has not paid the purchase price. But what if the parties have not included such a clause in their contract? Both the German (§ 346 BGB) and the Dutch Civil Code (Art. 6:271 BW) as well as Art. 1229 CC and the PECL (Art. 9:308) contain a specific provision according to which each of the parties is then obliged to return the received performance. The difference with Italian and Spanish law becomes clear if one realises that the duty to return the received goods is an obligation that in case of insolvency of the debtor must compete with claims of the other creditors (see however Box 13-2).

It is sometimes not very practical, or even impossible, to return the received performance. It is for example difficult to see how provided services (such as painting a house, treatment by a physiotherapist, or carriage of goods) can be 'returned'. The painter is not going to take off the paint, the physiotherapist will not kick her patient in the neck, and the carrier will not bring back the goods to the port of dispatch. In such cases the law allows a party to claim back the *value* of the performance. Article 9:309 PECL states what Art. 1352-8 CC, § 346 (2) BGB and Art. 6:272 BW also accept:

> On termination of the contract a party which has rendered a performance which cannot be returned and for which it has not received payment or other counter-

BOX 13.2

AN EXTRA STATUTORY RIGHT FOR THE UNPAID SELLER?

The seller of a good naturally expects to get paid by the buyer. If the buyer does not pay the price, the seller can ask for performance or eventually decide to terminate the contract. But this remedy may not always be the optimal one if the seller has already delivered the goods. Mere termination will not automatically lead to the seller regaining the property. If termination has no retroactive effect, the seller's claim to payment is only one of many in the case of the buyer's insolvency, meaning that the seller will probably remain empty-handed. It has already been seen that this is the reason why many sellers are only willing to sell goods under a retention of title clause. This ensures that they remain the owner of the goods until full payment has taken place. One could very well argue that a seller who refrains from adding such a clause, but still delivers the goods before payment, must face the consequences.

This does not prevent some jurisdictions from providing special protection to the unpaid seller who has already delivered movable goods. This extra protection finds its origins in legal history. Both in the law of Roman times and in the pre-codified laws of France and the Netherlands, the rule existed that the buyer only became the owner of a good upon payment. A jurisdiction in which this is still the case today is South African law (which is heavily influenced by seventeenth century Roman-Dutch law). The rule has long been abandoned in Europe, which makes the passing of property dependent on either the moment at which the contract is concluded (as in France) or when the goods are delivered (as in the Netherlands). However, the remains of the old rule are still detectable in French and Dutch law. Article 2332 CC, for example, allows the seller to '*revendicate*' (claim back the property in) the good within eight days after delivery (which is too short a period to make this right of great practical importance). Dutch law also allows the unpaid seller to claim back the good as his property, but allows a longer period of six weeks from the moment at which payment was due. This so-called *recht van reclame* (Art. 7:39 BW) provides the unpaid seller with a highly practical remedy: if the requirements for the termination of a contract are met, he can invoke this special right by way of a written declaration. The effect of this is that the seller, as the revived owner of the goods, is not bothered by the insolvency of the buyer.

performance may recover a reasonable amount for the value of the performance to the other party.

Long-term contracts

In the case of long-term contracts, the law provides a different solution. Long-term contracts are characterised by the fact that mutual performances take place over a longer period of time. The landlord for example is to provide the tenant with a liveable-in apartment in return for the tenant paying the monthly rent. The franchisor receives a regular remuneration from the franchisee, who in return has the right and obligation to use the franchisor's trade name, know-how and business method. In such contracts non-performance often only takes place after a number of months or even years. The effect of termination can then not be that the whole contract must be unwound back to the moment of conclusion. There is also no need for this as both parties have performed perfectly well until the breach. Termination in case of contracts providing for continuous performance is therefore only allowed for the future. In French law, this *résiliation* does thus not affect the period before the breach. The same is true for the German *Kündigung* (§ 314), which allows a party to terminate a contract for the future in case of performance of a recurring obligation if there is a good cause for doing so.

Partial termination

A final exception to the rule that termination leads to the end of the contract is when termination is only partial. If a contract is to be performed in separate parts and it is possible to apportion the non-performed part to a counter performance, the creditor can terminate for only this part (cf. Art. 9:302 PECL which in effect is an adequate description of the European common core). In other words: a partial non-performance could justify a partial termination. If the seller delivers 50 copies of the Swiss Civil Code instead of the agreed upon 200 copies, this is surely a non-performance that justifies termination, but if the buyer would like to keep the codes he received, he can terminate the contract for the remaining 150 codes and consequently pay one-quarter of the price. This is an easy example because the breach lies in a lesser *quantity* than agreed upon. It is more difficult to apportion a breach as to *quality* to a corresponding part of the counter performance. If the delivered bananas do not meet the expected quality, one must assess what would have been paid for bananas of the delivered type.

E.   Withholding performance

Termination is an extreme remedy that a party will only bring if it is no longer interested in the counterpart's performance. This is no small thing: parties conclude a contract to obtain a performance and the decision to bring this contract to an end is usually a bitter disappointment. This explains why a creditor usually prefers to postpone the moment of termination until he is absolutely certain that the debtor is unwilling or unable to perform. However, in a bilateral contract the mal-performing debtor is always also a creditor and may ask for performance *himself*. If the landlord of an office building refuses to repair the central heating, the tenant may want to wait to terminate the lease and hope for better times, but the landlord will still claim payment on the monthly rent. And if a seller delivers defective goods, he is likely to ask for payment from the buyer anyway. The question is whether this tenant and buyer (or any other debtor) can withhold performance until the other party has performed properly. One should note that withholding

Defence performance is in this sense not a true contractual remedy, but a *defence* of the debtor to a claim for performance by the creditor. Withholding performance (*exception d'inéxecution, Einrede des nichterfüllten Vertrags, opschorting*) is often a prelude to termination: the tenant and buyer will put an end to the contract if the landlord and seller end up being unwilling or unable to perform.

Any jurisdiction accepts that withholding performance is a valid defence against the creditor's claim for performance. Article 9:201 PECL is therefore a fair description of the European common core:

> (1) A party who is to perform simultaneously with or after the other party may withhold performance until the other has tendered performance or has performed. The first party may withhold the whole of its performance or a part of it as may be reasonable in the circumstances.
>
> (2) A party may similarly withhold performance for as long as it is clear that there will be a non-performance by the other party when the other party's performance becomes due.

In the situation mentioned subparagraph (1) there is already non-performance by the other party, while in the situation subparagraph (2)

Two types performance is not yet due but the party who is to perform first has a good reason to believe that the other party is not going to perform. The defence in the first case is also known as the *exceptio non adimpleti contractus* (literally: the exception of a non-performed contract), in the second case as the *defence of uncertainty* (which is the natural prelude to anticipatory breach). For example, if a party, after the conclusion of the contract, has good reason to fear that the other party will be declared bankrupt or will deliver the sold object to somebody else, he can invoke the defence of uncertainty. Both defences can also be found in the Arts. 1219 and 1220 CC, §§ 320 and 321 BGB and in the Arts. 6:262 and 6:263 BW while English law recognises them in case law.

BOX 13.3

THE RIGHT OF RETENTION

A special type of withholding performance is the so-called *right of retention*. This is a highly practical right: it allows a creditor to retain a good until the owner has met his obligations that relate to it. Thus, a garage is allowed to keep a repaired car in its possession as long as the owner does not pay the bill, a hotel can withhold the luggage of the guest, and a construction company can refuse to allow access to the finished building if the client does not pay. The right of retention is codified in the Arts. 1612 and 2286 CC (*droit de rétention*), § 273 BGB and § 369 German Commercial Code (*Zurückbehaltungsrecht*) and in Art. 3:290 BW (*retentierecht*). English law enacts a right of retention for the unpaid seller (*seller's lien*) in Sale of Goods Act 1979, s. 41, but also recognises such a lien in common law, equity and maritime law if further specific requirements are met.

TOPICS FOR REVIEW

Limits to termination in English, French and German law
Fundamental non-performance
Conditions and warranties
Method of termination
Efficient breach
The role of a second chance to perform
The role of notice
Anticipatory breach
The effect of termination
Retention of title clause
Termination of long-term contracts
Partial termination
Withholding performance
Exceptio non adimpleti contractus
Defence of uncertainty

FURTHER READING

– Hugh Beale et al, *Cases, Materials and Text on Contract Law, Ius Commune Casebooks for the Common Law of Europe*, 2nd ed., Oxford (Hart Publishing) 2010, Chapters 19 and 20.
– Dagmar Coester-Waltjen, 'The New Approach to Breach of Contract in German Law', in: N. Cohen and E. McKendrick, *Comparative Remedies for Breach of Contract*, Oxford (Hart) 2005, 135–56.
– Catherine Elliott and Frances Quinn, *Contract Law*, 10th ed., Harlow (Pearson) 2015, Chapter 14.
– Richard A. Posner, *Economic Analysis of Law*, 9th ed., New York (Wolters Kluwer) 2011, Chapter 4.
– Konrad Zweigert and Hein Kötz, *An Introduction to Comparative Law* (translated by Tony Weir), 3rd ed., Oxford (Oxford University Press) 1998, Chapter 36.

Part Six

Contracts and third parties

The last part of this book is devoted to the rights and obligations of third parties. Third parties are persons who are not a party to the contract and who therefore, in principle, do not incur rights and obligations under the contract. Although this principle of **privity** or **relativity** of the contract seems self-evident, a number of situations exist in which outsiders to the contractual bond are affected by the contract, either because they can sue or because they can be sued as a result of other people's agreement. This part (consisting of one single chapter) examines these situations.

14

Contracts and third parties

 CHAPTER OVERVIEW

Adding a third party to the equation often makes things more exciting. Contract law is not any different. This chapter studies a number of situations in which a person is affected by a contract although he is not a party to it. This can be the case because he derives a right from other people's contracts (in case of so-called **contracts for the benefit of a third party**), because he relies on an exemption clause in a contract to which he is not a party (**third-party effect of exemption clauses**) or because he can sue somebody other than his immediate party (in case of **linked contracts**). This chapter also investigates whether, next to these 'third party winners', the law must also recognise **'third party losers'** who suffer a loss as a result of a contract entered into by other people. Separate attention is paid to **agency**, in which a third party is involved in the conclusion of the contract, and **assignment**, which leads to the transfer of an existing right to a new creditor.

Privity

Nothing seems more natural than only the contracting parties themselves incurring rights and obligations under the contract. If contracts are based on the mutual consent of the parties, how could others ever be affected by the agreement? Lawyers speak of the doctrine of privity or relativity of contracts: not only can contracting parties not impose a burden on a third party, but a third party is in principle also unable to derive rights from other people's contracts. Art. 1199 s. 1 of the French Civil Code well reflects this line of thinking, where it states: 'A contract creates obligations only as between the parties.' Although this provision is perfectly consistent with the emphasis that contract law puts on the party agreement, it reflects neither the needs of commerce to sometimes benefit somebody else through the contract nor the brutal reality in which a contract can in fact harm others. The law must take this into account. It does so under the broad heading of 'contracts and third parties', a group of highly diverse situations in which others than the contracting parties are involved in the making of, or feel the effects of, the contract. This chapter considers six types of such third-party involvement.

Contracts for the benefit of a third party

The most important exception to the principle that contracting parties can only create obligations among themselves is the so-called contract for the benefit of a third party (*stipulation pour autrui, Vertrag zugunsten Dritter, derdenbeding*). In this case, the parties (A and B) agree that a third person (beneficiary C) obtains a right that is enforceable against one of them. Although it took most jurisdictions until the nineteenth century (and England even until 1999) to accept such a third-party right, there is a clear economic and societal need for it.

Examples

One straightforward example of a contract for the benefit of a third party is when two parties want to settle a debt owed by one of them to somebody else. If A owes C €200 and A decides to sell his bicycle to B, then A and B can agree in their contract that buyer B must pay the purchase price to C. C then acquires the right to claim direct payment from B. Next to C, A (sometimes called the promisee or 'stipulator') also can require promisor B to perform against third party C. Another common example is the contract of life insurance. This insurance entails that the insurer will pay a sum of money to a beneficiary upon the death of the insured person. If Mary buys a policy on Jim's life for the benefit of their common children, she has to pay premiums to the insurer while their children, obviously not parties to the contract, can claim the insured sum upon their father's death. In a similar manner, two football clubs transferring a player can agree that part of the transfer sum must be paid to the player himself, and a company taking over another company can agree to continue to employ certain employees.

These examples make clear that the benefit to be conferred on the third party can take a variety of forms. The broadly formulated statutory provisions in France, Germany and England confirm this:

> **Art. 1205 CC:** 'A person may make a stipulation for another person.
> One of the parties to a contract (the 'stipulator') may require a promise from the other party (the 'promisor') to accomplish an act of performance for the benefit of a third party (the 'beneficiary'). The third party may be a future person but must be exactly identified or must be able to be determined at the time of the performance of the promise.'

> **§ 328 (1) BGB:** 'Performance to a third party may be agreed by contract with the effect that the third party acquires the right to demand the performance directly.'

S. 1 (1) Contracts (Rights of Third Parties) Act 1999: 'Subject to the provisions of this Act, a person who is not a party to a contract (a 'third party') may in his own right enforce a term of the contract if –
(a) the contract expressly provides that he may, or
(b) subject to subsection (2), the term purports to confer a benefit on him.'

Right

One characteristic of a contract for the benefit of a third party is that the latter obtains an independent right against the promisor, meaning he can claim performance as well as damages in case of breach. In the examples above, the children, the football player and the employees obtain a right at the moment the contract is concluded. This is important because it means that the third party is not affected by the insolvency of the promisee, as the right is no longer part of the promisee's assets.

Intention inferred

It is obvious that the promisor and promisee must have the intention to create a right for the third party. Art. 6:110 PECL confirms that in all jurisdictions, this intention can also be inferred from the purpose of the contract or the circumstances of the case. In the German *Denied passenger* case (1985) a tourist had booked a charter flight from Frankfurt to Santa Lucia with a holiday tour operator, but the airline refused to give her a seat on the return flight. She had to book another flight herself and was able to successfully claim damages for non-performance from the airline, even though she and the airline were not in a direct contractual relationship. The court reasoned that it is typical for charter contracts that the individual holidaymakers are not known at the time the airline and the charterer conclude their contract, although the contract is clearly concluded in the interest of these individual passengers. This justifies that the latter have a direct contractual claim against the airline. The highest court in France went even further when it held that a hospital patient who had received blood contaminated with syphilis could directly sue the blood-transfusion service although this organisation had only contracted with the hospital in which the patient was treated and not with the unlucky patient herself. She was rightly considered a third-party beneficiary of the contract between the hospital and the supplier of the blood (*Centre National de Transfusion Sanguine v L*, 1954).

Renunciation

An important question is whether the third party should be told about, or even accept, the benefit before it becomes effective. Much speaks in favour of this: just like donation requires the donee to agree with receiving the gift – which he may decline because he does not like the donor or simply because he wishes to reject the gift for tax reasons – a third party should also in some way accept the benefit imposed upon him. The great majority of jurisdictions (confirmed by e.g. Art. 5.2.1 PICC and Art. II.-9:301 DCFR) realise this through the backdoor: they hold that the third party obtains the right at the moment the contract is formed, but he can renounce it if he wishes. An explicit acceptance or notification is not needed. It can happen, therefore, that a right is conferred upon a third party who does not know about the right and only finds out later that he is able to sue the promisor.

Dutch law

Dutch law is the odd one out. Art. 6:253 BW requires the third party to accept the clause in his favour before it can be enforced (be it that this acceptance can be implicit). This is an exceptional requirement from a comparative perspective. It has the distinct advantage that it is clear at which exact point in time the right comes into being, but the doctrinal quirk of this construction is that the beneficiary is no longer a true third party. This is indeed the position of Dutch law: Art. 6:254 BW states that after acceptance, the beneficiary is considered a party to the contract.

Third-party effect of exemption clauses

In commercial practice, it is not only important that a third party sometimes is given a direct right to performance, but also that the third party is able to defend itself against a claim. This is of particular importance in cases where the parties have included an exemption or limitation clause in their contract and a third party is involved in the actual performance, as is the usual situation in the field of shipping and transport. If the owner or shipper (the person who sends goods for transport) contracts a carrier to ship goods from Shanghai to Cairo, the carrier typically relies on contractors such as stevedores and sub-carriers to perform the contract. However, transport is a perilous activity and the carrier is likely to limit his liability for damage to the goods. What if the independent sub-contractor, for example, damages the goods when loading or unloading the cargo and is sued (usually in tort) by the owner or shipper? Can the sub-contractor rely on the limitation of liability in the original contract to which he is not a party?

Himalaya clause

It seems obvious that the sub-contractor can rely on the exemption clause if the parties have formulated it in such a way that it also shields third parties from liability. Inspired by the name of the ship in the court decision in which such clauses were first accepted under English law, these contractual provisions are usually referred to as *Himalaya clauses*. Such a clause could read like this: 'No agent or independent contractor employed by the carrier shall be liable to the owner of the goods for any loss or damage resulting from any act or negligence on his part while acting in the course of his employment.'

Third-party effect

The more interesting question is whether third parties can also invoke an exemption clause even if they are not explicitly mentioned in it. This is what most jurisdictions now accept. There is a good argument for this: the shipper who accepts the clause as part of his contract with the carrier must understand that the carrier will make use of sub-contractors, as this is the common situation. This is also exactly the argument the Dutch Supreme Court used in the well-known case of *Securicor* (1979). Bank Vlaer & Kol had agreed with Makro wholesalers that it would come to collect the cash money at Makro at the end of each working day. The bank subsequently contracted with the transport firm Securicor to carry out this task. One day in November 1972, Securicor's employees were robbed, losing some of Makro's daily proceeds, and Makro filed a claim against Securicor for negligence. However, the contract between Securicor and the bank contained an exemption clause to the effect that Securicor would not be liable for any losses while performing the contract. Even though Makro was not a party to this contract, the court held that Securicor could invoke the exemption clause; Makro should have understood that it would not be the bank itself that would collect the money and should have realised that contracts like these typically contain exemption clauses.

BOX 14.1

A GERMAN DOCTRINE: CONTRACTS WITH PROTECTIVE EFFECT FOR THIRD PARTIES

A famous case decided by the German Supreme Court in 1976 is the so-called *Vegetable leaf* decision. Here, a 14-year-old girl accompanied her mother when she went shopping at the local supermarket. The girl was seriously injured when she slipped on a vegetable leaf on the supermarket's floor. Although it seemed reasonable to hold the supermarket liable for the injury, the court could not rely on the limited scope of German tort law to realise this, in particular because it was not clear whether an employee or some other customer had dropped the leaf. It was equally impossible to found liability on contract as only the mother intended to contract with the supermarket and not the daughter. The victim was hurt when she was already on her way out of the supermarket, while her mother was paying at the checkout. And yet, the court held the supermarket liable by ingeniously assuming that the pre-contractual duty to take into account the interests of the customer (the victim's mother) also extended to the victim. The daughter, as a third party, was thus drawn into the contractual sphere in order to enjoy the same benefits as the (pre-)contractual party itself.

This separate head of liability is now known as the doctrine of 'contracts with protective effect for third parties' (*Verträge mit Schutzwirkung für Dritte*). The doctrine is particularly helpful in cases where a professional expert provides the wrong

➡

information or poorly performs its tasks under the contract, such as an accountant or tax advisor unjustifiably declaring a company financially fit or a surveyor writing an unreliable valuation report. If the information contained in these statements is inaccurate, the other contracting party can surely sue for non-performance, but the question is whether a third party (such as a bank relying on the false information when providing a loan) also has a claim. French, English and Dutch law would allow a claim in tort, but German law regards the third party as being protected under the contract. A well-known situation is that of the disap-pointed inheritor: a solicitor (in England) or a notary public (in civil law) draws up a will, but does not do so on time or as instructed, leading to the unfortunate result that the intended beneficiary (a third party to the contract between the professional and the testator) does not inherit. In *White v Jones* (1995) the English House of Lords held that the solicitor owes a duty of care to the intended beneficiary, potentially leading to liability in negligence (a type of tort). In German law, the court would hold that the contract between the notary and the testator has protective effect towards the third party.

Linked contracts

A contract seldom comes alone. As was already seen in the discussion about the third-party effect of exemption clauses, transport contracts are often part of a broader network of connected contracts. Other similar examples include the many contracts required to build a supply chain in the garment industry (see Box 1.2) or build a house. Typical for these linked contracts (*groupe de contrats, verbundene Verträge, samenhangende overeenkomsten*) is that, although they consist of different contracts among different parties, the contracts are economically or factually connected. While the natural tendency of the law is to treat these contracts as separate, it sometimes takes their interconnectedness into account. Two questions can illustrate this. The first one is whether a party to a contract can be held liable for a lack of conformity by a party in another (linked) contract. The second is whether a contract can share the fate of another contract in the sense that the end of one (through termination or withdrawal) automatically leads to the end of another.

Direct action

Any product being sold is likely to be the subject of many individual contracts before it reaches its end user. The manufacturer can sell its products to a foreign importer, the importer to a distributor, the distributor to a retailer and the retailer to a consumer. The first question is whether a party can bring a claim against someone further up or down the chain than his immediate contracting partner. Only a few jurisdictions accept such a contractual short-cut. The best-known example is French law, which allows a so-called *action directe* of the final purchaser against the original manufacturer or subsequent seller for a lack of conformity in the goods. If a buyer is confronted with a defect in the purchased product, he cannot bring a claim for non-performance only against the seller from which he bought the goods, but also against the producer of the goods. The French courts justify this blatant infringement of the principle of relativity of contracts by reasoning that the contractual remedies for non-performance are intrinsically linked to the defective goods as they move down the contractual chain. The claim of the buyer is seen as an accessory of the good itself and is therefore transferred to all subsequent buyers. This clever construction evades any further complex doctrinal reasoning necessary to justify this contractual shortcut.

Policy
arguments

Good policy arguments exist in favour of this direct liability of the manufacturer. In the great majority of cases, the seller is nothing but a mere supplier who is unable to influence the quality of the product. It then makes much more sense to hold the manufacturer liable. This also puts the incentive where it belongs: if the goal of contractual liability is to incentivise a person to minimise possible defects, the manufacturer is the right party to consider. This explains why in recent decades other jurisdictions, including Finland, Spain and the Netherlands (cf. Art. 7:25 BW), also introduced liability for a lack of conformity of a party further up the chain. A European variation of this direct action can be found in Art. 4 of EU-Directive 1999/44 on Sale of Consumer Goods, a provision that is rather useless as it leaves Member States the freedom to implement it or not.

Shared fate

The second question is whether the end of one contract can automatically imply the end of another contract. A standard situation is when a consumer buys a car or another valuable object and at the same time concludes a second contract with a money lender to finance the purchase, possibly with the lender directly paying the purchase price to the seller, and with this financing option being offered by the seller on behalf of the lender at the time of the purchase. What if the buyer discovers major defects shortly after delivery and successfully avoids the sale for mistake or terminates it for non-performance? It would be highly undesirable if the buyer would then still be bound to the credit agreement. Courts around Europe therefore held that in such a situation, the credit agreement shares the fate of the sales contract, even though it is concluded with another party. Legislators enacted similar rules for cases in which a consumer exercises his withdrawal right, as is for example apparent from Art. 15 s. 1 EU Directive 2008/48 on consumer credit:

> Where the consumer has exercised a right of withdrawal, based on Community law, concerning a contract for the supply of goods or services, he shall no longer be bound by a linked credit agreement.

Third party losers

In the three situations mentioned above, persons stand to benefit from being a third party to the contract: they are 'third party winners'. A key question is whether contract law also allows a claim to 'third party losers', those who suffer a loss as a result of a contract entered into by other people. The traditional answer is that a contract can never impose a direct duty on a third party to do something: contracting parties cannot force someone without his consent to send them flowers every morning or build a wall around their gardens. However, if one looks beyond legal doctrine, to the reality of contract practice, it becomes abundantly clear that individual contracts can affect other people in many different ways. The mere fact that I buy a painting and hang it on my wall deprives many others from enjoying it. When two business partners agree to open a restaurant, they are likely to lure customers away from existing eateries in the area. In the same vein, my decision to buy a Volkswagen or any other car will increase pollution to the detriment of others. It was seen before (Chapter 8) that parties must to some extent take into account each other's interests; however, the law generally does not require parties to also take into account the interest of third parties. The high threshold here is that of liability in tort: only the intentional or negligent infringement of a party's interest will merit a claim in damages.

CSR

A policy question legislators and courts will have to answer in the years to come is whether this view of contractual liability is not too narrow in case of gross violations of labour standards in the supply chain or threats to the environment. In one American case, employees of Wal-Mart Stores Inc.'s foreign suppliers in China, Bangladesh and Indonesia filed a claim against Wal-Mart to improve local labour conditions. They claimed that they could benefit, as third parties, from the contract concluded between Wal-Mart and its suppliers, requiring the suppliers to comply with set labour standards. The claim failed: even though Wal-Mart was eager to advertise to its home market that it only used responsible suppliers, the California Court of Appeal found it impossible to regard its foreign suppliers' employees as third-party beneficiaries of the standards Wal-Mart obliged its suppliers to use (*Doe v Wal-Mart Stores*, 2009). This is an exemplary application of existing contract law principles, but the question is whether these principles should not be adapted to better accommodate the externalities the contract entails. One argument in favour of this is that if a multinational company profits from the use of cheap labour within the supply chain, it must also be responsbible for the working circumstances of the labourers employed by its sub-contractors. This argument is even stronger if the company publicly adheres to a code of corporate social responsibility (CSR) on compliance with fair labour standards. Fresh thinking is required to translate this argument into a legal rule on when and how to involve the effects of contracts outside of the direct circle of the parties.

Agency

Modern economic life requires that contracts be made with the help of others. As soon as an entrepreneur no longer has the time or energy to buy all the equipment he needs himself, to carry out his own negotiations or to sit at the till of the supermarket he owns, the only way to expand his business is to find people willing to act as intermediaries and conclude contracts for him. The law facilitates this by recognising that not all persons involved in the conclusion of a contract are in fact considered contracting parties. Shop managers, directors, CEOs and cashiers are only some examples of people acting on behalf of other (usually legal) persons. In addition, one can commission someone to perform a specific task on one's behalf, as is the case if I pay a friend on holiday in La Paz to buy me a copy of the Bolivian civil code. In the English language, the broad term 'agency' is used to refer to all cases in which one person (the principal) agrees that another person (the agent) contracts on his behalf with a third party.

Civil law

Civil law recognises two different ways in which one can act on behalf of another person. One method is to simply ask an intermediary (B) to contract himself ('in his own name') with a counterpart (C) and then provide the principal (A) with the benefits of the contract. B himself is then bound towards the party C, but on the basis of the agreement between A and B, B also is bound to provide A with the economic benefit of his transaction with C. The sales commission agreement is the best-known example of this so-called indirect representation. A commission agent (such as a broker trading commodities) typically acts in his own name, but for the account of another. Thus, the agent who receives an order from his client to purchase oranges will buy these himself (possibly with the money provided in advance) and subsequently transfer the oranges to his client. Article 3:102 (2) PECL describes this situation as 'where an intermediary acts on instructions and on behalf of, but not in the name of, a principal.'

Civil law jurisdictions distinguish this type of acting on behalf of another from genuine ('direct') representation (*représentation, Stellvertretung, vertegenwoordiging*). Direct representation is characterised by the fact that the agent acts in the name of a principal and is not bound towards the party he in fact deals with. Both the German and the French civil code put this well:

> **Art. 1154 s. 1 CC:** Where a representative acts within his authority and in the name and on behalf of the person whom he represents, only the latter is bound to the undertaking so contracted.

> **§ 164 s. 1 BGB:** A declaration of intent which a person makes within the scope of his own power of representation in the name of a principal takes effect directly in favour of and against the principal. (. . .)

This explains why in civil law, the intermediary is not regarded as a real third party: he is automatically eliminated from the relationship between the principal and his counterpart. This obviously requires that the counterpart knows that the agent is not acting in his own name (regardless of whether the principal's identity is revealed at the time the agent acts or later). This representation often follows from the circumstances: if one buys something in a shop, one can safely assume that the employee at the counter does not intend to bind himself, but only the shop owner. The same is true for the manager representing her company. In other cases, the agent will explicitly mention that he is not acting in his own name but was given the explicit power to act in the name of somebody else. This power is what the Germans refer to as *Vollmacht* (cf. § 166 (2) BGB) and the French as *procuration* (cf. Art. 1984 CC): the full power of the agent to bind his principal. This authority often coincides with a duty to act (as in case of mandate), but this need not be the case. The aforementioned commission agent will have to follow the instructions of the commissioning party, but he does not have the power to act in his name. Reversely, my wife may have given me the authority to use her credit card, and although I am much tempted to make use of this power, I am not obliged to.

English law

The distinction between indirect and direct representation is alien to the common law. While on the European continent (followed by Art. 3:102 PECL), the principal is only bound if the agent acts in the principal's name and the counterpart is aware of the fact that he is dealing with an agent, English law is more lenient. As long as the agent acts within the scope of his authority (even when contracting in his own name), he can bind his principal. A peculiar trait of English law is that the agent need not even tell his counterpart that he is acting for somebody else. In such a case of undisclosed agency, the agent himself is bound, but as soon as it becomes clear that he in fact acted for a principal who authorised him, the counterpart can decide to also hold the principal liable. The interesting consequence of this – unthinkable in civil law – is that the other party can sue someone of whom he had not heard at the time of contracting and with whom he did not want to contract at all. This may explain why English lawyers have no difficulty calling the principal a third party: he intervenes in an already perfectly valid contract between the agent and the counterpart.

A central problem in the law of agency is how to protect the counterpart who deals with an unauthorised agent. If I ask you to negotiate in my name about a house I am interested in buying but not make any offers exceeding €250,000, it seems self-evident that I am not bound when you offer the seller €290,000. You acted as a *falsus procurator* and it would infringe upon my contractual autonomy if I were to pay €40,000 more than I had agreed. However, what if the seller had no reason to doubt that you had the power to make the offer? Should the seller's reasonable reliance be protected? If so, it means the seller cannot only sue the mal-performing agent (which is not of much use in the above example because he does not own the house), but also the principal. The affirmative answer provided by Art. 3:201 (3) PECL reflects what is accepted everywhere:

> A person is to be treated as having granted authority to an apparent agent if the
> person's statements or conduct induce the third party reasonably and in good faith
> to believe that the apparent agent has been granted authority for the act performed
> by it.

It is obvious that the agent himself cannot create this so-called apparent authority (*mandat apparent, Rechtsscheinsvollmacht, schijn van vertegenwoordingsbevoegdheid*). The counterpart needs to have acted in reasonable reliance on a declaration or conduct of the *principal*. This is not difficult to establish if the powers given to the agent are laid out in a publicly accessible document, as in the case of directors of legal persons whose competences are registered with the Chamber of Commerce. The counterpart is supposed to know about this information and can therefore never legitimately rely on a middleman exceeding his competences. However, there is abundant case law showing that things are not always so clear. What if the principal does not react to a confirmation of the order by the counterpart who acted with an unauthorised agent? And what if one lets someone work at the office, or provides someone with stationery containing the company's letterhead? Courts around the world have indeed held that the principal remaining silent or putting someone in a certain position can induce a reasonable person to think that the agent had the necessary authority to bring about a contract.

Assignment

A party to a contract not only can decide to provide a third person with an enforceable right (contracts for the benefit of a third party) or involve an intermediary in the conclusion of the contract (agency), it can also transfer an already existing contractual right to somebody else. Assignment (*cession, Abtretung, cessie*) is the transfer of a right (e.g. to the purchase money in a sales contract) by one person (the assignor) to another (assignee), resulting in the assignee being able to claim from the debtor (*debtor cessus*). If A sells his car to B for €3,000, A can assign his right to payment (enforceable against B) to C in a separate contract between A and C. C is not a third-party beneficiary or an agent, but can claim payment from B simply because he has taken the place of A as the creditor. B is no longer allowed to pay A: in case he does, he is not discharged of his obligation and must pay a second time (to C).

Assignment being possible seems the logical result of freedom of contract. If one is able to transfer physical objects, why should one not also be able to transfer rights to claims? However, there is an important obstacle to simply applying contractual freedom to the transfer of rights: as long as a contract is seen as a personal relationship between the creditor and the debtor (as it was in Roman law), it is unacceptable that the creditor can unilaterally decide to change the person towards whom the debtor needs to perform. This argument is still valid today in cases where the performance hinges on the personal characteristics of a party: a debtor obtaining a new creditor against his will is fine if the claim is for payment of money, but the landlord need not accept a new tenant in the existing lease or the publisher another author in the previously concluded publishing contract. Also, in the above example, buyer B may have had good reasons to choose A as the person to buy the car from. This explains why, although assignment is universally accepted (see e.g. Art. 1321 CC, § 398 BGB, Art. 3:94 BW and S. 136 Law of Property Act 1925), many jurisdictions allow parties to include a non-assignability clause in their contract. Such a clause limits or even prohibits the creditor from transferring his claim to somebody else. This is a distinct difference compared to tangible goods, where the interest of commercial intercourse requires that these remain freely transferable, and parties usually cannot exclude their transferability with effect against third parties.

A highly important question is at which point in time is the assignment complete. This question can receive two different answers depending on what one considers as 'complete.' On the one hand, one can say the assignment is accomplished only when the new creditor can claim from the debtor, and the debtor will only be discharged of his obligation if he pays the new creditor. In order to achieve this consequence, it is essential that the debtor be informed about the change of creditor. Next to the written form for the contract between assignor and assignee in French (Art. 1322 CC) and Dutch law (Art. 3:94 s. 1 BW), notification of the debtor is therefore a universally accepted requirement for the assignment to be completed. The requirement can be found in Art. 1324 CC, §§ 407, 409 BGB and Art. 3:94 BW as well as in S. 136 of the English Law of Property Act 1925.

Between assignor and assignee

On the other hand, one can consider the assignment as completed when the right to claim has left the assets of the assignor and the assignee is the new 'owner' of the claim. This other meaning of 'completed' is important because of the role that assignment plays in economic life, where it is often used as a means to provide security to creditors. The wealth of a company is to a large extent made up of claims. A moneylender (such as a bank) is usually only willing to provide credit if these claims serve as collateral security for payment of the debt. The moneylender will therefore require these claims to be assigned so that it can turn towards the company's debtors in case the company is unable to pay back the loan. However, both assignor and assignee have an interest in not having to inform the debtor about the assignment: this is not only impractical in the typical case of an assignor having hundreds of debtors, but it could also lead to doubts in the market about the solvency of the assignor. This explains why several legislators hold that assignment is already complete between assignor and assignee at the time of conclusion of the contract, without the need for notification of the debtor. While this is even the main rule for assignment in German (§ 398 BGB) and French (Art. 1323 CC) law, Dutch law accepts – next to the assignment, with notification of the debtor – a so-called 'silent assignment' (*stille cessie*) in Art. 3:94 s. 3 BW. It requires either a notary deed or a private deed registered at the tax office. Only S. 136 of the English Law of Property Act 1925 still requires a written notice sent to the debtor before the assignment is valid between assignor and assignee, but this requirement is not important in practice now that the transfer is valid in equity even before notification. Art. 11:202 (1) PECL thus has no difficulty in stating the following provision as the common core:

> An assignment of an existing claim takes effect at the time of the agreement to assign or such later time as the assignor and assignee agree.

BOX 14.2

FACTORING

Assignment plays an important role in commerce, in particular in the financing of a company's daily business. One often-used technique is factoring, which is a contract in which the assignor sells a large amount (or all) of its claims to a factoring company (factor) at a discount. This allows a company to obtain immediate cash. In particular, small and medium-sized enterprises may lack the cash flow to run their business while waiting for payment from their debtors. If they do not wish, or are unable, to borrow money from a bank, they can sell all their present and future claims (known as 'receivables' in American terms) to the factor. Because the factor buys these claims below their value (that is, the amount due by the debtor), it can make a profit when collecting the claim.

Obtaining finance is not the only reason a business may transfer its claims to a factor. Apart from the fact that it also conveniently shifts the risk of defaulting debtors away from the assignor, factoring allows the assignor to focus on his core business. He no longer needs to worry about administration and credit control and can leave the sending of invoices and collection of claims to the factor specialising in this type of work. This explains why factoring is not only popular among businesses in need of immediate finance, but also among healthcare providers such as doctors and dentists – rarely enthusiasts of paperwork.

The success of factoring stands and falls with the possibility to assign bulk claims. The instrument would not be very useful if each claim on an individual debtor should have to be separately assigned. It was already seen in the main text that legislators facilitate this by relaxing the notification requirement. They also allow for bulk assignment and even have come to accept that the assignment can cover future claims without the need for a new act of transfer every time a claim comes into existence. The only requirement is that the future rights are identifiable as rights to which the act of assignment relates (cf. Art. III.–5:106 DCFR and Art. 5 of the 1988 UNIDROIT Convention on International Factoring). For example, if metal manufacturer M supplies pipes to retailers, it can effectively assign factoring company F all its future claims to payment as listed in schedules regularly sent to F. This is sufficient to make the claims identifiable.

 TOPICS FOR REVIEW

Privity or relativity of contract
Contracts for the benefit of a third party
Third-party effect of exemption clauses
Contracts with protective effect for third parties
Linked contracts
Third party losers
Agency
Representation

Undisclosed agency
Apparent authority
Assignment
Factoring

 FURTHER READING

- Hugh Beale et al, *Cases, Materials and Text on Contract Law, Ius Commune Casebooks for the Common Law of Europe*, 2nd ed., Oxford (Hart Publishing) 2010, Chapters 26-28.
- Michael Joachim Bonell, 'Agency', in Arthur Hartkamp et al (eds.), *Towards a European Civil Code*, 4th ed. Nijmegen (Ars Aequi) 2011, Chapter 22.
- Jan Hallebeek and Harry Dondorp (eds.), *Contracts for a Third-Party Beneficiary: A Historical and Comparative Account*, Leiden-Boston (Martinus Nijhoff) 2008.
- Hein Kötz, *European Contract Law Vol. 1* (translated by Tony Weir), Oxford (Oxford University Press) 1997, Chapters 12-15.
- Ilse Samoy and Marco B.M. Loos (eds.), *Linked Contracts*, Cambridge (Intersentia) 2012
- Hendrik Verhagen and Laura Macgregor, 'Agency and Representation', in: Jan M. Smits, *Elgar Encyclopedia of Comparative Law*, 2nd ed., Cheltenham; Northampton Mass. (Edward Elgar) 2012, Chapter 3.
- Stefan Vogenauer, 'Contract in Favour of a Third Party', in Jürgen Basedow et al (eds.), *The Max Planck Encyclopedia of European Private Law, Vol. I*, Oxford (Oxford University Press) 2012, 385.

Glossary

Acceptance
The unconditional agreement of a party with the terms of an offer, bringing about the contract.

Agency
A relationship under which one party (the agent) agrees to act as an intermediary to conclude contracts on behalf of the other party (the principal).

Anticipatory breach (or anticipatory repudiation)
The situation in which, before performance is due, a party indicates that it will not perform the contract or is unable to do so.

Apparent authority
The situation where a person is treated as having granted authority to an apparent agent if this person induced a third party to reasonably believe that the agent had been granted authority to enter into a transaction.

Assignment
Transfer of a right by one person (the assignor) to another person (the assignee), resulting in the assignee being able to claim from the debtor.

Assumpsit
A form of action at common law that gives a right to sue someone for damages who claims that a contract has been breached.

Avoidable contract
A contract that suffers from such a defect that it allows one party or both parties to invalidate it. See also: void contract.

Avoidance
Invoking a ground of invalidity of the contract.

B2B contract
Business-to-business contract.

B2C contract
Business-to-consumer contract.

Barter
A contract under which each party agrees to transfer the ownership of a good in return for receiving the ownership of another good.

Battle of the forms
The situation in which each party to a contract uses its own general conditions and the law must decide which set of conditions applies to the contract, if any at all.

Bilateral contract
A contract under which each party assumes an obligation in order to obtain the performance to which the other party obliges itself. See also: unilateral contract.

C2C contract
Contract between two individuals not acting as a business.

Canon law
The law of the Catholic Church.

Capacity
The ability of a natural person to enter into a valid legal transaction.

Causa
A proper reason to be bound to a promise, codified as a requirement for the valid formation of a contract in most civil codes in the French legal tradition.

Caveat emptor
A maxim under English law literally meaning 'let the buyer beware': the buyer must investigate the goods himself in the absence of a duty of the seller to volunteer information. The maxim applies when buyer and seller are in an equal bargaining position.

Civil code
A comprehensive and systematic collection of the rules of private law that is promulgated by a formally empowered authority such as a state.

Closed system of contracts
A description of a system of contract law in which only some well-defined

contracts are recognised as binding. For example: the system of Roman contract law before the general principle of binding force of contract was accepted.

Condition
A type of contractual term that, in case of non-performance, justifies termination of the contract under English law.

Conflict-of-laws
The rules of law that deal with relations between persons across different jurisdictions. Conflict-of-laws (also known as private international law) deals mainly with the question which law applies to a cross-border relationship and which national court is competent to decide a cross-border case.

Consensus ad idem
The agreement of the parties to a contract (a 'meeting of the minds').

Consideration
The requirement for the valid formation of a contract under English law that each of the parties to the contract must provide or promise something of value to the other party.

Consumer credit
A contract under which a business (the lender) agrees to provide a private individual (the borrower) with credit and by which the borrower is obliged to repay the loan.

Consumer sale
Sale of goods by a business to a private individual for private consumption or use.

Contra proferentem rule
If the words of a contractual clause are ambiguous, the clause must be interpreted against the party who drafted it.

Contract
A legally binding agreement.

Corpus Iuris Civilis
The sixth century compilation of Roman law commissioned by Emperor Justinian.

Culpa in contrahendo
The violation of a duty to negotiate in good faith about a contract.

Deed
A written and signed document attested by a witness.

Default rules
Contract law rules that are automatically applicable to the contract if the parties do not provide otherwise.

Defect of consent
A flaw in the contractual consent that is of such a nature that it allows a party to invalidate the contract.

Directive
A European legislative instrument that is binding on the Member States as to the result to be achieved, but that leaves the form and method of implementation to the national legislatures.

Dissensus
The situation in which intention and declaration of a party differ from each other.

Distribution contract
An agreement under which one party (the supplier) agrees to supply another party (the distributor) with products on a continuing basis, and the distributor agrees to pay for them and to supply them to others in the distributor's name.

Donation
A contract under which one party (the donor) gratuitously undertakes to transfer the ownership of a good to another party (the donee) with the intention to benefit the donee.

Exceptio non adimpleti contractus
The right of a party to a bilateral contract to withhold its performance until the other party has duly performed its obligations under the contract.

Efficient breach
The view that a party is allowed not to perform a contract and pay damages instead if this is economically more efficient than performance.

Equity
The body of English law that supplements and mitigates the common law where the latter leads to harsh results.

Estoppel
The English doctrine that precludes a person from denying or asserting anything to the contrary of his own previous conduct.

Exclusion clause
A term in a contract that seeks to exclude liability of a party for non-performance of the contract.

Executed consideration
Something given or accepted in return for a promise, where the promised act is performed.

Executory consideration
Something given or accepted in return for a promise, where the promised act is still to be performed in the future.

Expectation interest
The interest of a party to be put in the position that it would have been in had the contract been performed.

Expedition theory (or dispatch theory, postal rule or mailbox rule)
The theory according to which a contract is concluded when the offeree sends the acceptance to the offeror.

Employment contract
A contract under which one party (the employee) is to perform contractually agreed work and another party (the employer) is to pay a remuneration for this.

Factoring
A contract in which a party assigns its claims to a factor with a view to obtaining finance and/or to outsourcing administration and credit control.

Feudalism
The political and economic system in large parts of Europe between the ninth and the fifteenth century in which vassals were protected and maintained by their lords and received land tenure in return for homage and legal and military service. The rights and obligations of people primarily followed from their status and not from contracts voluntarily entered into.

Fiduciary relationship
A special relationship of trust and confidence that requires a higher duty of care from both parties. Examples include the relationships between bank and client, solicitor and client, doctor and patient, principal and agent, guardian and ward, and shareholders and directors.

Franchise
A contract under which one party (the franchisor) grants another party (the franchisee), for a fee, the right to conduct a business, whereby the franchisee is to use the franchisor's trade name, know-how and and business system.

Fraud (or deceit)
Wilful deception of another party, inducing this party to enter into a contract.

Frustration
A doctrine in English contract law that is used to set aside a contract in case an event makes performance impossible or radically changes a party's principal purpose with the contract.

General conditions (or standard terms)
Terms that have been formulated in advance to be used for more than one contract and which have not been individually negotiated by the parties.

Good faith
Objective good faith is a standard of conduct prescribing a party to take into account the justified interests of the other party. Subjective good faith is a mental state of mind of a party characterised by a justified absence of knowledge about a certain situation.

Gratuitous transaction
A transaction in which one of the parties obliges itself to another without (the promise of) receiving anything in return.

Heads of agreement
A document outlining the main points of agreement relevant to the contract.

Hire-purchase
A contract under which one party (the 'hirer-purchaser') pays the price of a good in parts (usually every month) while enjoying the use of it, and the other party (the seller) transfers ownership when the instalments equal the total price.

Inequality of bargaining power
The situation in which one party has greater inherent 'power' (ability to influence the terms of the contractual agreement, information, expertise, financial means, etc.) than the other party.

Inertia selling
Sending unrequested goods to people, followed by demanding payment if they do not return them.

Injunction
A court order that requires someone to perform, or to refrain from performing, a specific act.

***In pari delicto* rule**
In cases where both parties are equally at fault, they cannot recover anything and will remain in the same situation they were in before one of them brought a court action claiming that the contract is prohibited.

Ius commune
The common system of legal thought and practice that was developed in large parts of continental Europe between the twelfth and nineteenth centuries and that found its basis in Roman and canon law.

Iustum pretium
The idea that a contract should have a 'just price'.

Juridical act
A declaration or agreement having legal consequences because these are intended by the person who acts.

Keep-open covenant
The clause in a commercial lease that requires the tenant to keep the premises (such as a shop or supermarket) open for trade during an agreed upon period.

Lapse
An offer coming to an end, meaning that it is no longer open for acceptance.

Lease
A contract under which one party (the lessor) grants another party (the lessee) a right of use for a specific period in return for a periodic payment (the rent).

Limitation clause
A term in a contract that seeks to limit liability of a party for non-performance of the contract.

Linked contracts
Contracts that, although concluded separately, are economically or factually connected.

Liquidated damages clause
A clause in a contract that requires the defaulting debtor to pay a specified sum to the creditor that is a reasonable pre-estimate of the likely damages.

Minimum harmonisation
The type of European harmonisation of law that sets a threshold which national legislation must comply with, leaving it to each individual member state to offer more protection.

Minor
A person below the age of majority.

Misrepresentation
An untrue statement of fact, which induces a party to conclude a contract.

Mistake
The erroneous belief of one or both contracting parties that certain facts are true and that allows one or both parties to invalidate the contract.

Multi-level legal system
A legal system in which rules are created at different (local, national, European or supranational) levels of government.

Non-compliance penalty
The sanction that a court can impose on a party for failure or refusal to comply with a court order.

Obligation
A usually enforceable duty to perform of one person (the debtor) vis-à-vis another person (the creditor).

Offer
A proposal that is intended to result in a contract if the other party accepts it and that contains sufficiently definite terms to form a contract.

Offeree
The person to whom an offer is made.

Offeror
The person making an offer.

Pacta sunt servanda
The principle that agreements must be kept. It is often mentioned to denote the end-result of the development from a closed system of contracts to the recognition of a general principle of binding force of contract.

***Parol* evidence rule**
A rule of evidence under English law, which prevents a party to a written contract from providing evidence extrincic to the written agreement.

Party agreement
The terms of the contract that the parties expressly agreed upon.

Past consideration
An act carried out before a promise is given and that therefore forms no good consideration for the promise.

Penalty clause
A clause in a contract that requires the defaulting debtor to pay a specified sum to the creditor that is not a reasonable pre-estimate of the likely damages.

Prenuptial agreement
A contract entered into prior to marriage or civil union, providing for the division of property and possibly other things in case of divorce or breakup.

Private law
The branch of law that defines the rights and duties of private actors (such as individuals and companies) as they relate to each other.

Privity
The principle that a contract can only bind the parties and does not confer rights or impose duties on others.

Procedural fairness
The view that a contract is fair if the parties were free from constraints that prevented their exercise of freedom of contract at the time of conclusion of

the contract (such as defects of consent, incapacity, lack of full information or inequality of bargaining power). See also: substantive fairness.

Promisee
The person to whom a promise is made.

Promisor
The person making a promise.

Promissory estoppel
The doctrine in English law that if a party changes its position by acting in reliance upon a promise lacking consideration, this party can enforce the promise even though the requirements for a valid contract are not met.

Receipt theory
The theory according to which a contract is concluded when the offeror receives the acceptance of the offeree.

Real contracts
Contracts which require the handing over of a good in order to be valid.

'Red hand' rule
The rule that a party who seeks to exclude or limit liability for non-performance of the contract must take reasonable steps to give notice of the clause to the other party. The more unreasonable the clause is, the greater the measures the party must take to draw attention to it.

Regulated contracts
Contracts of which the contents is substantially prescribed by law or regulatory measures.

Reliance interest
The interest of a party to be put in the position it was in before it acted in reasonable reliance on the contract.

Representation
A statement under English law, which asserts the truth of a given state of facts encouraging a party to enter into a contract.

Representation (direct)
The situation in which an agent acts in the name of a principal and is therefore not itself bound to the transaction.

Restraint of trade clause
A clause in a contract that restricts a party's freedom to conduct business or a profession.

Retention of title clause
A clause in a contract for the sale of goods that states that the property in the goods remains with the seller as long as the buyer has not paid the purchase price.

Revocation
The act of recalling an offer so that it no longer has any effect.

Sale of goods
A contract under which one party (the seller) obliges itself towards another party (the buyer) to transfer the ownership of a good against the payment of a price.

Second chance to perform
The requirement in German law that a claim for damages or termination must sometimes be preceded by first allowing the debtor to remedy his late or defective performance.

Services contract
A contract under which one party (the service provider) agrees to supply a service to another party (the client) in exchange for a price.

Stare decisis
The common law doctrine of binding precedent, obliging a court to respect the precedent established by previous decisions.

Stipulatio
A form of contract in Roman law based upon a question-and-answer ritual.

Subject to contract
A clause used to avoid that a party is bound to a contract before it is put into writing and signed.

Substantive fairness
The view that the fairness of a contract must be judged by the extent to which the outcome of the contracting process is in conformity with some view of fairness (such as social justice). See also: procedural fairness.

Suretyship
A contract under which one party (the surety or guarantor) obliges himself in favour of another party (the creditor) in order to secure a right to performance of an obligation of a third party (the debtor) owed to the creditor.

Surrogacy
The contract by which a woman agrees to carry and deliver a child for another person or couple.

Termination
Bringing an end to the contract for reason of non-performance.

Timeshare
A type of contract that allows a party to use the property (usually a holiday house or an apartment) for a certain period of time, often combined with shared ownership.

Tort (or delict)
A civil wrong causing loss or harm and allowing the victim to claim damages.

Undisclosed agency
A relationship between an agent and its counterpart where the counterpart does not know that the agent is acting on behalf of a principal.

Unilateral contract
A contract in which only one of the parties assumes an obligation.

Venire contra factum proprium
The legal maxim that no one is allowed to act contrary to their own previous conduct.

Void contract
A contract that suffers from such a defect that it is of no effect from the beginning ('*ab initio*'). See also: avoidable contract.

Warranty
A contractual term under English law, which if broken allows a claim for damages but not for termination of the contract.

Withdrawal
The overtaking of a declaration by another declaration that reaches the addressee before or at the same time as the first declaration.

Withdrawal right
The right of the consumer to end a contract within a limited period without having to give any reason for doing so.

Index